W9-DEV-554

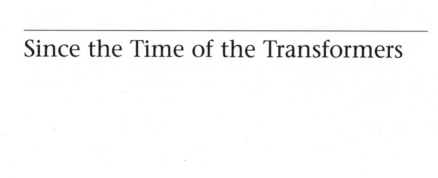

Since the Time of the Transformers

Pacific Rim Archaeology

This series is an initiative of UBC Laboratory of Archaeology and UBC Press. It provides a source of scholarly reporting on significant new archaeological research along the entire Pacific Rim – spanning the region from Southeast Asia to western North America and Pacific Latin America. The series will publish reports on archaeological fieldwork in longer monograph form as well as edited volumes of shorter works dealing with contemporary themes.

The general editors of the series are Michael Blake and R.G. Matson, both faculty members in the Department of Anthropology and Sociology at the University of British Columbia.

Since the Time of the Transformers is the second volume in the series. The first was *Hidden Dimensions: The Cultural Significance of Wetland Archaeology*, edited by Kathryn Bernick.

Alan D. McMillan

Since the Time of the Transformers: The Ancient Heritage of the Nuu-chah-nulth, Ditidaht, and Makah

UBCPress / Vancouver

© UBC Press 1999

Printed in Canada on acid-free paper ∞

ISBN 0-7748-0700-8

Pacific Rim Archaeology (ISSN 1483-2283)

Canadian Cataloguing in Publication Data

McMillan, Alan D. (Alan Daniel), 1945-
  Since the time of the transformers

  (Pacific Rim archaeology, ISSN 1483-2283)
  Included biblographical references and index.
  ISBN 0-7748-0700-8

  1. Nootka Indians – History. 2. Nootka Indians – Antiquities. 3. Makah Indians – History. 4. Makah Indians – Antiquities. I. Title. II. Series.

E99.N85M36 1999   971.1'2004979   C99-910015-7

This book has been published with the help of a grant from the Humanities and Social Sciences Federation of Canada, using funds provided by the Social Sciences and Humanities Research Council of Canada.

UBC Press also gratefully acknowledges the ongoing support to its publishing program from the Canada Council for the Arts, the British Columbia Arts Council, and the Multiculturalism Program of the Department of Canadian Heritage.

Set in Stone by Artegraphica Design Co.
Printed and bound in Canada by Friesens
Copy editor: Joanne Richardson

UBC Press
University of British Columbia
6344 Memorial Road
Vancouver, BC V6T 1Z2
(604) 822-5959
Fax: 1-800-668-0821
E-mail: orders@ubcpress.ubc.ca
www.ubcpress.ubc.ca

Contents

Figures, Maps, and Tables

Maps

Tables

Acknowledgments

I am grateful for the support of several Nuu-chah-nulth First Nations during my years of fieldwork on western Vancouver Island. In particular, I thank the Toquaht Nation and Chief Bert Mack for their constant support and for assistance in many aspects of the fieldwork. Jackie Godfrey and Pat North were particularly helpful in the Toquaht Band Office, handling most of the administrative details. Bert Mack and Archie Thompson also generously shared their knowledge of traditional Toquaht culture as part of the ethnographic component of research. I also thank the Tseshaht Nation for support during earlier fieldwork, and I fondly remember the late Chief Adam Shewish and the late Margaret Shewish for their hospitality and companionship during our stay with them. Return visits for potlatches and other events have provided welcome opportunities to continue to feel connected to the community. The Makah Cultural and Research Center authorized use of the illustrations related to their traditional territory and the Mowachaht/Muchalaht band granted permission to use the Yuquot excavation photograph.

My doctoral dissertation (McMillan 1996a) forms the basis for this book, although much of it has been rewritten and updated here. Accordingly, I owe a debt of gratitude to the original committee members, Roy Carlson and Philip Hobler. Both offered invaluable advice and assistance during the writing of the dissertation. With their extensive experience and knowledge in Northwest Coast archaeology, both served as inspirations for my work. In addition, David Burley and Madonna Moss kindly took time from their busy schedules to evaluate the dissertation as external examiners and offered valuable suggestions. I thank them all for their efforts.

The British Columbia Heritage Trust is gratefully acknowledged for providing the primary funding for the Toquaht Archaeological Project from 1991 to 1996. Additional funding was provided by the Toquaht Nation, student employment grants administered by Douglas College, and an Access to Archaeology grant administered by the Toquaht Nation. The 1996 fieldwork was also partially funded by a grant to the Toquaht Nation from the Nuu-chah-nulth Tribal Council under Interim Measures Funding through the BC Treaty Commission. The Department of Archaeology, Simon Fraser University, provided lab space, boats and motors, surveying equipment, and much of the field gear. The Toquaht Nation loaned the project its herring skiff for the last two field seasons. Other equipment and administrative support were provided by Douglas College, which also funded several periods of educational leave, allowing me to pursue doctoral studies and, later, to do the rewriting required for this book. The University of Manitoba also provided funding and support related to the analysis of faunal remains.

Any synthesis rests, of necessity, on the works of others. I would like to acknowledge my colleagues in Nuu-chah-nulth studies, with whom I have had numerous discussions and exchanges over the years. These include Richard Brolly, Dale Croes, John Dewhirst, Morley Eldridge, Gay Frederick, Jim Haggarty, Dave Huelsbeck, Richard Inglis, Al Mackie, Yvonne Marshall, Denis St. Claire, Arnoud Stryd, and Gary Wessen. In response to my requests while preparing both the dissertation and this book, Dale, John, Morley, and Gary kindly provided unpublished data, photographs, and/or other assistance. Particular gratitude is owed to Denis St. Claire, the co-director of the Toquaht Archaeological Project, for his numerous contributions during our long association in Nuu-chah-nulth fieldwork. Greg Monks should also be acknowledged for providing the Toquaht project with his expertise in faunal analysis. Randy Bouchard kindly provided transcriptions of various Nuu-chah-nulth place names and other words, using the practical orthography he developed for writing the Nuu-chah-nulth language (Bouchard 1971). I thank all the above for their contributions and apologize for where my summary or interpretation of their work differs from their own.

More generally, various friends and colleagues have influenced my thoughts on Northwest Coast archaeology through numerous discussions over the years. In addition to the people mentioned above, I would like to credit Knut Fladmark, Dave Burley, Bjorn Simonsen, Ken Ames, and R.G. Matson.

As always, I thank the members of my family for their tolerance of my absences during fieldwork and my preoccupied state during writing. My wife, Gillian, has my gratitude for her constant support and encouragement as well as for preparing most of the artifact drawings that appear in this book.

Finally, I thank the folks at UBC Press, particularly senior editor Jean Wilson and managing editor Holly Keller-Brohman, for encouragement and assistance.

Since the Time of the Transformers

1
Setting the Stage

Introduction

As is known from archaeological research, the record of human presence on western Vancouver Island spans at least the last 4,200 years. From an indigenous perspective, human history extends back to mythic times, when the transformers, such as Kwatyat among the central Nuu-chah-nulth, put the landscape and the animals in their present forms. This study examines the long culture history of the three related groups known today as the Nuu-chah-nulth, Ditidaht, and Makah, whose historic territories encompass western Vancouver Island and the northwestern portion of the Olympic Peninsula.

Long a "frontier area" to archaeologists, the precontact culture history of this region was essentially unknown until 1966, when large-scale excavations began at Yuquot in Nootka Sound and Ozette on the Olympic Peninsula. In subsequent decades several major excavation projects and intensive regional surveys, in addition to a number of smaller-scale archaeological investigations, have taken place at various locations within the general region. Sufficient data now exist to outline general diachronic trends and to perceive regional differences within the larger picture. For later time periods, this large body of information allows insight into a relatively wide range of past cultural practices. Linguistic and ethnographic data, as well as Native oral traditions, also provide substantial contributions to our understanding of Aboriginal culture history in this area.

Although this study examines and integrates such data from throughout the study region, the emphasis is on the Nuu-chah-nulth, with particular attention paid to the Toquaht of western Barkley Sound. This little-known Nuu-chah-nulth group is the focus of study for the ongoing Toquaht Archaeological Project (McMillan and St. Claire 1991, 1992, 1994, 1996). Throughout the following chapters, data from the Toquaht Project investigations are used as specific examples of more general issues. Ethnographic and archaeological information from Toquaht territory contributes to an emerging understanding of the broad patterns of Nuu-chah-nulth culture history, while at the same time being illuminated by, and interpreted within, a growing body of knowledge from the wider region.

As part of this general study, the West Coast culture type, the present model of cultural continuity proposed for western Vancouver Island by Donald Mitchell (1990), is examined and assessed. This construct was proposed as part of a general review of the prehistory of southwestern British Columbia, yet it was based almost entirely on the excavated results from Yuquot and Hesquiat Harbour. Cultural continuity evident in the Yuquot sequence led Mitchell to place the entire known precontact history of western Vancouver Island, covering at least 4,200 years, into a single culture type. He claims that the artifacts recovered, even from the earliest levels at Yuquot, are recognizable in the ethnographic material culture of the Nuu-chah-nulth and concludes that "the post-3000 B.C. period can be characterized as one of relatively little change in subsistence and other aspects of technology" (Mitchell 1990:357). This model of cultural conservatism and continuity, however, masks significant changes that occur through time. More recent archaeological data are used here to assess issues of temporal change and regional variation in the culture type.

The West Coast culture type, as generally applied, tends to project ethnographic Nuu-chah-nulth culture back in time in order to interpret the archaeological evidence. Certainly sites such as Yuquot demonstrate a remarkable cultural continuity. It is argued here, however, that significant changes did occur over time and that the cultural restructuring required by the traumatic events of the early contact period preclude any simplistic projections of the ethnographic culture into precontact times. Ethnographic data must be assessed with knowledge gleaned from archaeology in order to determine which traits have a lengthy continuity among the Nuu-chah-nulth as well as the nature and extent of culture change.

The theoretical approach underlying this study is found in the concept of "holistic archaeology," as advocated by Bruce Trigger (1989a, 1989b, 1991). Central to the search for a "holistic understanding of human behavior" (Trigger 1991:562) is a historical perspective that integrates data from a number of distinct fields. As Trigger (1989a:377) states: "This humanistic outlook also reinforces the view that it is reasonable to employ a direct historical approach and to use non-archaeological sources of data, such as oral traditions, historical linguistics, and comparative ethnography, in order to produce a more rounded picture of prehistoric cultures." Such a perspective has a lengthy history in North American anthropology, but it is put into its fullest modern form by Trigger. Unlike processualism, until recently the dominant interpretive framework in North American archaeology, this integrative and humanistic approach validates an interest in the cosmologies, religious beliefs, art forms, and other symbolic aspects of individual cultures. Trigger (1991:562) states that the search for culturally specific meaning in the archaeological record "requires additional information, which can only be acquired from non-archeological sources by means of the direct historical approach." Holistic archaeology, one of the many strands embedded in contemporary post-processual archaeology, also calls for the recognition of the dynamic and symbolic nature of material culture.

Trigger (1989b:22) notes that traditional culture history, which tends to attribute culture change to such external factors as migration and diffusion, has little in common with true history except for a concern with chronology. Processualists came to view historical concerns as the opposite of science, as descriptive rather than as explanatory, as particularistic rather than as capable of evolutionary generalizations. Trigger (1980:673, 1989a:373) rejects this "false dichotomy" between history and science. Through a holistic approach, he maintains (1991:562), where cultural traditions are examined as closely as are ecological and systemic constraints, archaeologists can gain a more rounded and humanistic understanding of the past.

Trigger has questioned the colonialism inherent in academic fields that have treated indigenous peoples as unsuitable subjects for historical study. People of European descent were perceived as the "prime movers" of historical analysis, while indigenous populations were perceived as "people without history" and were relegated to the subject matter of anthropology (Wolf 1982; Trigger 1980, 1984, 1985, 1989b). A misleading image of the "unchanging Native" was further enhanced by such anthropological concepts as the "ethnographic present." Trigger (1985:34) describes the differentiation of history and anthropology as "a product of colonialism and ethnocentrism."

Traditionally, as a subfield of anthropology, North American prehistoric archaeology has had weak ties with history. More recently, the processualist use of Aboriginal heritage to formulate and test general hypotheses on human behaviour was resented by First Nations for failing to address their own distinct identities and histories (Trigger 1980, 1985:29-32, 1989a:376, 1989b:24-25). Archaeology, if it is to meet the needs of the people it studies, must provide specific information on unique culture histories. This is particularly vital in the modern political climate, as collaboration for mutual benefit is a prerequisite for archaeologists working with First Nations. Potential contributions archaeologists can make to Aboriginal groups include documenting ancient ties to the land and demolishing the myth of the unchanging Native. In addition, the new emphasis on studying cognitive and symbolic aspects of the past has the potential to enrich our understanding of Aboriginal accomplishments. Recognition of the "Native voice" through study of oral traditions and collaborating with modern descendant populations also enhances our understanding.

The West Coast People: Nuu-chah-nulth, Ditidaht, and Makah

Languages

The rugged west coast of Vancouver Island, from Cape Cook in the north to around Point No Point in the south, is the traditional homeland of people known historically as the Nootka (Map 1). This name was applied by the famed British explorer Captain James Cook, who mistakenly thought he was recording a term the Natives of the area used to describe themselves. In fact, the term "Nootka" stems from a word meaning "to come around" or "to circle about" (Sapir and Swadesh 1939:276; Moser 1926:160), apparently reflecting Native attempts to direct Cook and his vessel into the sheltered harbour in front of the nearby village of Yuquot (Efrat and Langlois 1978a:55; Folan 1972:32; Arima et al. 1991:6-7). Although largely rejected by the people to whom it was applied, the name "Nootka" was widely used by anthropologists and others to describe not just the people of Nootka Sound but all the culturally related groups along Vancouver Island's west coast. The Aboriginal languages of the area lacked any such broad collective term, keeping self-designations at the more local level.[1] As a result, the English phrase "the West Coast (or Westcoast) peoples" came into widespread use to encompass all the people formerly known as Nootka. The name "Nuu-chah-nulth" is a relatively recent innovation, being formally adopted by the tribal council in 1978, fully 200 years after Cook erroneously used the term "Nootka." Loosely translated, "Nuu-chah-nulth" means "all along the mountains," referring to the mountain chain of central Vancouver Island, which forms the backdrop for the west coast villages.

To the south, along the storm-lashed coast of the Olympic Peninsula, were the culturally and linguistically related Makah. Their most southerly village, Ozette, was at Cape Alava, on the outer coast. In their own language, these people referred to themselves as the *Kw'idishch7aa7tx*, meaning "people who live at the cape" (Swan 1870:1; Colson 1953:76; Taylor 1974:43). The Nuu-chah-nulth called them the *Tl'aa7as7ath*, or "people of the outside coast" (Sapir and Swadesh 1939:148, 310; Arima 1983:7; Renker and Gunther 1990:429). This term frequently appears in early historic accounts as "Classet" or "Klazzart." The name "Makah," in common use since the mid-nineteenth century, is derived from a term applied to these people by the Clallum, their Salishan neighbours to the east.

---

1 Individual political groups generally have names ending in *-7ath* (Nuu-chah-nulth) or *-7aa7tx* (Ditidaht and Makah), meaning "people of." This led Sproat (1868) to refer to the Nuu-chah-nulth as the "Aht" Indians. Nuu-chah-nulth terms are rendered here in the practical orthography developed by Randy Bouchard of the British Columbia Indian Language Project, Victoria (Bouchard 1971). The symbol "7" represents a glottal stop (or "catch in the throat"), while underlining indicates that the sound is produced further back in the mouth.

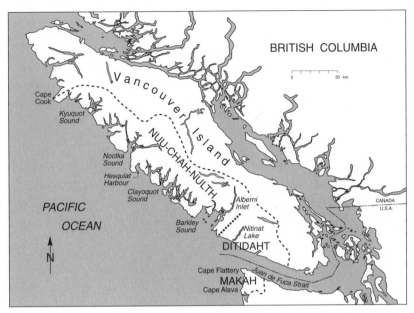

Map 1 Traditional territories of the Nuu-chah-nulth, Ditidaht, and Makah in the nineteenth century.

Although linguists today identify three separate languages, the Aboriginal peoples of this area have a strong sense of sharing a common culture. Certainly the late eighteenth-century European observers perceived them all as a single people, with only minor regional differences. Meares (1790:165) found "the language of King George's [Nootka] Sound ... to prevail from thence to the district of Tatootche," a reference to the powerful chief of the Cape Flattery area. Haswell, among the Ditidaht in 1789, was "glad to find that they spoke a dialect of the Nootka Language" (Howay 1941:71). When the Spanish established the settlement of Nuñez Gaona at Neah Bay in 1792, they thought the surrounding Makah closely resembled the inhabitants of Nootka Sound, differing only slightly in speech (Wagner 1933:189). Jewitt (1967:75), at Nootka Sound from 1803 to 1805, said of the Makah ("Kla-iz-zart") visitors to the sound: "Their language is the same as spoken at Nootka, but their pronunciation is much more hoarse and guttural."

Although these early observers had no linguistic training, the first anthropologists to work in this area came to the same conclusions. In his pioneering work among the "Nootka," Boas (1891:583) referred to three "closely allied dialects of the same language," which were "all intelligible to each other." Sapir, in his linguistic studies of the Barkley Sound groups, also comments on the three "Nootka dialects" (Sapir and Swadesh 1939:10). In her ethnographic study of the Makah, Colson (1953:4) states that they "spoke a dialect of the Nootka language." Similarly, Drucker (1951:3) refers to three "dialectic divisions," noting: "These dialects seem to differ through a few fairly simple and consistent phonetic shifts, so that although at first mutually unintelligible, a person who speaks one form can soon understand the other and make himself understood. At least that is what informants say." Several Tseshaht elders I interviewed during fieldwork in Port Alberni were adamant that they are a single people from Cape Cook to the Olympic Peninsula and that they could make themselves understood despite any linguistic differences.[2] More recently, Thompson and Kinkade (1990:39-40) have noted this tension between Aboriginal views and the linguistic evidence: "Nootka, Nitinaht [Ditidaht], and Makah are reported to be considered a single language by the Indians, sometimes referred to as the Westcoast language, after the native expression; however, as they are not mutually intelligible, they are considered here to be three separate languages."

The northernmost of the three languages, formerly termed "Nootka," is usually now referred to as "Nuu-chah-nulth." The Language Committee of the Nuu-chah-nulth Tribal Council uses the term *T'aat'aaqsapa* for this language (Nuu-chah-nulth Tribal Council 1991; see also Thomas and Arima 1970). *T'aat'aaqsapa* exists as a series of intergrading dialects, from the Kyuquot in the north to the Huu-ay-aht at the southern end of Barkley Sound. Local differences in speech are clearly evident but do not hinder communication. For example, the Tseshaht are said to "talk very fast"; if someone speaks rapidly in a conversation, the others will joke that he must be a Tseshaht (Sapir 1915:194).[3] Similarly, Drucker (1951:4) contrasts the sonorous drawl of the Mowachaht with the rapid speech of the Kyuquot.

The language spoken by the Vancouver Island groups south of Barkley Sound is Ditidaht (formerly Nitinaht, but this reflects Nuu-chah-nulth, not Ditidaht, pronunciation).[4] Like the Makah language, Ditidaht has a relatively small number of speakers and little dialectal variation (Thompson and Kinkade 1990:39). Although linguists consider Ditidaht and Makah to be two separate languages, a high degree of mutual intelligibility is evident (Bates 1987:54; Arima 1988:23). They are more closely related to each other than either is to Nuu-chah-nulth (Renker and Gunther 1990:422; Bouchard and Kennedy 1991:4; Nuu-chah-nulth Tribal Council 1991:3). Based on glottochronology, the divergence of Ditidaht and Makah may have occurred about 1,000 years ago (Jacobsen 1979:776).[5]

2 Bouchard and Kennedy (1991) report a different experience among the Ditidaht, who insisted that their language was distinct from Nuu-chah-nulth.

3 I was also told this joke on several occasions during research with the Tseshaht in the 1970s.

4 *Diitiid7aa7tx* is the term used by those who speak this language, while *Niitiinaa7ath* is the term used by their Nuu-chah-nulth neighbours.

5 Glottochronology was developed as a method of calculating the time elapsed since the split of two related languages. It compares word lists for each language and calculates length of separation based on the assumption of a constant rate of change. As this assumption is clearly flawed, glottochronology has had only limited acceptance.

1 John Webber watercolour of a Nuu-chah-nulth man at Nootka Sound in 1778. He is wearing a cape of woven cedar bark, his face is painted, and his hair is braided. *Peabody Museum, Harvard University, photograph by Hillel Burger*

Despite these linguistic differences, the three groups consider themselves to be a single population, distinct from their Kwakwaka'wakw, Salish, and Quileute neighbours. Ties of intermarriage and reciprocal attendance at social and ceremonial events enhance this shared identity. Even today, the Makah are frequently honoured guests at potlatches held by Ditidaht or Nuu-chah-nulth groups, and Nuu-chah-nulth chiefs are welcomed visitors at Makah festivals. At such occasions, speakers stress their kin ties with such statements as: "We are related up and down the coast" (Bates 1987:151).

The three Nootkan languages comprise the southern branch of the Wakashan language family. Like "Nootka," the term "Wakashan" comes from Captain James Cook's observations in Nootka Sound in 1778. He proposed that the people be called Wakashians, after "wakash," an expression in common use: "The word *wakash* ... was very frequently in their mouths. It seemed to express applause, approbation, and friendship. For when they appeared to be satisfied, or well pleased with any thing they saw, or any

incident that happened, they would, with one voice, call out *wakash!*
wakash!" (Cook 1784:337). The northern (or "Kwakiutlan") branch of the
Wakashan family also contains three languages: Kwakwala (spoken by people formerly called the Southern Kwakiutl who today are known as the
Kwakwaka'wakw), Heiltsuk (spoken by people at Bella Bella; the Oweekeno
of Rivers Inlet speak a distinct dialect but are usually included), and Haisla
(spoken at Kitamaat).

The recognition that the northern and southern branches of the Wakashan
language family are related was one of Franz Boas's early discoveries
(1891:678-679). Sapir (1911:15), however, noted that the differences between the two branches are "very great." Swadesh (1953, 1954) employed
glottochronology in an attempt to establish the time depth separating northern and southern Wakashan, arriving at an estimate of about 2,900 years.
Although there are numerous problems with glottochronology as a dating
technique, Jacobsen (1979:769), in a review of the Wakashan language family, considers this estimate "plausible." More recently, however, Embleton
(1985) has recalculated this divergence, using a technique that takes into
account borrowing and prolonged contact between members of the family,
and has arrived at the considerably earlier estimate of about 5,500 years.

Some linguists have sought more distant relationships. In his pioneering
linguistic work, Edward Sapir (1929) suggested that all the Aboriginal languages of North America could be encompassed within six broad super-
stocks. He linked the Wakashan languages to Kutenai and the widespread
Algonkian family, creating the Algonkian-Wakashan super-stock. One of
the three divisions within this super-stock he termed "Mosan," which consisted of the Wakashan, Chimakuan, and Salishan families. The Mosan grouping was further studied by Sapir's former student Morris Swadesh (1953). He
considered the Wakashan languages to be most closely related to Chimakuan
(consisting of only two languages, Quileute and Chemakum, widely separated on the Olympic Peninsula) and calculated that the time depth separating them was about 6,500 years. Differences between Wakashan and
Salishan languages were seen as even greater, requiring a time depth of about
9,000 years for Mosan as a whole (Swadesh 1953:27, 42). If such distant
relationships could be substantiated this would have obvious implications
for the early occupation of a vast area of what is now central and southern
British Columbia and northern Washington. This scheme, however, receives
very little support from modern linguists. The Algonkian-Wakashan link
has been completely abandoned, and the Mosan grouping has been largely
dismantled. Although Powell (1993) has attempted to demonstrate a relationship between Wakashan and Chimakuan, most modern linguists consider the former members of Sapir's Mosan to be three separate language
family isolates (Kinkade 1990:104).

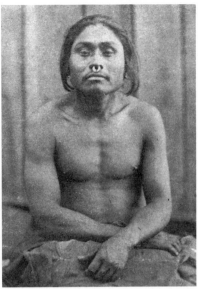

2   Nuu-chah-nulth (Tseshaht) man in Barkley Sound (top left), Ditidaht man (top right), Makah woman (above). Photographs taken in late 1860s. *Royal BC Museum PN4814, PN4807, PN8738*

Ethnographic Background

Throughout their entire territory, from Cape Cook to Cape Alava, the Nuu-chah-nulth, Ditidaht, and Makah occupied a landscape of majestic grandeur. Frequently shrouded in clouds, the rainy coast bears a lush green mantle of cedar, fir, hemlock, and spruce. Along the outer coast huge waves break against long sweeping sandy beaches broken by rocky headlands. Rugged mountains descend precipitously to the sea along the fjord-like inlets, which stretch far inland. Large sounds and numerous smaller bays and inlets, studded with island clusters, result in a convoluted coastline that offers a diversity of local environments and a great variety of resources. From the outer coast these people took whales, sea lions, seals, halibut, and shellfish; the protected waterways of the sounds and inlets offered salmon, herring, and other fish; and the forests provided deer, elk, bear, and various plant foods.

Large dugout cedar canoes once traversed these waterways, allowing people to exploit resources throughout their territories and to travel to distant villages for feasts, ceremonies, or raids. Permanent villages of large cedar plank-clad houses faced the sheltered waterways at important locations, although temporary housing was also used at short-term resource camps. The beaches in front of the houses bustled with activity, as the canoes of fishers, sea mammal hunters, and traders arrived and departed. Here people gathered to clean and dry fish, make and mend tools, and visit. The basic activities of everyday life, such as sleeping, cooking, and caring for children (as well as major ceremonial activities), took place primarily within the houses, the cluster of people occupying a house forming one of the basic

3   The village of Yuquot in Nootka Sound, as seen by Cook's officers in 1778. Drying racks stand outside the plank-clad houses along the beach. Engraving from a watercolour by John Webber. *Canadian Museum of Civilization J-2427*

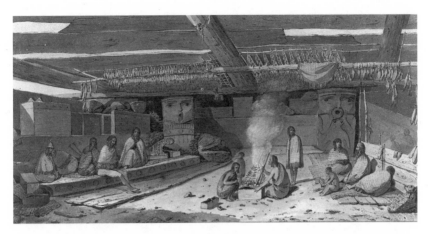

4 Interior of a house at Yuquot. This picture provides a wealth of information on Nuu-chah-nulth life at the time of first contact with Europeans. John Webber watercolour, 1778. *Peabody Museum, Harvard University, photograph by Hillel Burger*

levels of Nuu-chah-nulth social organization (Figure 4) (Marshall 1989a; Golla 1987:98-102; Wike 1958:219).

Throughout much of the Historic Period the numerous politically independent local groups along the west coast of Vancouver Island were coalescing into larger and more complex political units. By the nineteenth century rapidly declining populations, largely due to introduced European diseases and intense internecine warfare, resulted in amalgamations that led to the formation of the modern Nuu-chah-nulth and Ditidaht groups (Map 2). Sproat (1868:308) lists twenty "tribes" for western Vancouver Island in 1860; similarly, Boas (1891:583) lists twenty-two "tribes," including the Makah, in the late nineteenth century. Several of these ceased to exist, their surviving members being incorporated into other bands, in a process that continued well into the twentieth century. Today there are fifteen legally recognized bands of Nuu-chah-nulth and Ditidaht. The Makah, formerly composed of five semi-autonomous villages (with the people at Ozette being the most politically separate) (Taylor 1974:37, 66; Riley 1968:70, 79-80; Singh 1966), have amalgamated into a single political unit based at Neah Bay.

The basic social and economic unit in the Nuu-chah-nulth political system was the local group. As Drucker (1951:220) describes it: "The fundamental Nootkan political unit was a local group centering in a family of chiefs who owned territorial rights, houses, and various other privileges. Such a group bore a name, usually that of their 'place' (a site at their fishing ground where they 'belonged'), or sometimes that of a chief; and had a tradition, firmly believed, of descent from a common ancestor." Kenyon (1980:84) adds further details: "The Nootka local group was conceived of as

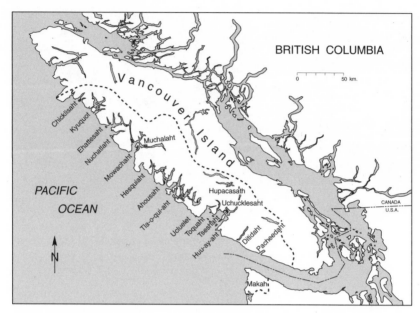

Map 2   Location of Nuu-chah-nulth, Ditidaht, and Makah political groups by the early twentieth century.

an idealized family, expanded over time, which owned a distinct territory and shared common ceremonial and ritual property. Members of this family were ranked on the basis of primogeniture and it was the highest ranking member who was regarded as the owner of most of the group's property." Such social units had clearly defined territorial boundaries, and access to economic resources within those boundaries was strictly controlled. As a result, each local group would have exploited a slightly different pattern of available resources, thus making individual local groups potentially detectable in the archaeological record (Calvert 1980; Haggarty 1982; Huelsbeck 1989).

Although the local group was the basic political entity in Nuu-chah-nulth society, it was composed of varying numbers of subgroups, called *ushtakimilh*. Anthropologists have designated these subgroups as "lineages," "houses," or "family groups." Members of a local group considered themselves to be the descendants of a common ancestor, and the various *ushtakimilh* represented the different lines of descent from that ancestor. Primogeniture prevailed; the senior member of the line of descent stemming from the eldest son would be the head chief of the entire local group (St. Claire 1991:22; Wike 1958:220). This person would bear the name of the ancestor-founder and act as custodian of all group property. Within the local group, each *ushtakimilh* was likely to have its own house, with that of the head chief being the largest and grandest (Golla 1987:111).

Marriage, particularly among high-status individuals, served to promote alliances between social groups. Membership in several different local groups was possible through ambilateral descent (Arima and Dewhirst 1990:399). Broad networks of kin ties meant that individuals could shift local group affiliation by changing residence and participating in a new social unit. Considerable movement of people between local groups was common. Although patrilocal residence was the preferred form, in practice there was no set rule (Drucker 1951:278; Arima and Dewhirst 1980:399).

In many regions, such as along Muchalat Arm and in Hesquiat Harbour, autonomous local groups survived into quite recent times. In other regions, however, more complex social structures emerged through political alliances between formerly separate groups. Drucker (1951:220) uses the term "tribe" to refer to allied local groups that shared a common winter village. Each local group owned and occupied at least one of the large permanent house structures at the winter village, where important ceremonial activities involving the entire tribe took place. The people of such a tribal union shared a name, frequently taken from one of the component groups, and had a pattern of fixed ranking for their assembled chiefs. The local groups still maintained their distinct identity, however, and retained exclusive ownership over important seasonal resource locations.

Warfare also played a major role in the formation of such larger groupings. Often hostilities were driven by a desire to appropriate the territorial holdings of another group, particularly if these contained such vital economic resources as rivers with salmon runs (Swadesh 1948; Drucker 1951:333; Arima 1983:105). The conquerors killed or enslaved the area's occupants and took possession of the territory. Families that escaped the destruction of their villages sought refuge among relatives in neighbouring groups. Some groups, reduced in population through such hostilities, sought protection through voluntary fusion with stronger neighbours. A well-documented example of such wars of conquest is the expansion of the Ahousaht, formerly restricted to a small area of the outer coast, who, in the early nineteenth century, nearly exterminated the Otsosaht and absorbed their territory along with its rich salmon streams (Drucker 1951:344-353; Arima 1983:107-117; Webster 1983:59-64; Bouchard and Kennedy 1990:224-241). Similarly, the Ucluelet, who also lacked a good salmon river, destroyed the Nahmintaht, an apparently independent local group on Alberni Inlet, and took possession of the rich fishery in the Nahmint River (Sapir and Swadesh 1955:362-367). Various other traditions of territorial conquest for economic gain have been recorded (Sapir 1910-1914; Swadesh 1948). The expanded territories of the victorious groups forced a shift in settlement pattern, involving seasonal movements between widely separated locations.

The northern Nuu-chah-nulth – the Mowachaht, Ehattesaht, Nuchatlaht, and Kyuquot – formed confederacies, some of which apparently predated

European contact. The members of such political units shared a name, generally taken from one of the constituent groups; a fixed series of chiefs, whose relative ranks were reaffirmed through ritual prerogatives (such as the order of seating for ceremonies); and a common village site occupied during the summer months (Drucker 1951:220; Arima and Dewhirst 1990:391; Morgan 1980). Constituent groups maintained their distinct identities and territories, and they acted as ceremonial units within the confederacy. At other times of the year people still occupied their tribal winter villages and the local group resource sites.

Hereditary chiefs (*ḥawilh*) derived their power from inherited privileges. These included ownership of specific economic resources, such as salmon streams, offshore halibut banks, sea lion rocks, clam beds, or salvage rights to anything that drifted onto a particular beach. House sites and important ceremonial privileges were also included. Drucker (1951:247) described such rights as the "fountainhead of chiefly power": "The Nootkans carried the concept of ownership to an incredible extreme. Not only rivers and fishing places close at hand, but the waters of the sea for miles offshore, the land, houses, carvings on a house post, the right to marry in a certain way or the right to omit part of an ordinary marriage ceremony, names, songs, dances, medicines, and rituals, all were privately owned property." Ceremonial privileges had to be publicly displayed. Sapir and Swadesh (1955:3) explain the Nuu-chah-nulth concept of *tupaati* (hereditary display privilege), which is essential to chiefly power: "The term 'tupaati' ... is used in a narrow sense for a ceremonial trial of strength or skill in a guessing game, which constitutes an exclusive hereditary prerogative of a given lineage; those who are successful in such trials are rewarded with prizes and the host takes the occasion to reaffirm his family prestige, of which the tupaati is a token. Tupaati is also used in a broad sense for any hereditary privilege or any token of such a privilege, including territorial rights, songs, names, painted screens, carvings, which are the exclusive possession of a lineage."

Commoners were individuals who lacked claims to inherited privileges. In return for access to economic resources, they provided their services to the chiefs as fishers, hunters, and craftworkers; they also provided much of the menial labour. Chiefs required the labour of their commoners in order to "keep up their names"; that is, to live up to the expectations of their chiefly positions through lavish feasting and potlatching (Drucker 1951:273). Commoners had much greater mobility than did chiefs, who were tied to specific locations by their hereditary rights and traditions. If their leaders were overbearing or failed to provide feasts and security, then commoners could leave to assert their kin ties in the villages of other chiefs (Arima and Dewhirst 1990:401). In extreme cases commoners might kill their chief; in 1804, for example, a period of hunger caused by poor fishing and unsuccessful whaling led the Mowachaht chief Maquinna to fear for his life, forcing him to use his slaves to protect himself from his own people (Jewitt 1988:59-60).

Slaves occupied the lowest rung of the social ladder. Most slaves were captives taken in war and then sold to other groups along the coast. A slave was considered to be a chattel and could be sold or mistreated at the whim of the chief. Occasionally slaves were killed at a chief's mourning ceremony, and sometimes a chief would publicly dispatch them at a potlatch in order to demonstrate his great wealth. In most respects, however, their lives differed little from those of commoners. They carried out numerous menial but essential tasks and were important economic resources. They also played an important military and political role, as some chiefs used their slaves to wage war or to enforce their control over commoners (Wike 1958:223, 225; Donald 1983:113).

Nuu-chah-nulth economic life changed with the seasons, as many resources, such as salmon, herring, and various waterfowl, were only available at certain times of the year, while other species, such as halibut and sea mammals, could only be taken when the seas were relatively calm and people were living on the outer coast. Drucker (1951:36-61) describes the Nuu-chah-nulth economic cycle in some detail. Although considerable local variation existed, the basic pattern involved an annual round of movement from a sheltered winter village site on the inner coast, to spring and summer fishing and sea mammal hunting locations on the outer coast, to various rivers and streams for fall salmon fishing, and back to the winter village. This seasonal movement between "inside" and "outside" locations typifies the ethnographic cultures. Much of the warfare and political manoeuvring historically recorded can be understood as attempts to secure territorial rights in both of these settings (Dewhirst 1978:7; Arima and Dewhirst 1990:394). Prior to the extensive historic amalgamations, however, many local groups appear to have relied year-round on the resources locally available, perhaps augmenting them through patterns of trade and ceremonial exchange with their neighbours.[6]

In early spring, as stores of dried salmon and other winter provisions were exhausted, Nuu-chah-nulth groups began the move towards the outside portions of their territories. Schools of herring, the first important resource to appear, were eagerly taken in the inlets through the use of dip nets and herring rakes (long wooden poles studded with sharp bone points on which the fish were impaled). Spring salmon also appeared to feed on the herring and were taken by trolling with a sharp-angled hook, usually baited

---

6 George Clutesi (1969), a Nuu-chah-nulth author, provides an example of food exchange in a ceremonial context. In *Potlatch*, he describes a Tseshaht ceremony at Port Alberni early in the twentieth century, to which the people of the inland lakes brought fresh deer and elk meat and roasted camas bulbs, while the people of the outer coast brought seal oil and chunks of smoked fur-seal and whale blubber.

with whole herring (Drucker 1951:40). These were cooked and eaten fresh. When the herring spawned, the Nuu-chah-nulth collected the thick egg masses on sunken hemlock boughs and dried them for later consumption. Spring was also the time when large flocks of migratory waterfowl arrived and were taken by various methods, including hunting from canoes, netting, and snaring. A large net strung across the mouth of the Nitinat Narrows, at the Ditidaht village of Whyac, was particularly effective, yielding hundreds of ducks at each use (Turner et al. 1983:131).

As the weather improved, groups that owned outside village locations dispersed there to fish for halibut and cod and to hunt sea mammals (Drucker 1951:48; Calvert 1980:83; Arima and Dewhirst 1990:394). Halibut were taken on U-shaped hooks of dense wood, usually baited with octopus tentacle, that were sunk to the ocean floor. The halibut banks were often considerable distances offshore; the Barkley Sound groups reported that they would paddle their canoes all night in order to reach their destination by dawn (Sapir and Swadesh 1955:41). People also harpooned seals, sea lions, and porpoises from their canoes and clubbed seals when they hauled up on the rocks.

This was also the time when migrating whales became available, and these mammals could be hunted throughout the summer. Grey whales (*Eschrichtius robustus*) and humpback whales (*Megaptera novaeangliae*) were the two main species taken ethnographically (Sapir 1924; Drucker 1951:49-50), although the latter may have been the most important in earlier times (Kool 1982). Only chiefs could hunt whales, an activity that required ritual preparation and careful training for both the whaler and his crew (Sapir 1924; Gunther 1942; Curtis 1916:16; Densmore 1939:47; Drucker 1951:169-170). The whaling canoe had to be paddled alongside the whale so that, just as the whale submerged, the whaler could thrust the heavy harpoon deep in behind its flipper. As the whale dove and the paddlers frantically tried to get the canoe out of the way, it took with it a long line attached to the harpoon head, to which floats of inflated sealskins had been added. As the whale resurfaced, other canoes could move in to implant additional harpoon lines and floats. Finally, when the weakened whale could no longer escape by diving, it was dispatched with a long lance and towed to shore. The "saddle" from the back of the whale was reserved for ritual treatment by the chief, while the rest was distributed according to rank and participation, with the blubber going to the entire group (Drucker 1951:55; Swan 1870:21-22; Waterman 1920:45; Koppert 1930:58-60; Densmore 1939:63).

Drucker (1951:49) argues that whaling was primarily a prestige activity and that successful hunts were relatively rare events. Certainly, Jewitt's observations among the Mowachaht between 1803 and 1805 show a low success rate for Maquinna's whaling expeditions. Nevertheless, whaling clearly played a major role in the Nuu-chah-nulth, Ditidaht, and Makah

5 Nuu-chah-nulth whaler attaching the harpoon head
to the shaft. Note the thick rope of twisted cedar root
and the floats of sea-lion hides visible in the foreground.
Photo by E.S. Curtis, National Archives of Canada C30205

economies. Even a relatively small number of kills would provide a substantial quantity of oil to the Aboriginal diet (Inglis and Haggarty 1983; Cavanagh 1983; Huelsbeck 1988a, 1988b; Arima 1988). The southern groups emphasized whaling to a greater extent than did the Mowachaht and other northern groups studied by Drucker. Riley (1968:72) quotes an Indian agent among the Makah in 1865 as stating: "What the buffalo is to the Indians on the plains, the whale is to the Makah."

The outside sites also provided excellent access to marine invertebrates. A variety of clams, mussels, and other shellfish were collected and eaten (Clarke and Clarke 1975, 1980; Ellis and Swan 1981; Calvert 1980). Women were the primary collectors, using digging and prying sticks of hard wood (such as yew) and open-weave carrying baskets (Figure 6). In addition to shellfish, the intertidal zone held an array of edible invertebrates, including several species of chitons, sea urchins, sea cucumber, crabs, and octopus (Ellis and Swan 1981).

6   Nuu-chah-nulth women, wearing cedar bark clothing
in this posed photograph, wait on the beach with the
open-weave baskets and digging sticks used in collecting
shellfish. *Photo by E.S. Curtis, National Archives of Canada
C20845*

From late spring to fall, a wide variety of plant foods was collected (Drucker
1951:56-57; Turner and Efrat 1982; Turner et al. 1983). In spring, the fresh
green stalks of salmonberries, cow parsnip, and several other species were
eagerly eaten raw. Several types of roots and bulbs were also dug for roasting
or steaming. Camas and tiger lily bulbs were dug in summer. In late summer the Nuu-chah-nulth dug and steamed clover rhizomes, their most important root food, and feasted on the numerous berries that ripened at that
time. People also continued to fish and hunt sea mammals throughout the
summer. A variety of rockfish, lingcod, Pacific cod, greenling, and other
fish were taken on hooks and lines around rocky reefs and headlands, while
halibut, cod, and red snapper were caught offshore.

By late summer the sockeye salmon run brought many people back into
the bays and inlets to the mouths of their salmon streams. As the season
advanced, particularly when the important chum or dog salmon run began
in the fall, most groups were back inside at their fall fishing stations. Wooden

7 Part of the Makah village of Neah Bay, photographed by E.S. Curtis about 1916. Note the old-style plank house in the left foreground. *National Archives of Canada PA202002*

stake weirs enclosing traps were constructed in coves by river mouths or in the rivers (Drucker 1951:58). As the runs began to thin, harpooning became the dominant method of capture. Most salmon taken at this time were smoked and dried for winter consumption. The chum salmon had spawning runs in nearly every sizable stream and river. Its relatively dry flesh made it easy to preserve, and the late timing of its runs made it an ideal resource for winter provisions (Drucker 1951:36).

The West Coast people spent the wet, stormy months of winter at their major villages, generally located on the sheltered inside portion of their territory. Large multifamily houses, consisting of permanent cedar log frameworks covered with removable split cedar planks, lined the beaches at such locations (Figure 7). House posts and ridge beams might be carved with images that were the inherited rights of important chiefs. When torrential rains and rough seas kept the people indoors, they were able to feast on such preserved foods as dried salmon and halibut, dried clams, dried salal berry cakes, and sea mammal blubber and oil. When the weather cleared, men set off to fish for cod, while women gathered shellfish, other marine invertebrates, and winter huckleberries (Drucker 1951:37-39), adding variety to the steady diet of dried foods. Hunting for land mammals, such as deer, elk, and bear, was conducted opportunistically throughout the year, but winter was a favoured time for many, when inland groups such as the

Muchalaht and Hupacasath used snowshoes to run down deer and elk in deep snow and dispatched them with yew lances (Drucker 1951:38; Arima and Dewhirst 1990:397). The reduced food-gathering requirements of this season allowed people to spend more time indoors, manufacturing and repairing their tools, weapons, and clothing as well as producing objects and regalia to be used in ceremonies.

The grey rainy winter days, when large numbers of people were gathered in the villages, were enlivened by major ceremonial events. Chiefs displayed their wealth, generosity, and ceremonial privileges at major feasts and potlatches to which guests from other villages were invited (Figure 8). The major winter ceremonial was the *tlukwana (tlukwaali* in Ditidaht and Makah), literally, the "Shamans' Dance" (although it is widely referred to as the Wolf Ritual). A wealthy chief would sponsor such an event, which might last for

8   Chief Joseph of the Tla-o-qui-aht wears a Thunderbird headdress in this 1929 photograph. *National Archives of Canada PA 140976*

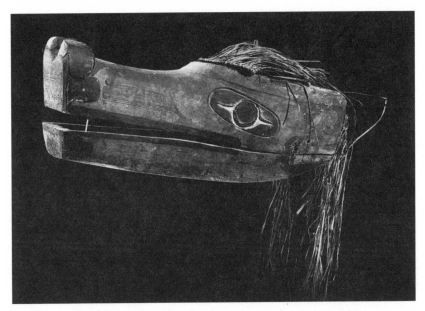

9 Nuu-chah-nulth wolf headdress, of the type used in the *tlukwana* ceremony. *Royal BC Museum CPN10707*

ten days or more, in order to initiate a son, daughter, or other younger relative. Nearly all the people of the village participated in some fashion, many having roles that were hereditary rights. At the beginning of the ritual, as the people were seated for a feast, whistles from the woods signaled the arrival of the Wolves. Men dressed as Wolves burst into the house and abducted the children who were to be initiated (Figure 9). These children were kept in isolation for several days and were then recaptured, "tamed," and restored to human society. The final event was a potlatch, at which the initiates danced to display the ceremonial prerogatives they had received from the Wolves. Elaborate costumes and theatrical illusions enhanced the dance performances, and the entire event was punctuated with feasting and speeches (Ernst 1952; Drucker 1951:386-443; Curtis 1916:68-91; Sapir 1922:320-321; Densmore 1939:102; Moogk 1980).

The technology of the three "Nootkan" groups, like that of all Northwest Coast Aboriginal peoples, relied extensively on the western red cedar. House beams and planks, carved figures, canoes, and boxes were all of cedar, as were most masks, whistles, and other ritual objects. Yellow cedar and alder were also important in various manufactures, and the tough wood of the yew provided spears, paddles, digging sticks, and other implements. Although ethnographic studies list a relatively limited range of woods, analysis of the late precontact material culture at the Makah village of Ozette demonstrates that almost every available species was employed (J. Friedman 1975, 1976).

In addition to wood, the roots, bark, and withes from cedar and other trees were important technological raw materials. Women spent much of their time collecting, preparing, and weaving cedar bark and other materials into a wide range of useful products, such as basketry, matting, blankets, and items of clothing (Drucker 1951:92-99; Sapir 1922:305). Drucker (1951:93) points out that such vital products permeated all stages of Nuu-chah-nulth life, from the shredded cedar bark pads used to clean infants to the cedar bark mats used to wrap the dead. The overwhelming importance of wood, bark, and roots in the technology is, unfortunately, reflected in the archaeological record only at the few waterlogged sites known in the area. At all other archaeological sites, factors of preservation have removed most of the material culture that once existed, leaving only such remnants as sharpened slivers of bone that were once parts of composite fishing gear.

Although ethnographic studies have provided a fairly detailed picture of traditional Nuu-chah-nulth culture, they have to be used with caution. Numerous differences existed between the various Nuu-chah-nulth, Ditidaht, and Makah communities, and even between families in the same village. Differing beliefs and behaviours attributable to rank and gender distinctions are also minimized in these normative descriptions. Furthermore, they present an idealized account of cultural practices, largely ignoring exceptions or variations in behaviour. The late date at which this information was collected means that it refers primarily to the mid-nineteenth century and cannot be extended uncritically to earlier periods. Practices documented ethnographically may reflect historic adaptations to declining populations and the European presence, while many earlier traits may have been abandoned and forgotten. The accuracy of the ethnographic record can now be evaluated only through archaeological research, which also provides the synchronic ethnographic picture with a temporal perspective.

The Nuu-chah-nulth of Barkley Sound: The Toquaht and Their Neighbours

Barkley Sound may have supported one of the densest populations in Nuu-chah-nulth territory. This, at least, was the opinion of the Spanish officers of the Eliza expedition, who explored Barkley Sound in 1791 and expressed the opinion that the villages they observed "contained more Indians than Nuca [Nootka] and Clayocuat [Clayoquot]" (Wagner 1933:149). Spanish chroniclers over the next several years estimated the population of Barkley Sound to be more than 8,500 people, compared to 4,000 at Nootka Sound (Boyd 1990:145). By the mid-nineteenth century five major groups – the Toquaht (*T'ukw'aa7atḥ*), Ucluelet (*Yuulhuu7ilh7atḥ*), Tseshaht (*Ts'ishaa7atḥ*), Huu-ay-aht[7] (*HuuẒii7atḥ*), and Uchucklesaht (*Huuchukwtlis7atḥ*) – shared the

---

7 Formerly known as Ohiaht, the spelling of this name was officially changed in 1996.

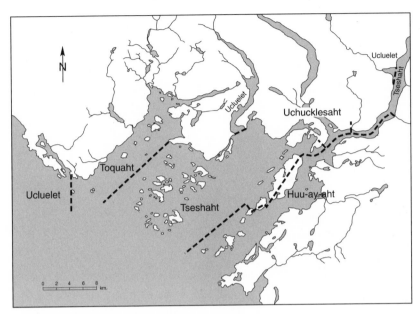

Map 3 Barkley Sound, showing nineteenth-century Nuu-chah-nulth group territories (after St. Claire 1991:175).

sound and its resources (Map 3). Unlike more northerly areas, no single polity dominated the entire sound. Each of the five groups maintained distinct and jealously guarded territories, with clearly established boundaries.

The islands and shoreline of Barkley Sound fall within the Estevan Coastal Plain, a comparatively low-lying strip of outer coast immediately backed by the rugged topography of the Vancouver Island Range (Figure 10). Numerous islands dot the sound, the main concentrations being the Broken Group in the central area and the Deer Group along the eastern edge. Steep-sided inlets extend from the upper sound far into the mountainous interior of Vancouver Island; the most extensive, Alberni Inlet, reaches about 40 km into the centre of the island. The lush, predominantly coniferous, forest that covers the land is sustained by the rainy climate, which provides an average annual precipitation of over 300 cm (Canada, Atmospheric Environment Service 1982). Winters are relatively warm and wet, with much of the annual rainfall occurring during that time. Snowfall occurs on average only about six days per year.

Recent oral history research in Barkley Sound has involved interviews with contemporary elders and has focused particular attention on such topics as place names, site usage, territorial boundaries, and group composition. Place name research has been particularly fruitful, with nearly 700 Nuu-chah-nulth names recorded for Barkley Sound locations (Inglis and Haggarty 1986:112). Studies of place names allow insight into how Aboriginal

10   Aerial view of Barkley Sound, with the islands of the Broken Group in the foreground and the mountains of Vancouver Island in the background. *Royal BC Museum PN17844-15A*

occupants perceived their landscape as well as providing specific details of site and resource use.

The central sound, including the islands of the Broken Group and the upper shoreline, is the traditional territory of the Tseshaht (Map 3). Numerous large shell midden sites in the protected setting of the Broken Group attest to the density of past occupations. By the time the ethnographic descriptions were collected, the Tseshaht also controlled most of Alberni Inlet and the lower Alberni Valley, including the rich salmon fishery of the Somass River. To the east are the Huu-ay-aht, who formerly held the entire eastern shoreline of the sound and the adjacent islands of the Deer Group. Uchucklesaht territory is also on the eastern sound, although by the Historic Period this had been reduced to Henderson Lake, Uchucklesit Inlet, and the adjacent portion of Alberni Inlet.

The western Barkley Sound groups are the Toquaht and Ucluelet. The traditional territory of the latter lay primarily outside the sound, in Ucluelet Inlet and along the outer coast. In the wars of the nineteenth century, however, they conquered additional territories, including Effingham Inlet in the northern sound and the mouth of the Nahmint River, off Alberni Inlet (Map 3). The quest for Nahmint River salmon and other seasonal resources required travel right across the sound. Toquaht traditional territory encompasses all of the western sound, including Toquart Bay and Mayne Bay. The Toquart and Maggie Rivers are also included, with the former having major fishing locations a considerable distance upriver. Smaller rivers and creeks

11 The boundary rock between Ucluelet and Toquaht territories, located near the site of T'ukw'aa, at the entrance to Ucluelet Inlet. *Photo by author*

also support important salmon runs. Several clusters of small islands provide some protection for the few major village sites, but much of the coastline is exposed to winter storms. As this area lacks the resource diversity and abundance of sheltered locations characteristic of the Broken Group Islands to the east, it has a much lower site density.

At the western edge of Toquaht territory, a short distance into Ucluelet Inlet, a prominent white-faced bluff marks the boundary with the Ucluelet (Figure 11). From there the boundary line ran out to the open ocean through the George Fraser Islands. These islands, ethnographically the location of a Toquaht whaling village, were shared with the Ucluelet (Blenkinsop 1874:33). On the east, Lyall Point forms the boundary with the Tseshaht. Even as late as 1874, however, Blenkinsop described the "dispute and contention" over this boundary (St. Claire 1991:55, 167). From there the boundary extended out to sea, cutting through the middle of Hankin Island at the western edge of the Broken Group. Such precisely demarcated territorial boundaries were a characteristic feature of Nuu-chah-nulth concepts of exclusive rights to lands and resources.

By the latter half of the nineteenth century a sixth Nuu-chah-nulth group was making seasonal use of the sound and its resources. This was the Hupacasath[8] (*Hup'ach'is7ath*), an amalgamation of several local groups

8 Formerly known as Opetchesaht, the spelling of this name was officially changed in 1997.

occupying the lakes and rivers of the Alberni Valley. Their ancestors were apparently Salishan-speaking, prior to the late prehistoric or early historic movement of Tseshaht subgroups up Alberni Inlet (McMillan and St. Claire 1982:13-16; St. Claire 1991:76-81). By the late nineteenth century the Hupacasath and Tseshaht were highly intermarried and lived in nearby communities in the lower Alberni Valley. The lucrative late nineteenth-century trade for dogfish and seal oil provided at least part of the incentive for Hupacasath movement into the sound. In 1869, Reverend J.X. Willemar lamented the disappearance of all the Native groups from around the mission at Alberni, stating: "Even the Opee-shesh-aht [Hupacasath] tribe, who have never been known to leave except for hunting deer in the interior, have given up their usual occupation and gone down to the coast in order to catch seals and make oil" (Willemar 1870). They had no established territories in the sound, and the reserve commissioner (O'Reilly 1883) did not assign them any reserves in this area.

By the mid-nineteenth century, all the Barkley Sound groups, with the possible exception of the Toquaht and the Uchucklesaht, were amalgamations of formerly autonomous local groups. Ethnographic accounts describe these late post-amalgamation societies. The Tseshaht consolidation continued into the late nineteenth century, when the Ekoolthaht (*Hikwuulh7ath*) of the upper sound joined their more populous neighbours (Blenkinsop 1874:41; St. Claire 1991:37-38). The territories of these amalgamated Barkley Sound groups shifted over time, as larger and more powerful groups seized valuable resource areas. Small groups, such as the Toquaht and the Uchucklesaht, may have held more extensive territories prior to the amalgamation and territorial expansion of their neighbours. These historic developments are discussed further in Chapter 6.

Several lines of evidence suggest that the Toquaht were once a large and dominant group in Barkley Sound. There is a tradition that they were the original Barkley Sound group, from which sprang all the others (Sproat 1868:19; St. Claire 1991:53). Their dominant position is also suggested by the location of T'ukw'aa, their major village, with its prominent steep-sided fortress controlling the entrance to Ucluelet Inlet. Bert Mack, the hereditary Toquaht chief, was told by his father that, prior to the formation of modern-day Ucluelet (through amalgamation), the Toquaht had protected the people of Ucluelet Inlet. In addition to dominating the Ucluelet Inlet groups, the Toquaht also held drift rights, from the surf line seaward, to the entire outer coast of the Ucluth Peninsula – all ethnographically Ucluelet territory. A Toquaht family apparently resided in one of the outer coast Ucluelet villages to watch out for Toquaht drift rights, quickly sending word when anything important was sighted, for once it reached the beach it was Ucluelet property. Such an arrangement also suggests that, prior to their near-disappearance during the catastrophic events of the early Historic Period, the Toquaht were the major political force in western Barkley Sound.

The Toquaht serve as a specific example at many points in this study, which strongly features the results of research conducted as part of the Toquaht Archaeological Project (see Chapter 3). Ethnographic and ethnohistoric information collected during that research greatly enhance the archaeological data. In addition, historic forces that affected the Toquaht feature prominently in the events described in Chapter 6. In their historic reduction by warfare and disease, the Toquaht illustrate processes that affected the broader Nuu-chah-nulth world.

2
Differing Approaches to the Nuu-chah-nulth Past

A considerable body of ethnohistoric and ethnographic data documents the recent Nuu-chah-nulth past. For earlier periods, however, the record is comparatively meagre. Archaeological research came late to the Nuu-chah-nulth area and even now provides only an incomplete picture. Many earlier studies relied on comparative analyses of ethnographic traits in order to place the Nuu-chah-nulth within broad models of the emergence of Northwest Coast cultures. Linguists have also played a major role in developing models of the origins and migrations of Northwest Coast cultures. More recently, biological anthropology and molecular biology have contributed new insights, particularly with regard to demonstrating genetic relationships between groups. For more recent periods, historians have examined and assessed the written observations of European explorers and settlers, thus providing vital insights into the changing nature of Native cultures following contact. Oral traditions of the Nuu-chah-nulth, Ditidaht, and Makah peoples add their own unique flavour to the study of this region's ancient inhabitants, providing rich detail to augment the meagre remains recovered by archaeologists and the limited information contained in early historic documents. Each of these diverse sources of knowledge provides unique insights into the past.

Oral Histories
Sharply differing views of the past are commonly held by archaeologists and Native groups. On the one hand, archaeologists have been preoccupied with determining the origins of Northwest Coast peoples and the development of various traits that characterize the ethnographic cultures; on the other hand, Native groups, through their oral traditions, perceive a past in which their ancestors have always been part of the land they presently occupy. Oral histories of the remote past refer to a time, prior to the arrival of powerful transformers who put all living creatures and many prominent features of the landscape into their present form, when humans and animals were not separate.

Edward Sapir (1959:106) noted the difference in Nuu-chah-nulth oral traditions between myths and legends, stating that the Nuu-chah-nulth

distinguish very strictly between myths proper and legends. Both are believed to be true, but the myths go back to a misty past in which the world wore a very different aspect from its familiar appearance of today. They go back to a time when animals were human beings, to be later transformed into the creatures we know, and the tribes of men had not yet settled in their historic places nor started upon their appointed tasks. The legends, on the other hand, deal with supposedly historic characters of human kind, are definitely localized, and connect directly with the tribes of today and what is of ceremonial or social importance to them. A myth ... is no one's special property. It may be told by anyone and is generally known to a large number. A legend, however, is family property. Only those may tell it who have an inherited right to it, who trace descent ... from the hero of the legend, the ancestor who has met one or more supernatural beings, has gained "power" from them, and has bequeathed to his descendants not only this "power" but a number of privileges, such as names, songs, and dances, which derive from the ancestral experiences.

Franz Boas (1974:159-160), working in the late nineteenth century with Tseshaht and Hupacasath informants in the Alberni area, collected a typical example of a Nuu-chah-nulth origin myth:

In the beginning only the ky'aimi'mit,[1] birds and other animals lived on the earth. They knew that they would one day be transformed into people and actual animals. Now when the rumour went round that two men, called kwe'kustEpsEp (the transformers), had descended from the sky and would transform them, they called a council to talk the matter over. A'tucmit, the Deer, said, "When they come and want to transform me, I'll kill them. I'm not afraid." He picked up a couple of seashells and sharpened them on the beach on a stone. While he was thus engaged he saw two people approach who looked just like his neighbours. They asked, "What are you doing there, A'tucmit?" He answered, "I'm making daggers for myself in order to kill them when they arrive." "Whom?" they queried. "The transformers, when they eventually come," replied Deer. "You've chosen really nice shells, let's have a look at them," they continued. When A'tucmit handed them over, they struck his forehead with them and shouted, "They shall always stay on your forehead, this one here and that one there! Now shake your head!" He had to obey. "Now once more," they called. After he had shaken his head

---

1 The translation of this term is not clear in the Boas manuscript, but in this context it refers to the animal people who occupied the world until the transformers arrived to create the animals that exist today.

for the second time the shells were transformed into antlers. Then they ordered him to prop his hands on the ground and smeared his rear-end with the dust which he had ground off the shells. Then they told him to run into the woods and he became a Deer. Then the transformers went to the village and changed all the inhabitants into animals and birds. The Land-otter had a long spear, the Beaver a long broad bone-knife and they fashioned them tails from these.

When the animals had thus come into being, the people came into the world, one couple in every village. The transformers created them and said, "Mankind shall speak different languages. Some tribes shall become powerful, others shall remain weak. We will give people everything they need: berries, clams and fish."

A similar version of this story was collected by Sapir from Tseshaht informants several decades later (Sapir and Swadesh 1939:45-51).

Stories of how the world was put into its present order varied along the west coast. Among the Barkley Sound groups, Kwatyat was the transformer and culture hero. He was said "to have been the creator of all things and to have had the power of transforming himself into anything" (Sapir and Swadesh 1939:217). Very similar stories were told among the Makah, where the trickster figure was called Kwahtie (Swan 1870:64). It was Kwahtie who arranged the present landscape, stealing the daylight from its owner and timing the tides so that people could gather shellfish (Colson 1953:47). Much later, another powerful transformer came along and changed all the people he met into animals. In some versions of the stories, Kwahtie was changed into a mink and, in this guise, continues to play his tricks.

Among the northern Nuu-chah-nulth, Kwatyat played a buffoon's role, while Andaokot was the primary transformer and culture hero (Drucker 1951:452). Also known as Mucus-Made or Snot Boy (Arima 1983:50), Andaokot was formed of the droppings from his mother's nose as she sobbed over having lost her child to a supernatural being. Growing rapidly to adulthood, Andaokot overcame the creature that had taken the children from the village and restored them to life. He eventually climbed on a chain of arrows to the sky world, where he received powers and instructions to return to Earth to transform all things into their present state (Arima 1983:50-54, 180-187; Boas 1916:903-913; 1974:188-192).

Such myths situate the people in their landscape and reaffirm their ancient connection with the land. Looking around their territory they can see prominent features that mark the transformer's exploits. An example is the story of Kwatyat and the Wolves, told to Sapir by a Tseshaht informant (Sapir and Swadesh 1939:33-34; Thomas and Arima 1970:15-19). After killing the Wolf chief, Kwatyat was forced to flee. When the Wolves were nearly upon him, Kwatyat set his comb in the ground, commanding it to become a mountain between him and his pursuers. When they again came close, Kwatyat poured some oil out of his pouch and it became a big lake, blocking his pursuers' path and allowing him to escape. When this story was told to Boas at Alberni late in the nineteenth century, it was specifically noted that the lakes and mountains formed by Kwatyat "can still be seen today between Sproat Lake and the central part of Alberni Canal" (Boas 1974:161). Similarly, in a modern retelling of this story, Hupquatchew (Ron Hamilton), a Hupacasath artist and writer, specifically links Kwatyat's flight with the creation of the Beaufort Range and the two large lakes, Sproat and Great Central, in the Alberni Valley (Hupquatchew 1981). Far to the south, Swan (1870:64-65) was told a version of this story by the Makah, who trace the origins of the Flattery Rocks and the Strait of Juan de Fuca to this mythic event.

Other stories were prized possessions of chiefly families. These stories traced people's origins, often from supernatural forces, and the history of how their ancestors acquired powers and associated privileges (such as names and songs) through encounters with supernatural beings (Golla 1987:85; Drucker 1951:157-161). Such stories, meant to be told verbatim, recount family histories in a Nuu-chah-nulth social context; they are, in Golla's (1991:108) words, "testaments in the native voice." Group names, founding histories, and traditions of remote times all reinforced the ties between the Nuu-chah-nulth and their physical and social landscape.

Several locations in Toquaht territory feature prominently in the oral traditions. According to Sproat (1868:19), Kwatyat (which he rendered as "Quawteaht"), during his time on Earth, lived at the Toquart River. In mythic times, Macoah, the main ethnographic Toquaht village, was the home of the Wolves (Sapir and Swadesh 1939:24-26; Thomas and Arima 1970:9-14). This is where the Thunderbirds went to play the hoop game, in which they were defeated by Kwatyat's tricks (Sapir and Swadesh 1939:51). After a dispute with the Thunderbirds, Kwatyat took revenge. He destroyed three of the four Thunderbirds by entering a vessel in the form of a whale and luring them from their mountaintop home, dragging them underwater and drowning them in Alberni Inlet, in the land of the Uchucklesahts (Sproat 1868:177-178; Carmichael 1922:29-30). The rocks in front of the site of T'ukw'aa are said to be the remains of this vessel, transformed by Kwatyat (Boas 1974:169-170). When the great flood covered the Earth, the Toquaht sought refuge on the large mountain called Quossakt, whose peak was one of the few places above the waters (Sproat 1868:184). A large rock in the intertidal zone at Toquart Bay is today known as *T'ikwuusim*, "an anchor," where the Toquaht tied their canoes with long ropes during the flood (St. Claire 1991:164; McMillan and St. Claire 1991:48). This association of modern landscape features with the beings and events of mythic traditions serves as a constant reinforcement of Toquaht identity and ancient ties to the land.

Other oral traditions are more straightforward historical narratives set in more recent times, describing wars, alliances, and other social and political events. Some traditions describe territorial changes, usually through conquest. Most involve internecine warfare among Nuu-chah-nulth groups, but some refer to Nuu-chah-nulth or Makah expansion at the expense of their neighbours. A specific example of such a historical narrative, recounting the events of the nineteenth-century "Long War" in Barkley Sound, is given in Chapter 6.

Historical Linguistics

Linguistic Models of Wakashan Origins and Expansion

Historical linguistics provides an important analytical framework from within which to assess prehistoric population movements. It provides insights that cannot be directly derived from archaeology, even where data are available. On the Northwest Coast, particular attention has been given to the Salishan-speakers, with their widespread distribution on the southern coast and in the interior plateau. Such noted anthropologists as Franz Boas (1905:96) and Alfred Kroeber (1923:17) had long maintained that the Salish were late arrivals to the coast from the interior. To counter these long-standing beliefs, Suttles and Elmendorf (1963; see also Suttles 1987a, 1987b) used linguistic data to argue that Salish origins were, in fact, coastal, with a later movement inland. They pointed to the greater variability in the coastal languages and postulated a formerly continuous distribution of Salishan-speakers along the coast as far north as the Nuxalk (formerly known as the Bella Coola) in the Bella Coola Valley. Such analysis suggested that the Salish homeland was around the lower Fraser River (Suttles 1987a:260; Jorgensen 1969:23; Thompson and Kinkade 1990:45), possibly extending as far south as the Skagit River (Kinkade 1991:148) or the southern end of Puget Sound (Suttles and Elmendorf 1963:45; Suttles 1987b:277).

As the immediate neighbours of the Salish, the Wakashans also figured prominently in these schemes. The proto-Wakashan homeland has been thought to encompass northern Vancouver Island (Kinkade and Powell 1976; Jacobsen 1979; Thompson and Kinkade 1990; Foster 1996). In their eventual expansion from that base, the northern (or Kwakiutlan) branch took much of the adjacent mainland coast, displacing or absorbing northern members of the Salishan continuum and isolating the Nuxalk from all other Salishan-speakers (Thompson and Kinkade 1990:47; Swadesh 1949:166). Around the same time, in this model, the southern (or Nootkan) branch moved down the west coast of Vancouver Island, ultimately reaching the northern Olympic Peninsula.

Using a somewhat different approach, Kinkade (1991) recently offered a variant of this established model. He states that it "seems fairly clear" that the Wakashans once occupied all of Vancouver Island and the south-central British Columbia coast (1991:151). His analysis of Salishan vocabulary reveals proto-Salishan words for animal species that do not occur on Vancouver Island, thus, in his opinion, "excluding Vancouver Island from the Salishan homeland" (1991:147). Similarly, his review of Nuxalk vocabulary indicates that names for typical coastal flora and fauna are borrowings from Wakashan, suggesting that the Nuxalk were, in fact, of interior origin (1991:149). He concludes that the Wakashans, in much of their former distribution, "were supplanted by Salishans moving north and by Bella Coolas moving across from the interior" (1991:151). Although an intriguing suggestion, this viewpoint provides a poor fit with the archaeological data and illustrates the equivocal nature of models drawn on linguistic data alone.

Sapir (1916), in his pioneering work in historical linguistics, proposed two principles for drawing inferences about the history of a group of related languages from their distribution. The first, the "greatest diversity" principle, asserts that linguistic differentiation increases with time, making the area with greatest linguistic diversity the original homeland; the second, the "centre of gravity" principle, asserts that the deepest cleavage between related languages will mark the homeland. Suttles (1987b), while challenging the inevitability of the first principle, used Sapir's methodology to argue for a coastal homeland for the Salish. Although the Wakashans lack the range of languages and the widespread territory of the Salishans, these principles could also be applied to them. Certainly the deepest cleavage in the Wakashan family is between the two major branches, Kwakiutlan and Nootkan, whose relationship is considered to be rather remote (Sapir 1911:15; Thompson and Kinkade 1990:39). Both branches have their greatest diversity near this split, as both the Nuu-chah-nulth and Kwakwaka'wakw have languages containing a series of dialects, while the other Kwakiutlan and Nootkan languages are more uniform. Both the "centre of gravity" and the "greatest diversity" criteria could then be interpreted as suggesting that the northern or northwestern portion of Vancouver Island was the original Wakashan homeland.

Some archaeologists have embraced these linguistic models and used them to interpret their own work. Mitchell (1990), for example, has argued that two distinct cultures once occupied the southern coast of British Columbia, the ancestral Wakashans along the west coast of Vancouver Island and the ancestral Salishans along the protected waterways of Puget Sound, the Strait of Georgia, and Queen Charlotte Strait. The Wakashans then expanded from the northern portion of their homeland into Queen Charlotte Strait and northward, absorbing or displacing Salishan-speakers and isolating the Nuxalk. He supports this linguistic model with archaeological evidence that suggests a population replacement in Queen Charlotte Strait around 500 BC. Similarly, Hobler (1990) adopts the Suttles and Elmendorf (1963) model of a continuous distribution of Salishan-speakers to the Bella Coola Valley, broken by an expansion of Wakashans from northern Vancouver Island. Examining his archaeological data from the Bella Coola Valley, he suggests that such population dislocations may be reflected in archaeological discontinuities around 2500 BC and in subsequent changes to about AD 1 (Hobler 1990:305).

Analysis of vocabulary, as Kinkade (1991) has shown for the Salish, provides evidence of the original environment and core elements of the culture that can be used to reconstruct ancestral homelands. No equivalent study exists for the Nuu-chah-nulth. Long ago, however, Sapir (1912:228) pointed out the extensive Nuu-chah-nulth vocabulary relating to various species of marine animals, and this suggests a long period of adaptation to the outer coast. Sapir (1912:238-239) also noted the common use of suffixes relating to potlatching, feasting, and gift-giving at girls' puberty ceremonies, claiming that this demonstrated the fundamental importance of such institutions in Nuu-chah-nulth culture.

Linguistic and Oral History Evidence for Territorial Shifts
Linguistic studies and oral histories also contain evidence of territorial shifts over time. A good example is the late arrival in the Alberni Valley of the Tseshaht from Barkley Sound. This event is well recorded in oral traditions and the ethnographic literature (Sproat 1868:179; Boas 1891:584; Carmichael 1922:51-64; Drucker 1950:157, 1951:5; McMillan and St. Claire 1982:14; St. Claire 1991:79-81). The ancestors of the Hupacasath, an amalgamation of three formerly separate local groups in the Alberni Valley, were apparently Salishan-speaking prior to the arrival of the Tseshaht. Boas (1891:584; 1974:208) reported informants who maintained that their grandfathers spoke only Nanaimo, a dialect of Halkomelem. Sapir's informants also claimed that some Hupacasath spoke a Coast Salish language until quite recent times (Sapir 1910-1914; St. Claire 1991:76), although Sapir related this language to the now extinct Pentlatch, another Salishan language of eastern Vancouver Island. In describing a girl's puberty ceremony, he stated that her original name was "apparently one of the stock of Coast Salish names that are current among the Hopatch'asath, who, according to reliable evidence, once spoke a now extinct Salish language" (Sapir 1913:77). In a later publication, Sapir (1915:19) described a unique linguistic trait (the confounding of "s" and "c" sounds) in Hupacasath, attributing this to "the fact that they carried over into Nootka speech a linguistic peculiarity found in the Salish dialect which they originally spoke."

Nuu-chah-nulth territory may have once extended somewhat further to the north. Boas (1891:608) recorded a tradition from the Kwakwaka'wakw of Quatsino Sound that describes the expulsion of the Nuu-chah-nulth from the region south of Quatsino Inlet. Galois (1994:347, 363) attributes this

Kwakwa̱ka'wakw expansion to the Klaskino and points to a Nuu-chah-nulth place name for the origin point of one of the Klaskino subgroups. The Klaskino are characterized by Drucker (1950:158) as a bilingual "mixed Kwakiutl and Nootkan" group.

As a third example, at the southern end of "Nootkan" distribution, Kinkade and Powell (1976) have argued that, according to linguistics, the Makah are relatively recent arrivals on the Olympic Peninsula. In earlier times, at least the northern portion of the Olympic Peninsula seems to have been the homeland of Chimakuan peoples, who are represented historically only by the Quileute (south of the Makah on the outer coast) and the now extinct Chemakum (at the northeastern end of the peninsula adjoining Puget Sound) (Curtis 1913; Kinkade and Powell 1976; Elmendorf 1990:438). The geographic separation of these two related languages carries obvious implications for the culture history of this region. Kinkade and Powell (1976) point out that a number of place names for significant features of the landscape, used by both the Makah and the Quileute, have Chimakuan origins. They also note the lack of strong differentiation between the Quileute and Chemakum languages, which indicates that these two groups had been separated by Makah intrusion in relatively recent times. Swadesh (1955:60) estimated a separation of twenty-one centuries between Quileute and Chemakum. Such glottochronological dates, however, are notoriously unreliable and, in any case, this need not refer directly to the arrival of the Makah. Kinkade and Powell propose that the Makah occupation of the Olympic Peninsula occurred about AD 1000, although the evidence for this specific date seems inconclusive at best. Wessen (1990:421), in reviewing the archaeology of this area, cautions that there is no evidence for such population replacement that late in the archaeological record. Whaling and fur sealing, long associated with the Makah, have much greater time depths on the Olympic Peninsula.

The Ditidaht may also have been relatively recent arrivals in their territory. According to an oral tradition told to anthropologists Mary Haas and Morris Swadesh in 1931, the Ditidaht originally stem from a group of people occupying Tatoosh Island off Cape Flattery (Clamhouse et al. 1991:288; Inglis and Haggarty 1986:200). Ditidaht Ernie Chester also recounted this story to Ann Bates (1987:293-294), although in his version only some of the Ditidaht ancestors arrived in this fashion. After a battle with the inhabitants of Ozette, the Tatoosh Island people moved across the Strait of Juan de Fuca and settled around the Jordan River, now in Pacheedaht territory near the boundary with the Salishan-speaking Sooke. There they lived for a long time, taking their name, *Diitiid7aa7tx̱*, from the name of the Jordan River, *Diitiida* (Bouchard and Kennedy 1991:3; Clamhouse et al. 1991:285). Continuous hostilities with their Salishan-speaking neighbours, the Sooke and the Clallam, eventually led them to abandon these lands and move north along the coast. They settled in a number of villages around Nitinat Lake, including the important fortress of Whyac at the lake's outlet. They remained a cluster of separate local groups, not coalescing into the modern Ditidaht band until, in the twentieth century, declining populations forced them to amalgamate.

Oral traditions tell of continued hostilities between the Ditidaht and the Makah. They maintain that at one time the Cape Flattery area was held by the Ditidaht and that it was forcibly seized by the Makah, who had been living in their more southerly villages (Irvine 1922). The Makah also defeated the Ditidaht in their own territory, taking possession of Nitinat Lake for the rich salmon fishery in the local rivers. The Ditidaht were scattered, many going to live with their relatives among the Pacheedaht. The Makah held the lake for a long time, assigning their own place names throughout the area (Clamhouse et al. 1991:299-309; Inglis and Haggarty 1986:204). Finally, the Ditidaht and Pacheedaht defeated the Makah and the Ditidaht reclaimed their territory.

The Pacheedaht (*Paachiid7aa7tx̱*) may have had different origins. Chief Peter of the Pacheedaht told Swadesh in 1931 that in earlier times they spoke the same Salishan language as did their Sooke neighbours (Clamhouse et al. 1991:289; Inglis and Haggarty 1986:215). Intermarriage with the Ditidaht led to the Pacheedaht adopting the Ditidaht language sometime prior to contact with Europeans.[2] They remained a component group of the Ditidaht for a considerable time before becoming politically separate. They took their name from a word meaning "sea foam," after great quantities of this material once appeared in their river (Jones and Bosustow 1981:21-22; Inglis and Haggarty 1986:214).

These traditions suggest that, until a relatively late period, Vancouver Island south of Barkley Sound was held by Salishan-speakers and that the northern Olympic Peninsula was home to Chimakuans. This may have lasted until roughly a thousand years ago, when Kinkade and Powell (1976) estimate the Makah arrived on the Olympic Peninsula. Despite the highly speculative nature of such dates, this corresponds with a linguistic estimate of about 1,000 years for the separation of Ditidaht and Makah (Jacobsen 1979:776). If the Ditidaht-Makah separation occurred when the Cape Flattery people moved to the Jordan River to become the Ditidaht, then we can roughly date this event. The Ditidaht movement around the still-Salish ancestors of the Pacheedaht to settle at Nitinat Lake occurred sometime later, as did intermarriage with the Pacheedaht and their absorption into Ditidaht culture. Arima (1988:23; Arima et al. 1991:289) speculates that it was the effective open-ocean technology, particularly with the development

---

2 This process is apparently still continuing. Bates (1987:128) notes that so many Ditidaht women have married into the Sooke band that the Sooke now speak Ditidaht as well as Sooke.

of whaling, that enabled the Ditidaht and Makah expansion. At present, however, the archaeological research required to assess these ideas is almost totally lacking in Ditidaht and Pacheedaht territories.

In summary, oral traditions and linguistic evidence suggest that, in early times, "West Coast" territory extended from slightly north of present distribution to somewhere around Barkley Sound. Later migrations took the ancestors of the Ditidaht and Makah south on Vancouver Island and to the Olympic Peninsula. The Tseshaht expansion from Barkley Sound into Alberni Inlet and the lower Alberni Valley took place even later, perhaps about the time of European contact. This information is in accord with linguistic suggestions of a Wakashan homeland on northern Vancouver Island, with a spread of the Nootkan branch south along Vancouver Island's west coast, leaving a string of dialects through Nuu-chah-nulth territory and a separate southern division that later split into two closely related languages.

Anthropological Theories
Prior to the availability of archaeological data, speculations on Nuu-chah-nulth culture history had to be drawn from ethnographic traditions or from distribution studies of material culture items. In an early example of the latter type of analysis, Ronald Olson (1927) concluded that the "Nootka" were the probable originators of such important Northwest Coast traits as the ocean-going "Nootka-style" canoe and the D-shaped adze. Later, Philip Drucker (1955a:79; 1955b:198) credited the Wakashans with the development of the D-shaped adze, the curved halibut hook, end-thrown sea-hunting harpoons with finger-holes or rests, sealskin floats for sea mammal hunting, the ritual use of human corpses and skeletons, and the development of the dancing societies and the elaborate masks used in rituals. However, Drucker also lamented the lack of archaeological data and the subjective nature of distribution studies: "There is a wealth of ethnographic information available plus a few linguistic and anthropometric data, and only a modicum of cold, hard, archeologic fact to refute one's interpretations ... One is tempted to rely far too heavily on ethnographic distributions in which subjective evaluations must be made ... and, further, arbitrary assumptions must be made as to the significance of those distributions" (Drucker 1955a:59).

Early views on the origins of coastal cultures were permeated with diffusionist and migrationist assumptions. Franz Boas, in his association with the Jesup Expedition, attempted to trace the spread of Asiatic traits around the Pacific littoral and down the Northwest Coast (Boas 1905). Although he felt that the Tsimshian and Salish were recent arrivals from the interior, he was willing to credit the Wakashans with a lengthier heritage on the coast, presumably supplying the model for Salish adaptation to their new environment (Suttles 1987a). Asiatic influences, in his view, continued to shape the development of the Northwest Coast ethnographic pattern until they were cut off by the intrusion of Eskimo-Aleut populations in the Bering Strait region (Drucker 1955a:60; Chard 1960:235; Suttles and Jonaitis 1990:81). Like so many early speculations, such ideas were rendered untenable by subsequent archaeological research (which, in this case, demonstrates considerable antiquity for the Eskimo-Aleut presence).

An alternative theory was that coastal cultures derived from interior groups, which moved down the major rivers to the coast. This idea was expressed in fullest form by Alfred Kroeber (1939:28), who proposed that "Northwest Coast culture was originally a river or river-mouth culture, later a beach culture, and only finally and in part a seagoing one." He pointed to the simpler societies found inland, along the Fraser and Columbia River drainages, as the logical prototypes for Northwest Coast cultures. Although crediting the northern coastal tribes with the "culture climax" in historic times, he thought that previously the Wakashans may have had the most developed cultures. He also speculated that in earliest times, as cultures emerged from the rivers to an ocean environment, the climax may have been centred around the mouth of the Fraser River (Kroeber 1939:30).

To assess these competing theories anthropologists sought the "earliest" and "purest" coastal cultures so that they could reconstruct the original form. These early speculative models prominently featured the Nuu-chah-nulth and their relatives. Looking at their relatively isolated location and lack of what he considered "interior cultural traits," Drucker regarded the Wakashans as "the most typical coastal peoples" (1955a:69), "the purest strain of Coast culture," and "the oldest strain of Northwest Coast civilization" (1955a:76). Borden (1951:39) referred to the Nuu-chah-nulth as "the Indians who have lived longest on the coast," while Gunther (1960:270) described them as "the base from which all coast cultures began." Such assessments of the Nuu-chah-nulth stress their perceived isolation and their marginality with regard to later developments on the coast. The emphasis was on their conservatism, as the Nuu-chah-nulth were believed to have retained most completely the basic form of the original coastal adaptation.

It was Nuu-chah-nulth whaling that attracted particular anthropological attention. Of all historic Northwest Coast peoples, only the Nuu-chah-nulth, Ditidaht, Makah, Quileute, and Quinault actively hunted whales, and the latter two groups most likely derived this practice from contact with the Makah. Along the coast to the north the nearest whalers were the Koniaq and Aleut peoples (of Eskimo-Aleut stock) in southern Alaska, and this left a distributional gap that cried out for explanation. In a diffusionist argument characteristic of the time, Lantis (1938) prepared a detailed list of parallels in whaling practices in the two areas and proposed a formerly continuous distribution that was later broken by the arrival of the northern Northwest Coast groups from the interior. The parallels that she noted were not simply technological traits but also such ritual practices as the use of human corpses to obtain supernatural power over the whale. This led Borden (1951:39) to state that the "close similarity" of whaling practices in the two areas "makes the assumption of a historic connection unescapable." He wondered whether "the Nootka found the Eskimo already on the scene upon their arrival on the coast" or if "the Nootka once lived much farther north than they do now" (Borden 1951:41). Swanson (1956) also noted a variety of shared traits between the Nuu-chah-nulth and Eskimoan groups, which led him to debate whether Nuu-chah-nulth whaling was derived from the Aleut and Koniaq of southern Alaska or from Eskimoan groups nearer Bering Strait. Duff (1965) added another aspect to the argument by noting similarities in construction and design between the Nuu-chah-nulth whaling canoe and the Eskimo-Aleut umiak, concluding that the open hide-covered boat was the parent form. Similarly, Suttles (1952) noted the use of a set formula for the division of sea mammal carcasses among the Wakashans, Salish, and Eskimo-Aleut, and he suggested that this reflects an ancient common origin.

Such ideas strongly influenced Borden's interpretations of his pioneering research in the Fraser Delta. Drawing on a presumed cultural continuum between the Nuu-chah-nulth and the Eskimo-Aleut in earlier times, Borden (1951) described the earlier cultures of his emerging Fraser Delta sequence as "Eskimoid," suggesting a common cultural base for much of the Northwest Coast – one that predates the arrival of the Salish from the interior. This view was then expanded by Drucker (1955a:64), who proposed the hypothesis that "the distinctive basic patterns of the Northwest Coast culture, from Yakutat Bay to northwest California, were derived from the same subarctic fishing-and-sea-hunting base of the coasts of Bering Sea and southwest Alaska that gave rise to the various Eskimo and Aleut cultures." Chard (1960) expanded even further the distribution of this proposed fishing and sea mammal hunting base, visualizing "an ancient arc of related culture and population around the entire rim of the North Pacific from Kamchatka to Puget Sound." Characterizing the Wakashans as "the purest and the most specialized Northwest Coast subculture," Drucker (1955a:78) concluded that "the groups of the Northern Province probably emerged on the coast after the Wakashan-speaking groups, and may actually have disrupted lines of communication of the latter with Eskimo-Aleut." The speculation of this early period is perhaps taken furthest by Duff (1965:30), who conjured up the image of "an umiak-borne migration of proto-Eskimo people down the coast."

Interpretations requiring the migration of peoples or the diffusion of cultural traits gradually fell into disfavour, partially because they failed to provide any real explanation of why such events occurred. Instead, many anthropologists shifted their attention to attempting to understand the ecological factors behind the distribution and evolution of cultural traits. Two hypothetical models for the development of Nuu-chah-nulth culture, based primarily on ethnographic data, are discussed below.

The model developed by Langdon (1976) follows the ecological functional school, popularized in the preceding decade by writers such as Suttles (1962, 1968), in that it emphasizes resource variability and occasional shortages as factors that shape cultural development. The potlatch was seen primarily as a mechanism for resource distribution. Similarly, warfare was viewed as a way of keeping populations and resources in balance.

The first of four stages proposed by Langdon was a long period of generalized coastal adaptation, based on fishing and sea mammal hunting. Sea-level stabilization about 5,000 years ago (Fladmark 1975) led to the second stage, which is characterized by increased dietary reliance on salmon and shellfish, semi-sedentary winter villages, modest population growth, and the development of feasting in order to enhance the power of emerging elites and to ensure the labour necessary for the acquisition of adequate supplies of salmon. In the third, or "classic," stage, the potlatch emerged from the feast as a mechanism for validating ownership rights to resource locations. An "ideology of extravagant giving and consumption" was generated, based on extensive resource surpluses and leading to further elaborations in ceremonial life and the power of the chiefly elite. In the fourth and final stage prior to European contact, continued population growth began to tax the energy requirements of this system, and this led to two very different results. In the north, the potlatch took on a unifying function, which resulted in an integrated system of ranking for chiefs and the emergence of confederacies. Among the central and southern groups, culturally induced shortages resulting from ritual consumption and competition led to extensive warfare over resource territories. Langdon views warfare as the "systemic alternative" that allowed such costly displays of chiefly power in ceremonial contexts.

An ecological approach also characterizes Morgan's (1980) study of Nuu-chah-nulth political organization. Donald and Mitchell (1975) had earlier shown that the potlatch rank of each local group among the neighbouring Kwakwaka'wakw ("Southern Kwakiutl") was strongly correlated with their population and the median size of the salmon runs in their territory. Morgan examined whether differential access to salmon could be a key variable in understanding why some Nuu-chah-nulth groups remained independent polities while others formed larger confederacies. Although salmon played a lesser role in the economies of many Nuu-chah-nulth groups than it did in those of the Kwakwaka'wakw, Morgan's analysis suggested that there was a significant relationship between salmon availability and the form of political organization. In general, politically independent winter village groups tended to occur in areas where there were productive salmon streams. Where the salmon resource was less dependable, it was likely that groups would form confederacies and share a common summer village.

Only where a group's population had dropped below levels required for defence and for participation in intergroup potlatching was this political union likely to be voluntary. Like Langdon, Morgan emphasizes the role of warfare in the growth of more complex political units. Rather than exterminating their opponents, militarily successful Nuu-chah-nulth chiefs could accept peace initiatives, usually consolidated through marriage, and absorb other groups, placing them in subordinate positions. In this way, such chiefs gained access not only to additional territory and resources but also to an enlarged pool of labour, which provided them with a military and economic advantage. According to Morgan, this resulted in the emergence of the hierarchically structured polities known ethnographically among the Nuu-chah-nulth.

Significant cultural change is clearly recognized in these ecological models, although the nature of this change was thought to be constrained by environmental variables. The earlier diffusionist models, on the other hand, effectively marginalized the Nuu-chah-nulth, viewing them as an isolated and conservative survival, tenaciously clinging to an earlier way of life. Modern scholars reject such a scenario, viewing whaling and other features of Nuu-chah-nulth culture as indigenous and ingenious adaptations to an open-ocean environment rather than as relic traits associated with a formerly more widespread distribution. Faint echoes of these early interpretations, however, may still reverberate through such modern archaeological constructs as the West Coast culture type, with its emphasis on cultural conservatism and continuity throughout time and its downplaying of change and innovation.

Archaeology

Archaeology, which involves the scientific recovery and interpretation of material remnants of past behaviours, plays a key role in understanding the human past. It has the ability to provide specific dates and a detailed temporal framework for past cultural developments. Such chronological information is largely lacking in oral traditions, which tend to float in time, or in approaches such as historical linguistics, which can provide only vague estimates of time. As it is based on material culture remains, however, archaeology is relatively silent on such important human concerns as beliefs and motives. In addition, the wet coastal climate and the overwhelming predominance of wood and other plant materials in the technology of the coastal peoples have meant that much of the evidence for earlier ways of life has not survived.

Interpretations of the archaeological record may be greatly enhanced by information from other approaches. Archaeology and historical linguistics are particularly compatible, providing different sets of data on past population movements. Anthropological views of cultural development draw on available archaeological data and also suggest ideas that can be investigated by further archaeological research. Increased archaeological knowledge may result in the abandonment of established ideas, as was the case with early diffusionist speculations. Native oral traditions also strongly complement the archaeological data, adding the human and spiritual dimensions to the material remains recovered by archaeologists, although it is only rarely that archaeology can directly confirm the information provided in these traditions. Further archaeological fieldwork will be required in order to address some of the issues raised earlier in this chapter. In particular, speculations based on historical linguistics regarding the nature and timing of population movements throughout Nuu-chah-nulth, Ditidaht, and Makah territories need to be evaluated and refined through additional archaeological research.

The West Coast culture type, the archaeological view of evolving Nuu-chah-nulth culture, was proposed by Mitchell (1990) as part of a broad synthesis of precontact history in southern coastal British Columbia and northern Washington. Excavated data from Yuquot and Hesquiat Harbour, the only major archaeological projects on the west coast of Vancouver Island at that time, provided most of the information on which the West Coast culture type was based. Claims for lengthy human continuity at these sites led Mitchell to propose that Nuu-chah-nulth culture history could be encompassed within a single culture type. In reviewing the archaeological data from these projects, he states that "the archaeological assemblages are so like described Nootkan material culture that a lengthy reconstruction of the technology is not necessary. There are artifacts interpretable as whale, small sea mammal, and salmon harpoons; parts of composite fishhooks; knives suitable for butchering salmon or herring or for preparing other fish and foods; woodworking tools; and tools for shaping the numerous bone implements ... These tools are represented even in the 2800-1200 BC levels at Yuquot Village" (Mitchell 1990:357). Mitchell concludes that the entire archaeological sequence known for the Nuu-chah-nulth area "can be characterized as one of relatively little change in subsistence and other aspects of technology."

Distinguishing features of this culture type are defined almost entirely in terms of artifacts. Mitchell (1990:356) lists the distinctive traits as "ground stone celts; ground stone fishhook shanks; hand mauls; abrasive stones; unilaterally barbed bone points; single barb points; bone fishhook shanks; unilaterally and bilaterally barbed bone nontoggling harpoon heads; bone single points; bone bipoints; large and small composite toggling harpoon valves of bone or antler, small ones with two-piece 'self-armed' variety with ancillary valve; sea mammal bone foreshafts; bone needles; bone splinter awls; ulna tools; whalebone bark beaters; whalebone bark shredders; perforated tooth and deer phalanx pendants; mussel shell celts; and mussel shell knives." The absence or rarity of flaked stone tools and detritus is also seen as an identifying trait. In fact, stone implements in general are relatively rare. The major exception is abrasive stones, which were essential in the technology used to produce the numerous ground bone artifacts found and which probably also served as a vital part of the woodworking toolkit.

Although a strong continuity through time is clearly evident at these sites, placement of the entire 4,200-year sequence into a single culture type, with a single list of identifying features, tends to project an image of an unchanging culture. This masks or minimizes the temporal aspect of Nuu-chah-nulth culture history. As is discussed in the following chapters, gradual changes in artifact forms and settlement patterns can be discerned in the archaeological record for this area. The ahistorical nature of the West Coast culture type regrettably tends to perpetuate the outdated stereotype of the unchanging Native, so strongly challenged by Trigger (1980, 1984, 1985).

The rarity of diagnostic artifacts in West Coast sites also poses a problem for such classification schemes. Most archaeological assemblages, particularly those from the small test excavations, consist primarily of abrasive stones and small bone points; chipped stone points and other diagnostic artifacts used to distinguish culture types in the Strait of Georgia are rare or absent on the west coast of Vancouver Island. Basketry and other perishable materials, in the few locations where these have been preserved, are much more sensitive indicators, providing clearer insights into past cultural change and affiliation than do implements of stone and bone (see, for example, Bernick 1987; Croes 1987, 1988, 1989, 1992). Where such organics are lacking, classifications based on artifacts may not adequately reflect cultural diversity and change.

Although the West Coast culture type was defined almost entirely on data from Yuquot and Hesquiat, it was intended to describe the culture history of the entire west coast of Vancouver Island. More recent excavations in Barkley Sound suggest a somewhat different picture. As is discussed in Chapter 4, the earlier occupation in this area may have involved a culture quite distinct from that of the contemporary inhabitants of Yuquot.

Archaeological research in Nuu-chah-nulth, Ditidaht, and Makah territory is still very limited. Only three geographic clusters of excavated sites exist: at Nootka Sound and adjacent Hesquiat Harbour, at Barkley Sound, and on the Olympic Peninsula. Only at Hesquiat Harbour and western Barkley Sound has a significant sample been excavated from the total number of archaeological sites in the region. Even in these better known areas, information is very limited, particularly for the crucial early period. Excavated data are particularly lacking for the area north of Nootka Sound and for the coastline of Vancouver Island south of Barkley Sound, in Ditidaht and Pacheedaht territory. These are crucial areas for assessing ideas about past population movements (such as those suggested by historical linguistics). The following chapter reviews the archaeological research that has been carried out in the territories of the Nuu-chah-nulth, Ditidaht, and Makah people, and it discusses the nature and limitations of the current archaeological record.

3
Archaeological Research in Nuu-chah-nulth Territory

Introduction

Prior to 1966, the west coast of Vancouver Island was virtually an archaeological terra incognita. In that year, the large-scale excavation at Yuquot in Nootka Sound began. At the same time, the large test trench through the Ozette village midden on the Olympic Peninsula initiated major archaeological work in Makah territory. Despite the considerable amount of archaeological fieldwork that has followed these projects, large areas of Nuu-chah-nulth, Ditidaht, and Makah territory remain uninvestigated. This chapter reviews the archaeological research that has been conducted and summarizes the current state of our knowledge.

In 1982, when Haggarty and Inglis (1983a) collated the distribution of Nuu-chah-nulth archaeological sites and their broad environmental settings, a total of 270 sites had been recorded. This number was swelled greatly by the rapid increase in archaeological fieldwork in the 1980s. By mid-1995, the recorded site inventory for western Vancouver Island (Nuu-chah-nulth and Ditidaht territories) had risen to 1,264. When separated by site types, the total increases to 1,536, as several different categories might be included under the same site number. Table 1 shows the site totals, classified by type, for this area.[1] Habitation sites, the vast majority of which are shell middens, account for 693, or about 45.1 percent, of this total. At least thirty-four of these are located on steep-sided headlands or islets, presumably serving as fortifications during times of hostilities or as lookouts for migratory sea mammals. Intertidal petroforms, with most identified as rock-wall fish traps or canoe skids, form another common category. Aboriginal burial sites are most commonly found in caves or rockshelters, but tree burials and canoe burials as well as historic cemeteries are also reported. Most of the "surface lithic scatters" were recorded in the lower Alberni Valley and may not be

1 Site inventory data came from site records in the Canadian Heritage Information Network (CHIN) system. The results of a computer search of the relevant areas were provided by the Archaeology Branch, Victoria. This information reflects the site files as they existed in August 1995.

Table 1

Site inventory totals for the west coast of Vancouver Island (ethnographic Nuu-chah-nulth and Ditidaht territories), 1995

Site type	Number
Habitation sites	693
Fish traps, canoe skids, other petroforms	266
CMTs	245
Burial sites	176
Historic Euro-Canadian sites	90
Surface lithic scatters	28
Rock art	23
Other	15
Total	**1,536**

directly related to Nuu-chah-nulth culture history. The Euro-Canadian presence is also represented in the site inventory by such historic ruins as shipwrecks, homesteads, canneries, and mines.

A large and rapidly growing, but still under-reported, site category is culturally modified trees (CMTs). These are all standing or fallen trees that show evidence of Native use (including bark-stripping, plank removal, and all stages of canoe manufacture). CMTs have only recently been given site numbers in the provincial system on a regular basis (and then primarily as clusters rather than as individual trees) and have been inconsistently recorded in regional surveys. Despite clearly being under-represented in the site records, CMTs have become one of the most common site types reported for western Vancouver Island. CMTs have also played a vital role in Aboriginal land-use studies that have been used for modern legal purposes. On Meares Island, for example, Nuu-chah-nulth claims to Aboriginal use of the entire island were strengthened by an intensive archaeological survey that focused on CMTs (Arcas Associates 1986). The survey identified almost 1,800 individual CMTs, with tree-ring dates indicating continuous use since the mid-seventeenth century, providing an estimate of 20,000 CMTs for the coastal portion of the island (Stryd and Eldridge 1993).

By the 1980s, a growing interest in non-destructive archaeological fieldwork and the application of new, more intensive, survey techniques helped focus attention on regional surveys, with a consequent rise in recorded site totals. These surveys, designed to record and map all sites at or near the modern shoreline, involved on-foot inspection of the entire shoreline area, including the intertidal zone. Soil probes were used to detect buried deposits. Rocky and inhospitable areas, unsuited to habitation uses, were examined for evidence of burials, rock art, or defensive locations. This method was first tested in the Brooks Peninsula survey (Haggarty and Inglis

1983b, 1997) and fully applied, with considerable success, in surveys through-out Pacific Rim National Park (Haggarty and Inglis 1984, 1985; Inglis and Haggarty 1986). Subsequently, these techniques were employed in the Meares Island survey (Mackie 1983), the Ohiaht Ethnoarchaeology Project (Mackie 1986), the Mowachaht/Muchalat Archaeology Project (Marshall 1990, 1992a; Marshall and Moon 1989), and the Toquaht Archaeological Project (McMillan and St. Claire 1991, 1992). Such regional surveys were also stimulated by the desires of First Nations communities to document heritage resources in their traditional territories and to assert legal claims to their traditional lands. At present, some portions of Nuu-chah-nulth and Ditidaht territory have been intensively surveyed and their heritage resources well documented, while other areas have received only cursory or unsystematic attention.

Despite the growing number of recorded archaeological sites in Nuu-chah-nulth and Ditidaht territory, excavated data are remarkably limited (Map 4). Although thirty-four sites have had some form of systematic excavation, most consisted only of very minor testing. The fifteen sites in Hesquiat Harbour that were systematically investigated as part of the

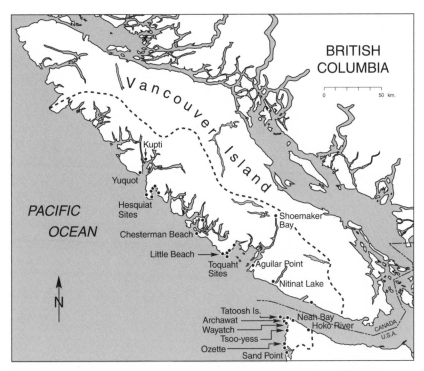

Map 4 Location of excavated sites in Nuu-chah-nulth, Ditidaht, and Makah territories. In the interest of clarity, only the major sites in Hesquiat Harbour are shown and only one site is indicated for the two present at Chesterman Beach, Aguilar Point, Nitinat Lake, and Hoko River.

Hesquiat Project account for almost half of this total, yet only four received more than minor subsurface examination. Major excavations, resulting in the recovery of fairly extensive cultural materials, are limited to those conducted at Yuquot, several of the Hesquiaht sites, two of the Toquaht sites, and Shoemaker Bay (at the end of Alberni Inlet).

Eleven sites have been excavated in the ethnographic territory of the Makah. Of these, only Ozette and the two Hoko River sites have been the locations of major excavation projects. A number of sites around Neah Bay and from Cape Flattery to just south of Ozette have had limited testing (Friedman 1976; Wessen 1990).

Major gaps are evident in the geographic distribution of archaeological research on western Vancouver Island. While Nootka Sound and Hesquiat Harbour in the north and Barkley Sound in the south have seen relatively extensive fieldwork, including both inventory and excavation, relatively little fieldwork has taken place in the intervening areas. The entire northern portion of Nuu-chah-nulth distribution, from Cape Cook to Nootka Sound, has been almost entirely ignored. To the south of Barkley Sound there have been several programs of site inventory but only limited excavation around Nitinat Lake. Such gaps in archaeological research greatly restrict our ability to understand past population movements and cultural developments throughout the region.

There are other problems with the archaeological record from the west coast. Differing sampling strategies hinder comparison of recovered materials from various sites. Only at Hesquiat Harbour has a systematic sample been taken of all site types in the study region and a significant number of the total sites tested. Elsewhere, archaeological attention has been limited to the large, ethnographically important village sites. At Yuquot, the presence of modern occupied houses put great constraints on where excavation could occur, limiting this to a single large block in an unoccupied portion of the village. Although an impressive collection of cultural remains was recovered, the extent to which this represents activities carried out over the total site area is unknown.

Differences in season of occupation may also hinder comparisons. Abbott (1972) has cautioned that the ethnographic pattern of seasonal movement would result in a single social group leaving distinctly different archaeological remains at various locations. He argues that this pattern has considerable antiquity, at least in the Coast Salish region. Dewhirst (1980:17-18), however, minimizes seasonal differences in Nootka Sound by noting the very similar nature of artifacts found at the ethnographic summer and winter villages. Also, as is argued in Chapter 6, archaeological and ethnographic research now indicates that the ethnographic seasonal round was a late adaptation and that year-round occupation is more likely to characterize the major shell midden sites prior to contact with Europeans. Detailed analyses of faunal remains provide the clearest indicators of seasonality, but such studies have been completed in relatively full form only for the three major Hesquiat Harbour sites (Calvert 1980) and Shoemaker Bay (Calvert and Crockford 1982).

Finally, a major problem in understanding the culture history of the area lies in the incomplete nature of the material remains recovered through archaeological excavation. Ethnographic sources on the Nuu-chah-nulth and their relatives emphasize the overwhelming importance of wood, bark, and root in the material culture – a fact fully borne out at the few sites (Ozette, Hoko River, and Nitinat Lake) where such materials are preserved in waterlogged deposits. These sites provide something of a "control," showing the nature and degree of loss in contexts that yield only objects of such relatively imperishable materials as bone, antler, shell, and stone.

The remainder of this chapter briefly describes the nature and results of all excavation projects in Nuu-chah-nulth, Ditidaht, and Makah territories. Tables 2 to 10 present all available radiocarbon age estimates based on wood or charcoal for sites in this region. At a few locations radiocarbon dates were also obtained from marine shell. Such dates, which were collected for comparative purposes from the same strata as were charcoal dates, are consistently too old and require correction for the marine reservoir effect (caused by upwelling of deep ocean waters containing ancient carbon). As they generally duplicate information obtained from charcoal, only the latter are reported here. These are given as radiocarbon lab dates, without any calibration or correction.

Nootka Sound and Hesquiat Harbour

These two adjacent regions have yielded similar archaeological remains. Ethnographically, however, Drucker (1951:4) considered Estevan Point, between Nootka Sound and Hesquiat Harbour, to mark a significant cultural break. The Mowachaht of Nootka Sound were placed in Drucker's "Northern Nootkans" category, which was characterized by frequent contact with the Kwakwaka'wakw and extensive cultural borrowing. Only the Northern Nootkans developed the confederacy level of social organization. Of these groups, only the Mowachaht have received any significant archaeological attention. Around the point, the Hesquiaht were the northernmost of Drucker's central division, which he described as having "little direct contact with foreigners." Drucker (1951:4) considered any outside influences among the central groups to be indirect, "brought in by their northern kin, or by the Makah, who plied busily back and forth across the Strait." The Hesquiaht and Toquaht are the only "Central Nootkans" to have received significant archaeological study through excavation.

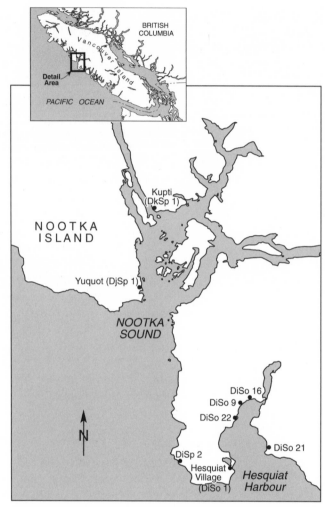

Map 5 Excavated sites in Nootka Sound and Hesquiat Harbour.
Only the Hesquiat sites mentioned in the text are shown.

Research in Nootka Sound

Nootka Sound has had considerable archaeological attention, including
intensive archaeological inventory throughout the entire region (Marshall
1992a, 1993) and excavation at two sites. The major excavation project
took place at Yuquot (*Yukwaat*), the historic summer village for the
Mowachaht confederacy, while more minor excavation was conducted at
Kupti (*Kwuupti*), the winter village of the dominant Mowachaht tribal unit
(Map 5). In addition, several small impact assessment studies have been
carried out by archaeological contractors (Eldridge 1989; Arcas Consulting
Archeologists 1993, 1994).

12 Aerial view of Yuquot, 1976. *Photo by John Dewhirst*

The outer coast village of Yuquot (DjSp 1) is one of the largest sites on the west coast of Vancouver Island and is the best known archaeologically (Figures 12 and 13). The 1966 excavation was conducted on a large scale, encompassing a trench 19.5 m long and between 3 m and 4.5 m wide. The excavation reached a maximum depth of 5.5 m, without encountering sterile deposits. The total volume of matrix removed is calculated at 231.8 m^3 (Dewhirst 1980:29). Over 4,000 artifacts of indigenous manufacture, as well as several thousand items of metal, ceramic, or other introduced historic materials, were recovered. Numerous faunal remains, consisting of about 217,000 fish, mammal, and bird elements as well as about 26,000 mollusc and barnacle specimens, were collected (Dewhirst 1980:33). However, only the avifauna, molluscs, and barnacles have been analyzed and reported in any detail (McAllister 1980; Clarke and Clarke 1980; Fournier and Dewhirst 1980).

The Yuquot strata are clustered into four zones, providing a continuous archaeological sequence that spans the period from sometime prior to 4200 BP to the modern era (Dewhirst 1978, 1980, 1988). Dewhirst stresses continuity throughout, maintaining that there are "no breaks and no extensive qualitative discontinuities" in the sequence, which culminates in historic Nuu-chah-nulth culture. Where changes are evident, they represent more complex forms emerging from their earlier prototypes. Dewhirst (1980:336) concludes: "In short, the archaeological record reflects a single culture in a process of improved adaptation to the outside coastal environment."

13   Excavation in progress at Yuquot, 1966. *Photo by John Dewhirst, courtesy of Parks Canada, 1T-52M*

Similarly, Folan (1972:x) interprets the archaeological evidence from earliest occupation as representing essentially the same way of life as that represented by the historic Nuu-chah-nulth: "In general, the picture provided by the archaeology ... is that the inhabitants of Yuquot through time have been a rather conservative people, fishing and hunting and collecting the same species of fauna (and probably flora) since their earliest discovered habitation of the site, and all the while utilizing basically the same fishing and hunting equipment and tools. Further, there is no reason to believe that they lived in structures differing much from some of those drawn by John Webber in 1778 during Captain James Cook's third and last voyage of discovery."

Zone I, dating from sometime prior to 4200 BP to about 3000 BP, encompasses the two lower strata. Sterile deposits were not reached; a test hole in the wet sand and pebbles of the lowest stratum still revealed fish vertebrae at a depth of about 60 cm below where the excavation terminated. During this Early Period, prior to the build-up of extensive midden deposits, the site was a low-lying gravel spit. Many of the artifacts and faunal remains are waterworn, suggesting that sea levels were slightly higher than they are at present. Poor preservation in these wet lower deposits meant that few faunal remains and only a small number of artifacts were recovered. These artifacts, however, reflect the types of tools and the range of grinding, pecking, and splitting technologies found in later stages. The artifacts characteristic of this period include stone abraders and abrasive saws; stone celts; bone points for composite fishing gear; and bone awls, needles, and barbed points or harpoons.

The Middle Period is encompassed within Zone II deposits, estimated to date between about 3000 BP and 1200 BP. These strata contain much more organic material, particularly crushed mussel (*Mytilus californianus*) shell, resulting in much better preservation of bone and antler. More intensive occupation of the site is also suggested by large rock-rimmed firepits, some superimposed, which may indicate that permanent house structures were in place. A wider range of artifacts may simply reflect the improved preservation conditions. Stone artifacts include abundant abraders, abrasive saws, and celts. In addition to the bone points, awls, and needles continuing from Zone 1, these deposits contain bone fishhook shanks, small barbed points for composite fishhooks, and bone bipoints that would have served as gorges for taking fish. Paired valves and arming points are the components of composite toggling harpoon heads (of the size used for taking salmon). Larger barbed harpoons would have been suitable for hunting sea mammals. Whalebone shredders and beaters indicate that the technology for processing and weaving cedar bark was established by this time. Canine-tooth pendants and other objects of personal adornment are also found.

Materials from Zone III deposits are assigned to the Late Period, dated from about 1200 BP to 200 BP. According to Dewhirst (1980:342), the Late Period, which ends with the Spanish occupation of the site in 1789, "largely reflects Nootkan culture as it is known from early historical and ethnographical sources." Although there are no large firepits in Zone III, the deposits seem to have formed from activities associated directly with habitations. Artifacts remain largely unchanged from the Middle Period, with the exception of several innovations that suggest increased efficiency in exploiting open-ocean resources. Stone fishhook shanks, indicating the specialized salmon-trolling hooks known ethnographically, appear late in this period. Technological changes associated with sea mammal hunting also become evident. Barbed non-toggling harpoon heads were replaced by large composite toggling harpoon heads, with bone valves slotted for mussel shell cutting blades, of the type known ethnographically as parts of sea mammal hunting gear (Waterman 1920; Drucker 1951:26-29). Several large valves have a punctate zigzag design, identical to historic specimens used in whaling, where the design had "magical virtue" (Drucker 1951:28). This trait led Dewhirst (1977; 1980:344) to conclude that Nuu-chah-nulth whaling emerged only in the Late Period.

Faunal remains were abundant in Zones II and III and, according to Dewhirst (1979), were "remarkably consistent" through time. Molluscan remains, which made up a large part of the site deposits, were overwhelmingly California mussel (Clarke and Clarke 1975, 1980; Dewhirst 1979). Fish bones dominate the vertebrate remains. Although analysis is incomplete, most elements were identified to species. These are roughly evenly divided between salmon (*Oncorhynchus* spp.); nearshore pelagic species, primarily rockfish (*Sebastes* spp.); and nearshore bottom dwellers, of which lingcod (*Ophiodon elongatus*) is the most abundant (Dewhirst 1979). Halibut (*Hippoglossus stenolepis*) appear to have played only a minor role in the economy, despite their ethnographic importance among the Nuu-chah-nulth. Avifauna were abundant, representing sixty-seven species, of which twenty-three occurred in significant numbers. The most abundant single species, representing 27 percent to 40 percent of all avian remains, is the short-tailed albatross (*Diomedea albatrus*) (Dewhirst 1979; McAllister 1980). McAllister (1980:133) describes the abundance of albatross bones as "astonishing," overwhelming all other species in the sample. Identification of mammals, based on a sample of about one-third of the elements recovered, indicated that land mammals were primarily coast deer (*Odocoileus hemionus*), while the most abundant sea mammal species was the northern fur seal (*Callorhinus ursinus*), followed by the harbour seal (*Phoca vitulina*) (Dewhirst 1979). Whalebones were found throughout the deposit, although their fragmentary nature inhibits specific identification and quantification. The presence in the midden deposits of a distinct type of barnacle (*Coronula reginae*), which lives almost exclusively on the skin of the humpback whale, provides indirect evidence for the procurement of humpback whales since at least about 2200 BP (Fournier and Dewhirst 1980:95-96). Based on this sample of elements, the ratio of sea mammals to land mammals appears to have increased by the Late Period (Savage 1973; Dewhirst 1978:14).

Seasonality studies based on the faunal remains are incomplete and tentative. Analysis of the avifauna indicates that the site was occupied from at least February to October during the Middle and Late Periods (McAllister 1980:169). The molluscan remains also suggest a spring-to-fall occupation for the Middle Period, with a shift to year-round residence by the Late and Historic Periods (Clarke and Clarke 1980:52).

Zone IV encompasses the Historic Period, from the beginning of intensive European contact around 1789 to 1966, the year of the excavation. Although Dewhirst (1978:17) maintains that "the basic character of Nootkan technology and subsistence remained unchanged until the late

19th century," substantial cultural shifts are evident. Metal, glass, and ceramic implements became abundant, replacing some categories of indigenous artifacts. Only a few classes of historic artifacts have been analyzed, however, and objects that can be shown to predate the late nineteenth century are relatively rare (Jones 1981:69; Lueger 1981:104). Small bone points and other tools persist, but they appear to have been whittled to shape with iron cutting tools (Dewhirst 1978:17; 1980:346). Substantial shifts also took place in the faunal species exploited. Among the avifauna, albatross remains are less numerous while the Canada goose (*Branta canadensis*) markedly increases in importance (Dewhirst 1979; McAllister 1980). In the molluscan remains, rock-dwelling species such as mussel, which dominate the prehistoric deposits, were largely replaced by sand-burrowing species, such as little-neck clam, butter clam, and horse clam (Clarke and Clarke 1975, 1980; Dewhirst 1979). Even the dominant species of barnacle found in Historic Period deposits differs from that characteristic of earlier periods (Fournier and Dewhirst 1980). Most of the scattered human skeletal elements, including three possible fragmentary burials, also came from Zone IV deposits (Cybulski 1980).

The archaeological sequence at Yuquot is supported by an extensive series of radiocarbon age estimates (Table 2). Not all are consistent, and several have been rejected by the excavator. The earliest radiocarbon date is 4230 ± 90 years, based on a sample collected from wet sand and pebbles near, but not at, the base of the cultural deposit.

As part of their 1966 fieldwork, Folan and Dewhirst also excavated four small testpits at the site of Kupti (or Cooptee; DkSp 1) on the protected inside of Nootka Sound at the entrance to Tahsis Inlet. Few faunal remains and no artifacts were found. Two years later, I conducted more extensive test excavations (McMillan 1969). A total of fifteen units, 1.5 m × 1.5 m, was excavated, removing approximately 35.4 m³ of matrix. Most test units were located on the relatively shallow lower terrace, but two were excavated on the upper terrace along the back of the site, where a maximum depth of 2.4 m was reached. This site was revisited in 1990 by Marshall (1992), who prepared a detailed map and collected additional artifacts from the beach.

Kupti was the winter village of Chief Maquinna's tribal group in the late eighteenth century. A 1792 Spanish engraving (Moziño 1970:Plate 11) shows houses on several levels, densely clustered together. The map prepared by Marshall (1992a:50; 1993:34) shows the numerous surface ridges and other features suggestive of closely spaced dwellings. This site was an occupied Mowachaht village well into the twentieth century.

Fewer than 200 artifacts of indigenous manufacture were recovered from the 1968 excavation, along with numerous introduced historic items and a substantial quantity of faunal remains. Bone points and abrasive stones were the most common implements; more diagnostic artifacts include a stone fishhook shank and several hand maul fragments. Although faunal analysis is incomplete, some observations can be made (Marshall 1990:109-111). The most numerous vertebrate remains are fish, which are dominated by

Table 2

Radiocarbon dates from Nootka Sound

^{14}C age	Lab no.	Zone	Comments
Yuquot (from Dewhirst 1980)			
1330 ± 80	GaK-2852	IV	date rejected, historic deposits
980 ± 50	GaK-2855	III	
1050 ± 80	GaK-2194	III	
1050 ± 100	GaK-2190	III	
1120 ± 80	GaK-2184	III	
1150 ± 90	GaK-2192	III	
1250 ± 80	GaK-2197	III	
1300 ± 80	GaK-2189	III	
1540 ± 110	GaK-2181	III	date rejected
1920 ± 100	GaK-2854	III	date rejected
1280 ± 90	GaK-2185	II	date rejected
1770 ± 90	GaK-2195	II	
1850 ± 90	GaK-2182	II	
1860 ± 90	GaK-2200	II	
1880 ± 110	GaK-2199	II	
2000 ± 80	GaK-2193	II	
2040 ± 90	GaK-2201	II	
2050 ± 90	GaK-2178	II	
2120 ± 110	GaK-2186	II	
2160 ± 100	GaK-2198	II	
2630 ± 110	GaK-2196	II	
3020 ± 220	GaK-2191	II	at interface with Zone I
3100 ± 120	GaK-2188	II	date rejected
3320 ± 90	GaK-2187	II	date rejected
3000 ± 100	GaK-2180	I	date rejected
3590 ± 190	GSC-1767	I	same sample as above, rejected
4080 ± 80	GaK-2179	I	
4230 ± 90	GaK-2183	I	near base of excavation
Kupti (from Marshall 1992a)			
490 ± 75	SFU-655		lower terrace, near base of deposit
680 ± 75	SFU-656		as above, at base of an adjacent unit (1.3 m)
700 ± 50	Beta-53090		from 2nd terrace unit, 0.8 m depth
1210 ± 50	Beta-53089		same 2nd terrace unit as above, ca. 1.6 m
1250 ± 50	Beta-50031		other 2nd terrace unit, ca. 0.9 m depth
3090 ± 90	SFU-654		date rejected, same sample as Beta-53089

salmon, along with smaller numbers of dogfish and rockfish. Among the birds, the common murre, loons, and cormorants are the most abundant. These were all common avifauna at Yuquot, although they were overshadowed by the great abundance of albatross, a bird that was very rare in the more inner coast environs of Kupti.

Based on the types of artifacts found, I initially suggested that all materials recovered were relatively late, probably within the last 1,000 years (McMillan 1969:109). Dewhirst (1978:19; 1980:16) considered all the Kupti artifacts to be contemporaneous with Zones III and IV at Yuquot, suggesting an occupation spanning the last 1,200 years. More recently, when a number of the original radiocarbon samples were analyzed, an early date of 3090 ± 90 BP was obtained (Marshall 1992a:49). This date, however, aroused enough suspicion that Marshall and I sent the remaining portion of the sample to another laboratory, which provided an age estimate of 1210 ± 50 BP. Thus the 3,000-year date was rejected, and the oldest radiocarbon age corresponds closely to what Dewhirst and I had originally predicted.

The earliest Kupti dates came from the two excavation units on the second terrace. Evidence of thick ash layers with rocks (presumably hearths), little shell, and few artifacts suggests that these are house deposits. No radiocarbon samples were obtained from the base of this terrace, so the date of earliest occupation is unknown. The initial occupation may have been limited to the upper terrace, while the lower deposits, which contain much more shell, accumulated through refuse disposal. The site appears to have grown rapidly in late precontact times, with evidence of house structures spread along the relatively shallow deposits of the lower terrace. Marshall (1993:156-157) attributes this to the use of Kupti as a winter village by the larger social group that emerged through the political confederacy formed by the Yuquot and Tahsis Inlet peoples.

In addition to the excavated data, stone artifacts have been found on the beaches in front of several sites in Nootka Sound (Marshall 1990, 1992a; Arcas Consulting Archeologists 1993). These consist primarily of small stone celts and chipped stone tools, including bifaces, flakes, and cores. The rarity of chipped stone in the excavated deposits of Yuquot and Kupti makes these beach discoveries of particular interest. One possible explanation is that they belong to an early occupation period in Nootka Sound – one that predates the excavated deposits. This is examined in more detail in Chapter 4.

The Hesquiat Project

The Hesquiat Project was initiated in 1971 through collaboration between archaeologists and Hesquiaht band members (Calvert 1980; Haggarty 1982; Haggarty and Boehm 1974). At first, the focus was on the protection of burial caves and rockshelters, which had been subjected to considerable theft and vandalism. The initial field season goals were to locate and to record all archaeological sites within Hesquiaht traditional territory and to remove all surface materials from the burial caves and rockshelters (Sneed 1972; Haggarty 1982). In all, human remains representing at least 108 individuals were removed from eleven such sites, probably all dating to the early Historic Period (Cybulski 1978). Over half came from DiSo 9, the largest burial cave in the region, which also contained thousands of surface artifacts, including cedar bark mats and baskets, cordage, wooden harpoon shafts, wood and bone combs, and a wooden dance mask (Sneed 1972:5; Haggarty 1982:19). About 7,000 trade beads were also included with the burials in this cave. In subsequent fieldwork, lasting until 1979, the Hesquiat Project evolved into an ambitious program of site survey and excavation as well as of linguistic and ethnographic research. In all, test excavations were carried out at fifteen habitation sites, sampling all site types from the study area. Substantial excavations, however, were limited to four sites: DiSo 1, the major ethnographic village of the Hesquiaht people; DiSo 9, the large burial cave that also had extensive precontact habitation deposits; DiSo 16, a smaller burial and habitation cave; and DiSo 22, a site consisting of both rockshelter and open midden deposits (Haggarty 1982) (Map 5). DiSo 9 is the oldest of the four sites, with precontact deposits dating between 1200 BP and 1800 BP underlying the historic burial materials. Hesquiat Village was occupied from about 1,200 years ago to modern times, while the remaining two sites are encompassed within the past millennium (Calvert 1980; Haggarty 1982). Radiocarbon age estimates are shown in Table 3.

Over 1,500 artifacts of Aboriginal manufacture were excavated from these four sites, with over 900 of the total coming from Hesquiat Village (DiSo 1) (Haggarty 1982:Table 18). Abrasive stones were numerous, as were a number of bone and antler artifacts, including various points and bipoints, awls, and composite harpoon valves. Less numerous but more diagnostic artifacts include stone fishhook shanks and mussel shell tools, including a cutting point for a composite harpoon head. As at other Nuu-chah-nulth sites, the simplicity of the assemblage and the low numbers of artifacts compared to the abundant historic items in the burial caves suggest that most objects were made from perishable materials. In general, the artifacts closely resemble those from Kupti and from Zones III and IV at Yuquot, which are contemporary with Hesquiat Village.

A strong focus of the Hesquiat project was the systematic collection and analysis of faunal remains. Calvert (1980) provides a detailed study of the fauna from three of the major excavated sites. Fish remains dominate the vertebrate fauna, but major differences between sites are evident. At Hesquiat Village, rockfish, lingcod, greenlings, and dogfish were the most numerous, while herring and salmon were particularly important at DiSo 9. Sea mammals, particularly northern fur seal, harbour seal, and sea otter (*Enhydra lutris*), were abundant at Hesquiat Village, near the outer coast, while DiSo 9

Table 3

Radiocarbon dates from Hesquiat Harbour sites

Site	¹⁴C age	Lab no.	Comments
DiSo1	520 ± 90	WSU-2286	
	520 ± 90	WSU-2287	
	540 ± 65	WSU-2290	
	720 ± 90	WSU-2291	
	820 ± 70	WSU-1542	
	1065 ± 70	WSU-2288	
	1220 ± 65	WSU-2289	
	2430 ± 200	GaK-4394	date rejected by excavators
DiSo9	1180 ± 60	GaK-4395	component II
	1200 ± 85	I-8109	component II
	1285 ± 85	I-8111	component II
	1740 ± 60	WSU-1543	component I
	1790 ± 90	I-8110	component I
	1800 ± 70	WSU-1544	component I
	1810 ± 115	I-8112	component I
DiSo16	575 ± 85	I-8114	
	685 ± 80	I-8113	
DiSo21	230 ± 90	WSU-2295	date rejected by excavators
	280 ± 90	WSU-2292	
	520 ± 120	WSU-2293	
	680 ± 90	WSU-2294	
DiSo22	580 ± 80	I-8115	open camp
	980 ± 70	WSU-2292	rock shelter
DiSp2	570 ± 90	WSU-2296	
	690 ± 90	WSU-2297	

Source: from Haggarty 1982: Table 20

and 16, on the inner harbour, had a mix of sea and land mammals. Sea mammals, however, overshadowed land mammals at the former site, while the latter site yielded almost entirely land mammal remains, primarily deer. Unidentified whalebone was also common at Hesquiat Village; the presence of a whale barnacle (*Coronula* sp.) suggests that at least some of this represents humpback whale. Avifauna were also numerous, representing a wide range of species. Loons, ducks, geese, cormorants, and gulls were common, with albatross dominating the assemblage from Hesquiat Village. The faunal pattern from that site strongly resembles that from Yuquot, which is located in a similar outer coast environmental setting.

Calvert (1980) suggests that the earliest remains at DiSo 9, dating to about 1800 BP, show unrestricted access to resources throughout the harbour. By about 1200 BP, differing faunal assemblages evident at each site suggest the emergence of politically autonomous local groups holding clearly defined territories that were exploited on a year-round basis. Haggarty (1982) also claims that such distinct patterns can be seen in artifact distributions in Hesquiat Harbour, as the technology of resource procurement would leave distinguishable assemblages in each local group territory. This form of political organization, which survived into historic times in Hesquiat Harbour, may have been the earliest adaptive pattern along the west coast of Vancouver Island, even in those areas characterized historically by larger tribal or confederacy groups.

Clayoquot Sound to Barkley Sound

Little archaeological research has been conducted between Hesquiat Harbour and Barkley Sound. Intensive site surveys have been carried out on Meares Island in Clayoquot Sound (Mackie 1983), including systematic searches for CMTs (Arcas Associates 1984, 1986), and along the Long Beach portion of Pacific Rim National Park (Inglis and Haggarty 1986). Excavation projects, however, are limited to minor testing at a historic house structure on Meares Island (Arcas Associates 1988) and two shell middens near Tofino (Wilson 1990, 1994).

Barkley Sound has received much more archaeological attention than has Clayoquot Sound. Intensive surveys have been conducted in the Broken Group Islands of the central sound (Inglis and Haggarty 1986), along western Barkley Sound (McMillan and St. Claire 1991, 1992), and near Bamfield on the eastern side of the sound. Major excavations are limited to the Shoemaker Bay site at the head of Alberni Inlet (McMillan and St. Claire 1982) and several of the ethnographic Toquaht sites along the western sound (McMillan and St. Claire 1991, 1992, 1994, 1996). Another important, although smaller-scale, excavation took place at the Little Beach site in Ucluelet (Arcas Consulting Archaeologists 1991; Brolly 1992). In addition, minor test excavations have been conducted at two sites on the Ittatsoo reserve near Ucluelet (Arcas Consulting Archeologists 1998) and at two adjacent sites at Aguilar Point in Bamfield, across the sound from the Ucluelet and Toquaht sites (Buxton 1969; Coates and Eldridge 1992).

Along with the Hesquiaht, in Drucker's scheme all the peoples of this region are considered "Central Nootkans." The Huu-ay-aht of eastern Barkley Sound are today the southernmost Nuu-chah-nulth speakers. The ethnographic boundary with the Ditidaht is at Pachena Point, on the outer coast just south of Barkley Sound.

The Toquaht Archaeological Project

The Toquaht Project, initiated in 1991, involved test excavation at Toquaht village sites, intensive surveying throughout ethnographic Toquaht territory, and oral history research with Native elders (McMillan 1992; McMillan and St. Claire 1991, 1992, 1994, 1996). Five sites, including the only three

14 Chief Bert Mack of the Toquaht discusses an
artifact found at Macoah with project co-director Denis
St. Claire. *Photo by author*

large villages recorded in Toquaht territory, have been excavated as part of
this project (Map 6). Radiocarbon dates for all excavated Toquaht sites are
listed in Table 4.

Macoah (*Ma7akwuu7a*; DfSi 5), near the upper portion of the sound, was
the ethnographic winter village. It features prominently in the nineteenth-
century traditions collected by Edward Sapir (1910-1914; Sapir and Swadesh
1939, 1955). During the Long War in Barkley Sound, which broke out at
Macoah as the result of a dispute over an escaped slave, the village was
apparently palisaded, as returning slaves noted "a fence all around the
Tukwaa [Toquaht] village" (Sapir and Swadesh 1955:437). Peter O'Reilly
(1883), the reserve commissioner, described Macoah as a winter village and
fishing station in 1882, as did the Royal Commission on Indian Affairs in
1914 (British Columbia 1916). Toquaht elder Jim McKay noted that some
people lived there throughout the year, as "a sort of headquarters for all the

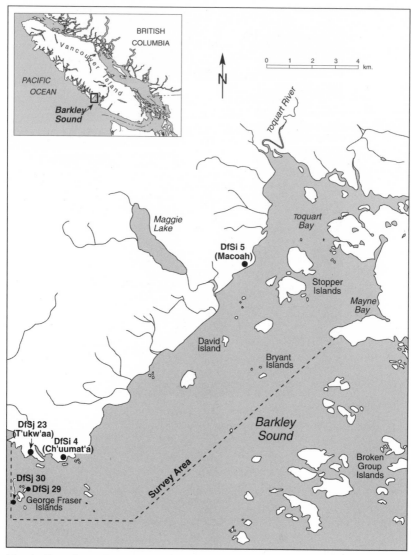

Map 6 Toquaht traditional territory in western Barkley Sound, showing locations of five sites excavated as part of the Toquaht Archaeological Project.

creeks around" (St. Claire 1991:163). The site name means "house on the point," referring to a rocky point at the north end of the modern reserve (Figure 15). O'Reilly's 1882 map shows four houses near this point, while five houses appear in the 1893 reserve surveyors' map (BC Ministry of Crown Lands 1894). By the 1920s the site was abandoned, as the Toquaht moved closer to Ucluelet.

15 Macoah (DfSi 5), looking north to the rocky point for which the site is named. Modern reserve housing is visible on the site. *Photo by author*

Today, Macoah is again an occupied Toquaht village. Construction of a gravel road to Toquart Bay provided access, and new houses began to appear at Macoah in the early 1980s. House construction continues at the site, and a new sawmill provides an economic base. Such activities, however, have resulted in considerable disturbance to the archaeological deposits. Objects recovered through such disturbance, now in the possession of Chief Bert Mack, include the handle of a whalebone club in the form of the Thunderbird, a complete flat-topped hand maul, and a bone gambling piece that once had a central copper band (McMillan and St. Claire 1991). A reserve resident near the south of the village has collected seven stone celts (most of which are the small rounded-poll "pebble celts" characteristic of the West Coast culture type), three basalt bifaces, and a number of shaped sandstone abraders from her property. House construction was monitored as part of the Toquaht Project, and all recovered materials have been recorded.

Systematic excavation at this site was limited, partially because of the disturbed nature of some site deposits. In all, five 1 m × 2 m units were excavated, removing a total of about 18.2 m³ of archaeological deposits. Of the sixty-two artifacts recorded for the site, forty-nine are of indigenous materials. Bone points and bipoints, along with abrasive stones, were the most common implements. A finely made complete stone fishhook shank, similar to late types from Yuquot, was found immediately under the sod. Most artifacts and faunal remains came from the upper midden strata, but some cultural materials continued into the deeper gravel and pebble layers. Two radiocarbon dates, collected from basal deposits in widely separated areas of the site, give varying estimates of the initial occupation, with the

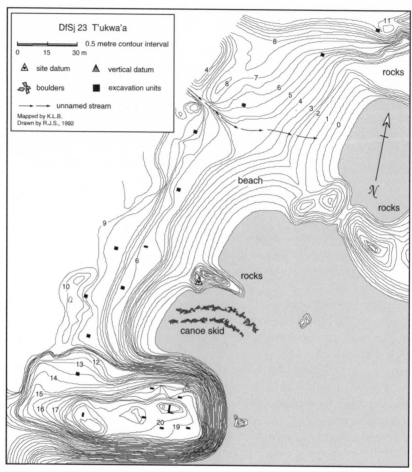

Map 7 Contour map of T'ukw'aa, showing location of excavation units. The 0 contour line refers to mean sea level. The rise from the upper beach to the site occurs at about the 4.5 m contour line.

earliest suggesting that the site was first occupied almost two millennia ago. Intensive occupation, however, would not have occurred until considerably later.

The largest and most impressive of the Toquaht archaeological sites is T'ukw'aa (DfSj 23), at the entrance to Ucluelet Inlet (Map 7; Figures 16 and 17). The importance of this site is evident in its name, for the Toquaht (*T'ukw'aa7ath̲*) are literally "the people of T'ukw'aa." It would appear, however, that its prominence had greatly declined by the mid-nineteenth century. Little mention of this site occurs in the extensive ethnographic accounts of Edward Sapir. When O'Reilly laid out the reserve in 1882, he described it as "a fishing station used only during the sealing season." The Royal

Commission on Indian Affairs lists this as a "village site and fishing station." Toquaht informants describe fishing for halibut and cod and hunting seals, sea lion, and whales from this location during spring and summer, moving to Macoah and other sites up the sound when the fall salmon runs began.

16 Aerial view of T'ukw'aa (DfSj 23). The defensive portion of the site is located on the rocky headland at the left. *Photo by Terry Spurgeon*

17 T'ukw'aa from the terrace at the eastern end of the site. The rocky promontory with the defensive location is at the far end. *Photo by author*

The impressive size of this site and the depth of archaeological deposits suggest much more extensive occupation in earlier times. The site extends for about 250 m along the beach, with a maximum depth of between 2 m and 3 m. Two distinct terraces are evident along the western portion of the village area, with ridges forming several house outlines clearly visible on the upper terrace. At the western end of the site, midden deposits extend out along the top of a steep-sided rocky promontory. This would be an ideal defensive location, with a drop of about 20 m off the steep cliffs. One narrow access route from the village area would have been relatively easy to defend. Ethnographic accounts of other defensive sites in Barkley Sound suggest that the narrow access point could have been closed with logs piled so that they could be released to roll down on attackers. The entire top of the promontory is covered with relatively shallow shell midden deposits,

18 Profiling a completed excavation unit at T'ukw'aa.
Dark house-floor deposits and the rocks of a hearth can
be seen behind the ladder. *Photo by author*

with numerous surface features. Several flat areas, at considerably different elevations, suggest house locations.

Excavation on both the village and defensive areas of this site took place during two field sessions. On the village area, a total of 38 m² was excavated, reaching a maximum depth of 2.75 m. Units scattered across the elevated defensive area accounted for another 30 m² of excavation, ranging from very shallow deposits over bedrock to a maximum depth of about 1.4 m. The total volume of archaeological deposit removed from the site is about 106 m³. Nearly 1,500 artifacts were recorded, of which 1,407 are of Aboriginal materials. All but a few of the introduced Euro-Canadian artifacts were surface discoveries associated with the ruins of an early twentieth-century house. Faunal remains from all levels of the deposit were abundant. A series of radiocarbon dates indicates that this site was first occupied about 1,200 years ago, although no evidence exists for use of the refuge area until about 800 years ago.

The third major excavated village site is Ch'uumat'a (DfSi 4), a large conspicuous shell midden in a small cove east of T'ukw'aa (Map 8; Figure 19). Large rocks on the beach in front of the site have been moved to create an access channel for canoes. This was the former village of the *Ch'uumat'a7ath*, a subgroup of the Toquaht. It takes its ethnographic name from the mountain behind it. A cave near the village was said to extend up the mountain, and from this cave emerged the Wolves, both natural and supernatural (St.

19 Ch'uumat'a (DfSi 4). Midden deposits extend into the forested area at the back of the site. A cleared canoe run is visible on the beach in front. *Photo by author*

Claire 1991:159). The village appears to have fallen into decline and disuse even earlier than T'ukw'aa. As it was apparently not being occupied at the time of the reserve commissioner's visit in the late nineteenth century, it is not held today as a Toquaht reserve. Except for objects associated with remains of a recent cabin on the site, the excavation showed little evidence of later historic occupation.

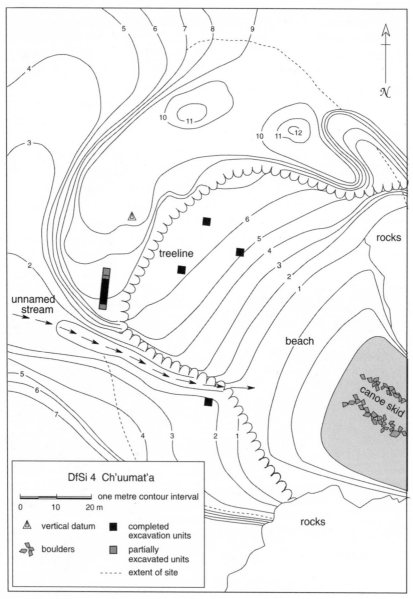

Map 8 Map of Ch'uumat'a, showing locations of excavation units.

The front, most visible, portion of the site is gently sloping and covered with salmonberry bushes. Three 2 m × 2 m units were excavated to the base of cultural deposits in this area. The two units furthest from the beach reached depths approaching 4 m, with basal dates of 2300 BP to 2500 BP. The third, closer to the beach and at somewhat lower elevation, had a depth of about 3 m and a radiocarbon date at its base of only about 1100 BP. This part of the site appears to have been occupied into the early Historic Period. In addition, another 2 m × 2 m unit was excavated on a low terrace near the front of the site, in an area of old-growth forest across the stream from the brush-covered Late Period village. Almost 2 m of deposit, with a basal date of about 2000 BP, overlaid bedrock at this location.

At the back of the site is an area of old-growth forest cover, with large coniferous trees and little undergrowth. Soil probes revealed a shell midden below a considerable overburden of forest deposit. In addition, a stream cutting through this area had exposed over 4 m of shell midden deposits. The potential for earlier dates than those obtained from T'ukw'aa and Macoah led to the decision to excavate a large trench above the edge of the stream bank. Although the trench had dimensions of 11 m × 2 m at its surface, the ends were stepped down for access and safety, so that only seven metres of the trench's length reached the base of cultural deposits, at a depth of about four metres. A radiocarbon date immediately below the thick humus layer revealed that this part of the site had been abandoned about 700 years ago. Below that, the upper shell stratum is dated to about 2500 BP. Underlying strata have consistently older radiocarbon estimates, with a cluster of dates between 3800 BP and 4000 BP at or near the trench's base (McMillan and St. Claire 1996; McMillan 1998). Ch'uumat'a and Yuquot are now the only two sites on western Vancouver Island to reveal a continuous record of culture history spanning the last four millennia.

The total volume of deposit removed from Ch'uumat'a, over three field seasons of excavation, is approximately 115.7 m³. Of the 750 artifacts recovered, only three are of introduced historic materials. Chipped stone tools and other objects from the trench excavation, dating prior to 2000 BP, differ considerably from contemporaneous materials at Yuquot. This earlier period at Ch'uumat'a is discussed further in Chapter 4, while the post-2000 BP materials are examined in Chapter 5.

In addition to the three major villages, two small midden sites (DfSj 29 and 30) were test excavated on the George Fraser Islands, a cluster of small islands off the tip of the Ucluth Peninsula. *Ch'uch'aa*, the Nuu-chah-nulth term for the George Fraser Islands, was also the name of a Toquaht summer whaling and halibut fishing village. Toquaht informants described the whaling village on these islands, although its exact location could not be determined. The islands are associated with a great whaling chief named *Wiihswisanap*, which means "filling or blocking the pass," who attempted

20   DfSj 30, a lookout site on the outer George Fraser Islands. *Photo by author*

to fill the channel between the two main islands with the bones from the many whales he had killed (St. Claire 1991:157). Blenkinsop (1874:33) stated that although these islands were Toquaht possessions, their use was shared with the Ucluelet. Any whale driven ashore on these islands was shared equally by both groups.

The most extensive excavation took place at DfSj 30, a small saddle-shaped rocky islet on the outer edge of the island cluster (Figure 20). At low tide there is a beach around it and it is joined to surrounding islands, while at high tide the water comes up to its steep sides. The shallow midden deposits that cover its surface are thickest in the centre of the saddle area, tapering off to almost nothing over bedrock at both ends. An excellent view from this site extends across a wide arc, allowing observation of the open ocean, from the entrance to Ucluelet Inlet on one side to the Broken Group Islands in Barkley Sound on the other. The elevated location and commanding view would suggest that this site served as a lookout, probably to watch for whales or other sea mammals.

Excavation at this site took the form of a 10 m × 2 m trench across the central saddle (Figure 21). The average depth of deposit over bedrock was about 70 cm. Approximately 13.9 m³ of deposit was removed. Of the 239 artifacts recovered, all but one, a rolled copper tinkler, were of indigenous materials. Despite the ethnographic association with whaling, the artifact assemblage contains no obvious whaling equipment, such as large slotted harpoon valves, nor was whalebone particularly common in the faunal remains. Ethnographic accounts, however, suggest that these locations were

21 Excavation in progress across the centre of DfSj 30.
Photo by author

used only to watch for whales and that the results of any successful hunt would be towed to the major village of T'ukw'aa. Two radiocarbon dates suggest that this site was occupied only in relatively recent times (i.e., within the last 400 years).

The second George Fraser Islands site (DfSj 29) is on several levels of an inner island, looking directly across to T'ukw'aa. A small excavation, consisting of four 2 m×× 2 m units, removed a total of about 4 m³ of deposit. The concentrated whole and crushed shell layer that made up most of the shallow site matrix showed little trampling, which suggests limited activity. Only ten artifacts, all of bone, were recovered. No radiocarbon samples have been processed for this site, but it would appear to be late, probably coexisting with DfSj 30. The presence of a thick humus layer and the absence of any historic objects, however, suggest that it has not been used in the last few centuries.

Faunal remains from all five excavated sites were abundant. However, analysis of this great quantity of material is still incomplete. Sea mammals, due to their large size, were particularly evident, with whale, sea lion, and porpoise bones frequently noted in the field. Fish bones were extremely numerous, dominating the assemblage from all sites when considered by number of identified elements. These ranged in size from herring (*Clupea harengus pallasi*) and other small fish to the giant bluefin tuna (*Thunnus thynnus*), which is more frequent in these sites than anywhere else on the Northwest Coast (Crockford 1997). Land mammals and birds are also well represented, as are shellfish.

The five sites yielded a total of 2,559 catalogued artifacts, of which 2,451 are of Aboriginal manufacture. Objects of bone and antler dominate the

Table 4

Radiocarbon dates from Toquaht sites

Site	^{14}C age	Lab no.	Comments
Macoah	580 ± 60	Beta-47310	sand at base of deposit
	1840 ± 80	Beta-67472	clay at base of site
T'ukw'aa	640 ± 60	Beta-67474	2 m depth
(village	690 ± 70	Beta-47312	upper terrace, 1.5 m
area)	870 ± 50	Beta-47314	upper terrace, basal clay at 2.3 m
	1150 ± 90	Beta-55803	from hearth in basal sand
T'ukw'aa	150 ± 50	Beta-47313	bottom of shell matrix
(refuge	380 ± 50	Beta-67473	lower shell matrix, near bedrock
area)	560 ± 50	Beta-47311	just above bedrock
	780 ± 90	Beta-50030	near bedrock
Ch'uumat'a	970 ± 60	CAMS-16625	0.2-0.3 m depth
(front	1140 ± 50	Beta-75884	basal sand in front unit, 3 m depth
area)	1990 ± 70	Beta-98010	creek mouth unit near base, 1.8 m
	2010 ± 60	Beta-55799	2.3 m depth
	2280 ± 60	Beta-75885	1.95 m depth
	2290 ± 80	Beta-55802	4.0 m depth
	2450 ± 60	Beta-75886	3.6 m depth, basal sands
Ch'uumat'a	720 ± 50	Beta-55798	just under humus
(back	2510 ±110	Beta-98007	1.0 m depth
trench)	2560 ± 70	Beta-98008	1.1 m depth, in pit of cairn burial
	3010 ± 70	Beta-98009	2.1 m depth
	3480 ± 80	Beta-55800	3.3 m depth
	3760 ± 80	Beta-98012	4.0 m depth, at base of trench
	3810 ± 90	Beta-55801	4.1 m depth, at base
	3900 ± 60	CAMS-3967	3.7 m depth, near base
	4000 ±140	Beta-98011	3.65 m depth, in sand near base
DfSj30	260 ± 60	Beta-75888	near bottom, eastern end of trench
	440 ± 70	Beta-75887	near bottom, western end

latter, comprising 88.6 percent of the total. By far the most numerous artifact categories are bone bipoints and a variety of bone points, assumed to
be parts of composite fishing gear. Other categories of bone objects include
harpoon valves, fishhook shanks, and awls. Whalebone artifacts are not
common but include a wedge, small handle, and comb preform from DfSj 30
and several rough clubs from T'ukw'aa. In addition, a complete bark beater
from T'ukw'aa and a fragmentary bark shredder from Ch'uumat'a, both of
whalebone, show that cedar bark was being prepared for weaving basketry
and clothing. Artifacts of stone account for 9.8 percent of the total. Abrasive stones are most numerous, but this category also includes fishhook
shanks and several small ground stone points, with celts and chipped stone
tools almost entirely limited to Ch'uumat'a, generally from deposits older
than those encountered at the other sites. Artifacts of tooth (1 percent of
total) consist primarily of pendants and other decorative items, along with
several beaver incisor tools. Shell implements (0.7 percent of total) consist
largely of mussel shell tools, such as knives and small celts, along with small
numbers of dentalium and Olivella shell beads and two abalone shell pendants found together at DfSj 30.

With some exceptions, artifacts of Aboriginal manufacture recovered from
the excavated Toquaht sites fall within Mitchell's (1990) West Coast culture
type. The exceptions consist, primarily, of a small number of ground stone
points found at several of the Toquaht sites and chipped stone tools and
detritus from the lower levels of Ch'uumat'a. The only significant absences
among the Toquaht sites from the list of traits established for the West Coast
culture type are deer ulna tools and hand mauls.

Shoemaker Bay and Little Beach
The Shoemaker Bay site (DhSe 2) is located at the end of the long Alberni
Inlet, which cuts through the Vancouver Island mountains from Barkley
Sound to a short distance from the eastern coast. Although this area is
today the political centre for the Nuu-chah-nulth Tribal Council, the Nuu-
chah-nulth presence in the lower Alberni Valley appears to be relatively
recent. Oral histories, discussed in Chapters 2 and 6, describe the forceful
seizure of the rich salmon fishery on the lower Somass River by groups
that later amalgamated to form the Tseshaht. The original occupants, who
apparently spoke a Salishan language, were acculturated as Nuu-chah-nulth.
Excavation at Shoemaker Bay shows close similarities throughout the Prehistoric Period to the Strait of Georgia to the east, confirming the late arrival of the Nuu-chah-nulth from Barkley Sound.

Excavation at Shoemaker Bay was conducted in 1973 and 1974. A total of
132 m³ of deposit was removed, resulting in the recovery of 2,558 in situ
artifacts (an additional 583 were obtained from the disturbed surface), 5
burials, and 20,210 vertebrate faunal elements (McMillan and St. Claire 1982;

Calvert and Crockford 1982). Three major stratigraphic zones are evident, with a fourth zone underlying these at one end of the site. A series of radiocarbon dates (Table 5) shows that the site was first occupied about 4,000 years ago and was abandoned sometime after about 1,000 years ago. No evidence of any historic occupation is evident at this location.

The most recent component, Shoemaker Bay II, is contained in a single stratigraphic zone (Zone A). This is the only zone with a high level of crushed shell, which results in far better preservation of bone and antler than do lower levels. Consequently, most artifacts of those materials and most faunal elements were obtained from this zone. Particularly common artifacts are the valves for composite toggling harpoons and the small wedge-based bone points that served as arming points for such harpoons. Other bone and antler implements include barbed harpoons and fixed barbed points, deer ulna tools, and bone splinter awls. Abrasive stones dominate the stone artifacts, but ground stone points and rectangular celts are also relatively numerous. Chipped stone artifacts are not common but include small chipped basalt points. Faunal remains suggest an emphasis on fishing, particularly for salmon and herring, as well as on hunting, primarily for coast deer (although the harbour seal was also relatively important). All would have been available in the immediate vicinity of the site. Radiocarbon dates suggest an occupation of roughly 1,500 to 1,000 years ago, although the fact that the surface of the site had been levelled off by a bulldozer prior to excavation makes any terminal date uncertain. Although differences are evident, the closest parallels for this component are with the Strait of Georgia culture type defined for the east coast of Vancouver Island (Mitchell 1971, 1990).

The earliest component, Shoemaker Bay I, encompasses materials from all the lower zones. Zone B, a very dark matrix with abundant fire-cracked rock, had only traces of shell. Bone and antler artifacts from Shoemaker Bay I came predominantly from near the top of this zone. Zone C, a lighter brown matrix with abundant pebbles, and Zone D, a light brown to grey sand that occurred only in one portion of the site, had few bone or antler artifacts or faunal remains. The predominance of stone objects in the artifact assemblage is at least partially attributable to the lack of bone preservation in the lower deposits. Numerous chipped stone artifacts include a variety of points and knives as well as abundant microblades and microflakes of quartz crystal and obsidian. Trade networks are indicated by the presence of obsidian from several distant locations, including central Oregon. Numerous abrasive stones dominate the ground stone tools, but points and celts also exist in considerable numbers. The relatively limited bone assemblage consists primarily of small points and splinter awls. Evidence of a large house structure and domestic activities from the lower levels consists of a row of three very large evenly spaced post moulds and numerous large hearths and

concentrations of fire-cracked rock. Several burials came from this component, including one cairn burial, where large rocks had been piled over a
shallow pit containing a partially disarticulated individual with artificial
cranial deformation. What faunal remains exist for these levels suggest an
economy similar to the upper component, based on fishing salmon and
hunting deer and waterfowl. No radiocarbon estimates are available for Zone
B, but several from Zone C suggest a time span of between 1,700 to nearly
3,000 years ago.

The earlier component at Shoemaker Bay could be further subdivided.
Almost all the bone and antler artifacts are found in Zone B, although this
distinction is primarily due to preservation factors. The abundant
microblades and microflakes of quartz crystal and obsidian are heavily concentrated in Zones C and D. In addition, nine water-rolled non-diagnostic
stone objects came from the top of Zone E (the original beach gravels) and
are included in this component as a matter of convenience. They are associated with a radiocarbon date of 4,000 years, presumably marking the initial
occupation of the site, and may considerably predate the other materials
from Shoemaker Bay I. In general, the abundance of chipped stone points
and knives, microblades, ground stone points, and small rectangular celts
in Shoemaker Bay I most closely resembles the temporally equivalent stages
in the Strait of Georgia, the Locarno Beach and Marpole culture types.

Shoemaker Bay's proximity to the east coast of Vancouver Island, along
with the ethnographic traditions of early historic Salishan occupancy of
the Alberni Valley, helps to support the conclusion that this locality was
culturally related to the Strait of Georgia until the relatively late arrival of
the Nuu-chah-nulth. Certainly the artifacts recovered are markedly dissimilar
from those characteristic of other Nuu-chah-nulth area sites. Much more
surprising is a similar claim that has been advanced for an open-ocean site
near Ucluelet.

The Little Beach site (DfSj 100) is in a small open-ocean cove near the end
of the Ucluth Peninsula. Development plans for the site area led to the
excavation of a small test pit in 1990 (French 1990) and more extensive
testing in 1991 (Arcas Consulting Archaeologists 1991; Brolly 1992). In a
brief (two-week) project, mechanical equipment was used to cut 180 m of
trenching across the site. Because a number of burials were encountered
during trenching and left in situ, not all trenches were excavated to basal
deposits. Four 1 m × 1 m units were laid out adjacent to the trenches and
hand-excavated, resulting in the removal of a total of just over 10 m³ of
cultural deposits. The main deposit, containing all the burials encountered
at the site, was a shell midden up to 3 m deep. Several radiocarbon estimates suggest that the midden dates from roughly 4,000 to 3,000 years ago.
An overlying layer of black silty loam yielded a radiocarbon date of about
2,500 years. No evidence of more recent occupation was uncovered, and no

ethnographic traditions of a village in this location could be obtained from Ucluelet informants (Arcas Consulting Archaeologists 1991).

Seventeen definite and six possible burial features, representing at least twenty-seven individuals, were encountered while trenching the midden deposit. Several were in shallow pits covered with low rock cairns and sometimes also with whalebone. Only sixty-eight artifacts were recovered, with forty-one coming from the controlled excavations. Bone points and abrasive stones dominate this small collection, although more diagnostic implements also occur. These include a leaf-shaped chipped stone projectile point, a crudely chipped cobble tool, a thick ground slate point fragment, and a fragment of what appears to be a large flanged labret. Fish elements dominate the vertebrate faunal remains recovered from controlled excavations, with the most numerous being lingcod, rockfish, and greenling, although a wide variety of fish species was present. The most common mammals were cetaceans, northern fur seals, harbour seals, and canids. Although only a small sample of the faunal remains has been analyzed, an economy oriented to open-ocean resources seems evident.

A number of similarities link Little Beach and the lower component at Shoemaker Bay, which are at least partially contemporaneous. Chipped stone projectile points, thick ground stone points, labrets, and cairn burials are found at both sites. Further, all these traits are absent from the West Coast culture type and most closely resemble the Locarno Beach stage in the Strait of Georgia. This led the excavators at Little Beach to suggest that a "major revision" was required in our knowledge of Nuu-chah-nulth prehistory (Arcas

Table 5

Radiocarbon dates from Shoemaker Bay and Little Beach

^{14}C age	Lab no.	Zone	Comments
Shoemaker Bay (from McMillan and St. Claire 1982)			
1130 ± 85	GaK-5432	A	
1450 ± 80	GaK-5108	A	
1730 ± 80	GaK-5107	C	near base of deposit, possibly too recent
1730 ± 90	GaK-5106	C	near base of deposit, possibly too recent
2860 ± 90	GaK-5104	C	from large trench feature
4030 ± 105	GaK-5105	E	top of underlying beach gravels
Little Beach (from Arcas Consulting Archaeologists 1991)			
2510 ± 60	Beta-47923		from humic black deposit, overlying the midden
3310 ± 70	Beta-47925		bone collagen from burial
4000 ± 90	Beta-47924		near base of deposit, overlying cobbles
4000 ± 170	Beta-47655		from base of deposit, overlying sandy beach

Consulting Archaeologists 1991). This is further examined in Chapter 4, along with similar evidence from the lower levels at Ch'uumat'a.

Other Archaeological Research

In Clayoquot Sound itself, the only controlled excavation to take place was in 1985 at the site of Tsacheesowus (DhSk 1) at the eastern end of Meares Island (Arcas Associates 1988). Narrow exploratory trenches were used in an unsuccessful search for buried features associated with an old-style house described for the site by a Tla-o-qui-aht informant. The trenches only extended to the upper levels of this deep midden, and a total of just over 3 m³ of deposit was removed. A large sandstone abrader was the only artifact of Aboriginal manufacture recovered from this site.

On the outer coast of the Esowista Peninsula, near Tofino, two shell midden sites on Chesterman Beach have had minor testing. Six 1 m × 1 m excavation units were spread across two terraces at the disturbed site of DgSl 61, near the south end of the beach (Wilson 1990). The lower deposits contained an abundance of shellfish remains, primarily of *Mytilus californianus*, suggesting that this was a shellfish processing area. The upper level, which may have been a seasonal camp, contained a wider variety of shellfish as well as numerous bones of fish, birds, and mammals. Fish were the most common remains, while the identified mammal bones were dominated by porpoise. These remains and the environmental setting suggest a summer fishing and sea mammal hunting camp. Only fifteen artifacts were found, with bone points and bipoints being most common. No historic materials were recovered. Two radiocarbon dates suggest that the site was first occupied at least 1,500 years ago.

More recently, minor test excavation was carried out at DgSl 67, near the north end of Chesterman Beach (Wilson 1994). Two 1 m × 1 m test pits were excavated in the disturbed and relatively shallow precontact deposits. A variety of fish species dominated the vertebrate faunal remains, while mammal remains consisted primarily of fur seal and sea lion. No artifacts were found. A single radiocarbon estimate indicates that this site was first occupied nearly a millennium ago.

Radiocarbon dates are also available for two sites further south on the outer coast of the Esowista Peninsula, at First Radar Beach (no site number) and at the northern end of Long Beach (Esowista village, DgSk 54). Although neither site has been excavated, auger tests of the middens provided organic materials for dating. A cluster of radiocarbon dates (Table 6) shows that this area was occupied between about 1900 BP and 1100 BP.

Two sites on the Ucluelet reserve of Ittatsoo have had minor test excavations (Arcas Consulting Archeologists 1998). A 2 m × 1 m excavation unit at the Touchie midden (DfSj 41) exposed 0.7 m of deposits. No artifacts were found and no radiocarbon dates are available. More informative was a

Table 6

Radiocarbon dates from other sites in Clayoquot and Barkley Sounds

Site	^{14}C date	Lab no.	Comments	Reference
Chesterman Beach (DgSl 61)	660 ± 80 1480 ± 100	not given not given	lower site, 30-35 cm depth upper bench , 80-85 cm depth	Wilson 1990
Chesterman Beach (DgSl 67)	890 ± 80	AECV-1937C		Wilson 1994
First Radar Beach	1090 ± 60 1100 ± 60 1920 ± 60	CAMS 14442 CAMS 14444 CAMS 14443	auger, 165 cm depth auger, 195 cm depth auger, 185 cm depth	Sumpter et al. 1997
Esowista (DgSk 54)	1390 ± 50 1570 ± 50 1720 ± 50 1850 ± 50	CAMS 29307 CAMS 29305 CAMS 29301 CAMS 29303	auger, 50 cm depth auger, 125 cm depth auger, 250 cm depth auger, 76 cm depth	Sumpter and Fedje 1997

Site	Date (BP)	Lab number	Notes	Reference
Ittatsoo North (DfSj 40)	820 ± 60	Beta-111563	ca. 1 m depth	Arcas Consulting Archeologists 1998
	1560 ± 70	Beta-111554		
	2190 ± 70	Beta-111555		
	2360 ± 140	Beta-111556	2.7 m depth, in possible tsunami sand	
Benson Is. (DfSi 16)	2260 ± 50	CAMS 28075	auger, 270-278 cm depth, just above sand	Sumpter et al. 1997
Aguilar Point (DfSg 3)	705 ± 95	I-4008	thought to date trench embankment	Buxton 1969
	1190 ± 95	I-4007		
Aguilar Point (DfSg 2)	40 ± 50	Beta-56669	top of undisturbed midden, 37 cm	Coates and Eldridge 1992
	170 ± 50	Beta-56668	base of deposit, 120 cm depth	

1 m × 1 m excavation at the Ittatsoo North midden (DfSj 40), in the centre of the modern Ucluelet village. Although this excavation unit, dug alongside a drainage ditch, was terminated for safety reasons at 3.5 m depth, probing demonstrated that the deposits are at least 4 m deep. Bone artifacts, which consist of such characteristic items as points and bipoints, awls, and unidentified fragments, make up 85 percent of the small (39 items) artifact sample, while stone tools (3 abraders, 2 flakes, and a siltstone bead) make up the remaining 15 percent. Lingcod and rockfish dominate the abundant fish remains, while fur seal is the most common of the numerous sea mammal remains. As at Yuquot and Hesquiat Village, albatross is the most common avian species identified. Four radiocarbon age estimates (Table 6), none of which come from the lowest levels, show that this location has been occupied for over 2,300 years.

Although the islands of Barkley Sound have been intensively surveyed, no excavations have taken place. Auger testing at a site on Benson Island (DfSi 16), however, provided materials for dating from the base of the nearly 3 m of deposit (Sumpter et al. 1977). The date of over 2,200 years presumably marks the earliest occupation of this site. This was the important village of *Ts'ishaa*, origin place of the dominant Tseshaht local group.

On the eastern side of Barkley Sound two adjacent sites have been excavated at Bamfield, in the ethnographic territory of the Huu-ay-aht. DfSg 3 is a defensive earthwork at Aguilar Point, near the entrance to Bamfield Inlet. Below this rocky promontory, on the outside of the peninsula, is the ethnographic village of *7O:ts'o:7a* (St. Claire 1991:99-100; Coates and Eldridge 1992:2), today represented by a shell midden designated DfSg 2. Although the two sites are slightly separated, they probably represent the same ethnographic location, which consists of a village and its associated refuge area. Also nearby, on the inside of the peninsula, is DfSg 47, the Bamfield Teacherage site, where semi-controlled excavation salvaged the disturbed burial of a Native female, probably dating to the Historic Period (McLeod and Skinner 1986).

The defensive earthwork at DfSg 3 was formed by the construction of a ditch and embankment, which stretch across the headland for about 15 m. A small test excavation in 1968, consisting of a 1 m × 8 m trench across the mound, confirmed that there had once been a ditch parallel to the mound, with the total height from the bottom of the ditch to the top of the mound being about 1.3 m (Buxton 1969). Only nine artifacts, all of bone, were found, with bone bipoints being the most common. Faunal remains consisted largely of sea mammals, particularly seals. Two radiocarbon dates suggest that people were living at the site about 1,200 years ago and that the ditch was cut through earlier midden deposits about 700 years ago (Buxton 1969:29).

The adjacent village site (*7O:ts'o:7a*; DfSg 2) has also had minor excavation, consisting of a series of shovel test holes and the excavation of three 1 m × 1 m units (Coates and Eldridge 1992). The 2.9 m³ of excavated deposit contained fifty artifacts, of which thirty-two are of Aboriginal manufacture. These are primarily of bone, consisting largely of points and bipoints, with the only stone artifact being an abrader. Faunal remains were relatively abundant, with fur seal and sea lion comprising most of the mammal remains and salmon comprising most of the fish. This is consistent with the open-ocean location of this site. The two radiocarbon dates are remarkably recent. Although both are within the Historic Period, the fluctuations within radiocarbon in recent times make it possible that the dates could actually be late precontact (Coates and Eldridge 1992:14). This would be more consistent with the depth of deposit and the lack of historic artifacts from those levels.

Although defensive sites atop steep rocky promontories are well known in Barkley Sound and elsewhere in Nuu-chah-nulth territory, the defensive earthwork at DfSg 3 is unique. Such trench embankments, however, are relatively common in the Strait of Georgia region. Buxton (1969) lists fifty-eight such sites in southwestern British Columbia and adjacent Washington. Mitchell (1990:348) refers to the "widespread distribution of sites with trench embankment features" as evidence of intergroup hostilities during the late precontact Strait of Georgia culture type. The excavated materials from the two Aguilar Point sites, however, fit comfortably within the West Coast culture type. No strong ties to the Strait of Georgia are evident in the excavated data, although the total sample recovered is very small.

Ditidaht Territory

This long stretch of coastline, from southeast of Barkley Sound to Port San Juan and Point No Point, has received little archaeological attention. Intensive survey has been carried out only along the portion in Pacific Rim National Park (Haggarty and Inglis 1985; Inglis and Haggarty 1986). More recently, the Ditidaht band commissioned an inventory and assessment of heritage resources on its reserve lands, along with the preparation of a management plan (Eldridge 1992). Discovery of significant archaeological resources, including waterlogged intertidal deposits, led to excavation at two such sites in 1994 (Eldridge and Fisher 1997).

The two excavated sites are large multi-terraced settlements on the same Ditidaht reserve, which is located at "The Flats" near the mouth of Nitinat Lake. The large shell midden of DeSf 9 corresponds to the former Ditidaht winter village of *Wikpalhuus*. Nearby, the site of DeSf 10 is so large that it has two ethnographic names, *Hitats'aasak̲* and *Hit'ilhta7sak̲*, corresponding to two clusters of houses (Eldridge 1992:26; Arima et al. 1991:273, 277).

According to Bates (1987:41), this "may have been the site of the largest population concentration in Ditidaht territory." Bouchard and Kennedy (1991:30) describe this as the home of the "original" Ditidaht, who were "said to be very numerous."

Two 1 m × 1 m units were excavated at DeSf 9 and three at DeSf 10 on the flat terraces at the front of the sites, where waterlogged deposits contained artifacts of perishable materials. In addition, shovel tests were taken from the back of the sites, where creeks had exposed deep erosion faces, in order to obtain organic samples for radiocarbon dating. A small sample of artifacts includes such typically West Coast culture type items as small bone points, mussel shell knife fragments, and abrasive stones, the latter being the only stone implements recovered. Objects of such normally perishable materials as basketry and wood dominate the recovered artifact assemblage. These include basket and mat fragments, cordage, bentwood fishhooks, wedges, small wooden points, and several unilaterally barbed wooden points. The barbed and unbarbed wooden points are nearly identical to those of bone from other West Coast sites. Although the sample is very small, the basketry styles show strong similarities to those known from Ozette, thus confirming the close ties between the Ditidaht and the Makah. Fish of a variety of species, including salmon, dogfish, halibut, and lingcod, dominate the faunal assemblages from both sites, followed by sea mammals, including seals, sea lions, and porpoise (Eldridge and Fisher 1997).

At DeSf 9 a series of seven radiocarbon dates was taken from the midden deposits at the back of the site (Table 7). Although the samples were taken from strata spanning about 2 m of deposit, the dates are essentially contemporaneous. This part of the midden appears to have built up very rapidly about 2,400 years ago. A sample of basketry from the waterlogged excavation area at the front of the site dated to about 600 years ago, raising the possibility that there were two discrete periods of occupation. Similar dates were obtained from DeSf 10.

Radiocarbon dates also exist for two sites (DdSe 11 and 23) near the mouth of the Cheewat River, only a short distance south along the coast from the Nitinat River mouth (Sumpter, Fedje, and Sieber 1997). Materials obtained through auger testing of the middens yielded relatively recent dates, providing evidence for only a few centuries of occupation.

One small excavation has occurred in Pacheedaht territory, near the southern end of Wakashan distribution on Vancouver Island. A single 1 m × 1 m unit dug into site DdSc 12, between Port Renfrew and Sombrio Point, revealed about 1.5 m of cultural deposits (Dahlstrom and Wilson 1996; Dahlstrom 1997). Fish, primarily greenling, herring, and rockfish, were the most common faunal remains, along with the abundant shellfish that made up much of the midden. Almost half (sixteen) of the thirty-three artifacts found are of chipped stone, including a projectile point and point preform

Table 7

Radiocarbon dates from Ditidaht territory sites

Site	¹⁴C age	Lab no.	Comments	Reference
Nitinat Lake (DeSf 9)	2390 ± 60	CAMS-14450		Eldridge and Fisher 1997
	2410 ± 60	CAMS-14451		
	2430 ± 50	CAMS-14445		
	2440 ± 60	CAMS-14449		
	2450 ± 60	CAMS-14446		
	2500 ± 60	CAMS-14448		
	2530 ± 60	CAMS-14447		
	610 ± 80	CAMS-14452	from basketry at front of site	
Nitinat Lake (DeSf 10)	2260 ± 60	CAMS-14453		Eldridge and Fisher 1997
	2030 ± 60	CAMS-14455		
	1920 ± 60	CAMS-14454		
	1000 ± 60	Beta-49003		
	690 ± 60	CAMS-14456		
	600 ± 60	CAMS-14457	from front of site	
Cheewat R. (DdSe 11)	240 ± 50	CAMS-28076	20 cm depth	Sumpter et al. 1997
Cheewat R. (DdSe 23)	170 ± 50	CAMS-28077	80 cm depth	Sumpter et al. 1997
DdSc 12	4120 ± 130	not given	1.5 m depth, base of deposit	Dahlstrom and Wilson 1996

(both of basalt) along with flake tools and debitage. Ground slate tools are also represented. A single date from the base of the cultural deposits is 4120 ± 130 BP, making this one of the oldest dated sites on the west coast of Vancouver Island.

Olympic Peninsula

The Makah, the southernmost Wakashans, occupy the northwestern portion of the Olympic Peninsula around Cape Flattery. Their nineteenth-century territory stretched east along the Strait of Juan de Fuca to the Hoko River, which was also claimed by the Clallam Salish, and south beyond

Cape Alava, where they bordered on the Quileute. Five semi-autonomous winter village groups, linked by ties of kinship and common traditions, made up the Makah people in the nineteenth century (Swan 1870; Taylor 1974; Renker and Gunther 1990). Although these major villages seem to have been occupied for much or all of the year, during the warmer months many people moved to more exposed locations, such as Tatoosh Island off Cape Flattery, to fish for halibut and to hunt sea mammals (Renker and Gunther 1990; Huelsbeck and Wessen 1995).

Ozette

Ozette (*Usee7ilh*; 45CA24), at Cape Alava on the Olympic Peninsula's open Pacific coast, was the southernmost and most isolated of the Makah villages. The huge shell midden that marks the village location stretches for over a kilometre along the beach, making this the largest site on the Washington coast. While providing immediate access to the resources of the open Pacific, the site itself was protected by offshore islands and reefs. Tskawahyah (Cannonball) Island, joined to the village by a sandspit at low tide, forms part of the Ozette site complex. Shell midden deposits atop this steep-sided rocky island indicate its use as a lookout or defensive location. Ozette was occupied for at least two millennia, continuing into the early twentieth century when the last inhabitants moved to the main Makah community of Neah Bay.

Research at this important site began in 1966, with the excavation of a trench through the midden deposits (McKenzie 1974; Samuels and Daugherty 1991). This 2 m wide trench extended for 70 m perpendicular to the beach, cutting through several distinct terraces and, in places, reaching depths of over 3 m. In total, about 200 m^3 of midden was removed (Huelsbeck 1994b:278). In the following year, further excavation took place south of the main trench, in an area where remains of recent longhouses could be seen decaying in the thick vegetation. Although most of the deposit removed was shell midden, essentially identical to that of the earlier trench, waterlogged deposits were encountered at lower levels in some of the excavation units. The corner of a well preserved wooden house was exposed in one unit, and such normally perishable materials as basketry and wooden wedges and box parts were common. These early excavations also included testing the offshore islands, including the deep midden deposits atop Tskawahyah Island. Later, additional excavation in the midden portion of the site was carried out by E. Friedman (1976), who dug two 2 m x 2 m units, with an average depth of about 1.5 m, on the uppermost terrace near the top of the earlier trench.

The results of the early excavations at Ozette have never been fully reported, although McKenzie (1974) provides an analysis of artifacts from the lower portion of the 1966 trench. Throughout the midden deposits, there was evidence of a highly maritime subsistence orientation. Gustafson (1968) estimated that nearly 80 percent of the numerous marine mammal bones recovered from the trench are those of northern fur seal and that reliance upon this mammal remained constant throughout the occupation of the site. E. Friedman (1976:109) found even higher percentages of fur seal in his upper terrace excavation. Fur seals are pelagic mammals, requiring the hunters to venture out to sea to procure them (Friedman and Gustafson 1975). Whalebones were also common in the midden deposits. Although fish bones from this part of the site have not been analyzed, the majority of the artifacts recovered are small bone and antler portions of composite fishing gear (McKenzie 1974:138). In her examination of the artifacts from the trench, McKenzie (1974:147) denies any "significant morphological change" throughout the period of site occupation and maintains that, "with few exceptions," all artifacts are "comparable with ethnographic forms." The "few exceptions" include some objects of chipped stone, which are concentrated in the earliest levels. These, and some "heavy ground slate knives," are the only artifact types from the Ozette trench that would be out of place in the West Coast culture type (as proposed for the Nuu-chah-nulth area).

   The time represented by these midden deposits is uncertain. Gustafson (1968:50) maintains that the site was occupied for about 2,000 years, based on stratigraphic evidence and four radiocarbon dates, and McKenzie (1974:26) follows Gustafson. These dates were never published or reported, however. The two earliest dates from the trench excavation are 1495 ± 300 BP (Daugherty and Fryxell n.d.:4) and 1835 ± 305 BP (J.C. Sheppard, WSU Radiocarbon Laboratory, pers. comm. 1995). All have very large margins of error. McKenzie (1974:27) submitted an additional sample from a lower level of the trench, which revealed a date of only 180 ± 70 years. This date seems unacceptably recent for the depth at which it was recovered, although it is associated with artifact types, such as stone fishhook shanks, which are known to be late at excavated Nuu-chah-nulth sites. Upper terrace deposits yielded age estimates of 440 and 710 BP (E. Friedman 1976:84). The oldest date yet available from this site, at about 2,000 years, comes from the base of deep midden deposits on Tskawahyah Island (Samuels and Daugherty 1991:11). It seems likely that the earliest deposits in the village area should be at least of equivalent age. All Ozette radiocarbon age results are listed in Table 8.

   The most spectacular discoveries at Ozette occurred after 1970. At the beginning of that year winter storms sent huge waves crashing into the bank along the edge of the village, causing slumps that exposed portions of a preserved wooden house and its contents (Figure 22). The importance of this discovery and the recognition that invaluable objects and information would be lost without immediate attention led the Makah Tribal Council to request archaeological salvage work, which began that summer (Kirk with

Daugherty 1974; Daugherty 1988; Samuel and Daugherty 1991). This salvage excavation soon expanded into a major year-round archaeological
project, with fieldwork continuing until 1981. When the project was eventually halted, over 800 m² of site area had been cleared, completely expos-
ing the floors of three houses and portions of several others (Samuels and
Daugherty 1991:23; Samuels 1989:143; Huelsbeck and Wessen 1994:3).
Hydraulic excavation techniques were developed, which involved the use

Table 8

Radiocarbon dates from Ozette

¹⁴C age	Lab no.	Location	Comments	Reference
180 ± 70	I-7175	midden trench	lower stratum, likely too recent	McKenzie 1974:27
585 ± 210	WSU-499	midden trench		J.C.Sheppard, pers. comm.
900 ± 305	WSU-506	midden trench		J.C.Sheppard, pers. comm.
1495± 300	WSU-507	midden trench		Daugherty and Fryxell n.d.
1835± 305	WSU-505	midden trench		J.C.Sheppard, pers. comm.
440 ± 65	WSU-1609	upper terrace	near base	Friedman 1976:84
710 ± 65	WSU-1610	upper terrace	near base	Friedman 1976:84
440 ± 90	WSU-1778	House 1	hearth	Samuels 1991:186
790 ± 80	WSU-1865	house area	stratum below houses	Samuels 1991:180
810 ± 70	WSU-1777	house area	stratum below houses	Samuels 1991:180
285 ± 180	?	south end of site		Daugherty and Fryxell n.d.
495 ± 330	?	south end of site		Daugherty and Fryxell n.d.
980 ± 180	WSU-1122	Tskawahyah Is.		Moss and Erlandson 1992:84
2010± 190	WSU-1123	Tskawahyah Is.	near base	Samuels and Daugherty 1991:11

22 Excavation in the main house area at Ozette, 1973. Note the two whale skulls and articulated vertebrae in the foreground. *Photo by author*

of high-pressure hoses to remove the thick clay deposit and smaller hoses with adjustable pressure to expose delicate perishable objects (Gleeson and Grosso 1976). Over 50,000 precontact artifacts, between 20,000 and 40,000 preserved wooden structural elements, and over 1,000,000 identified or identifiable faunal elements were recovered from the extensive excavations in this portion of the site (Wessen 1990:416; Samuels and Daugherty 1991:24; Samuels 1991:178; Huelsbeck 1994a:20).

These spectacular discoveries at Ozette were the result of a natural disaster, in the form of a massive mudslide. Sometime shortly before contact with Europeans a section of the hillside above the village gave way, possibly as a result of an earthquake. A mass of liquefied clay roared down the slope, crushing and burying at least four houses that stood in its path. Many of the roof planks and beams were swept out onto the beach by the force of the slide, but the lower portions of the houses and most of the contents were sealed beneath a layer of wet clay up to 3 m thick. The deposits immediately below the clay were kept permanently saturated by subsurface water flow, resulting in excellent preservation of all items of wood or bark. Broken and scattered architectural elements and almost the entire contents of the houses at the time the slide struck were exposed as excavation proceeded (Figure 23). Ozette provides an unprecedented opportunity to study the nearly complete material culture of a late precontact Northwest Coast society at a single moment of time.

23 This broken plank, carved with the images of the Thunderbird and Wolf, was exposed during excavation of one of the house floors at Ozette. Other planks visible in this picture are from the house walls. *Photo by Pete Rice, courtesy Makah Cultural and Research Center, Neah Bay*

The exact timing of this disaster is not certain. Initially, the slide was estimated to have occurred perhaps 450 or 500 years ago, or roughly AD 1500 (Kirk with Daugherty 1974:90; Daugherty and Friedman 1983:183; Wessen 1990:416). More recently, dendrochronological studies on the cedar planks of a house destroyed by the slide yielded dates of AD 1613 and 1719, respectively, although both planks are missing their outer rings and bark (Samuels 1991:186; Huelsbeck 1994a:20). The lack of European material items among the house contents indicates precontact occupation, probably prior to Captain Cook's arrival in Nootka Sound in 1778 (when the Nuu-chah-nulth first obtained a substantial quantity of European goods) and certainly before 1792 (when the Spanish built a short-lived fort at Neah Bay) (Swan 1870:4; Wagner 1933; Cook 1973). This slide, therefore, was an eighteenth-century event, occurring sometime after AD 1719 and prior to about 1778.

The house from which the planks came showed signs of use and repair, suggesting that it had been occupied for a considerable period, perhaps about 'entury, at the time of its destruction (Huelsbeck 1989:157; Samuels 1:186). A radiocarbon date of over 400 BP was obtained from a hearth at 'owest house levels, providing the earliest evidence for a house at this location (Samuels 1991:186). Underlying the deposits associated with the protohistoric houses affected by the slide are late precontact midden deposits, which provided two radiocarbon age estimates of around 800 BP (Samuels 1991:180; Samuels and Daugherty 1991:21). These are the earliest cultural materials from this portion of the site. Throughout the depositional sequence at Ozette, clay layers show that the eighteenth-century slide that covered the excavated houses was not a unique event and that the inhabitants of this village had been forced periodically to contend with the consequences of slope instability. Makah oral histories also tell of repeated mudslides that plagued the village inhabitants (Renker and Arnold 1988:303).

Although the force of the slide snapped upright support posts and scattered the planks, the great quantity of architectural elements preserved in the waterlogged deposits allowed the reconstruction of house forms (Mauger 1991). The three completely excavated examples were large, plank-covered shed-roof structures, closely resembling historic Makah dwellings. Drainage ditches, frequently lined with whalebone, ran along the house walls to take runoff from the hillside away from the house floors. One house, along the front row of the village, has a number of features (such as carved wall panels) that suggest it was occupied by a high-status household (Huelsbeck 1989; Samuels 1989).

The nearly complete contents of these houses were also preserved within the waterlogged deposits. Of the great quantity of artifacts recovered, over 85 percent are of perishable materials (Samuels and Daugherty 1991:4). Woven or twisted plant fibre objects, such as cordage, baskets, pouches, hats, capes, and mats, are numerous (Croes 1977, 1980a). The abundant wooden artifacts include fishhooks, clubs, wedges, bows and arrows, bowls, and kerfed-corner boxes (Gleeson 1980; Mauger 1982; Daugherty and Friedman 1983). Numerous finely carved wooden artworks, from decorated bowls and clubs to large incised panels, feature such motifs as the Thunderbird, Wolf, and Whale – all characteristic of historic Nuu-chah-nulth and Makah art (Daugherty and Friedman 1983). The exceptional circumstances of this site even led to the recovery of such ritual items as a large wooden effigy of a whale dorsal fin, inlaid with sea otter teeth forming the outline image of the Thunderbird, suggesting whaling ceremonies similar to those described ethnographically. The typical bone and antler artifacts that characterize Nuu-chah-nulth and Makah shell midden sites are present but are greatly reduced in importance. The small bone points that dominate most assemblages play only a minor role here and are often found as parts of composite tools, such as the barbs on wooden fishhooks. Small quantities of iron also appear in these protohistoric house deposits, generally as the cutting edges of woodworking tools and knives. The source of this metal is not known, but its origins must be in Europe or Asia and must have reached the people of Ozette shortly before direct contact with outsiders.

The excavated house floors and intervening midden deposits also yielded a vast array of faunal remains (Huelsbeck 1981, 1988a, 1994a, 1994b; DePuydt 1994; Wessen 1982, 1988, 1994a). The late precontact occupants at Ozette collected 90 species of shellfish, took 18 species of fish, and hunted 42 bird species and 27 mammal species (Huelsbeck and Wessen 1994:10). However, a relatively small number of species dominate each class. This is particularly the case with regard to mammals; when whalebones are excluded, 90 percent of all mammal remains come from a single species – the northern fur seal (Huelsbeck 1989:163; 1994a:28). Grey and humpback whales were also a major part of the Ozette economy, representing such a huge quantity of meat and oil that whale products were likely a significant trade commodity (Huelsbeck 1988a, 1988b, 1994b). Halibut, lingcod, and salmon were the principal food fishes. California mussel, little-neck clams, and chitons were among the most important shellfish in the diet. A highly maritime way of life is evident in an economy dominated by whaling, sealing, and halibut fishing.

Swan (1870:6) describes Ozette as being occupied during the winter, the people dispersing to various fishing locations in the other seasons. Faunal analysis, however, indicates that this was a year-round settlement. Although most fishing and sea mammal hunting took place from spring to fall (Huelsbeck 1994a, 1994b), the presence of various species of fish, birds, and shellfish indicates procurement throughout much of the year (Huelsbeck 1994a; DePuydt 1994; Wessen 1988, 1994a). Population levels may have fluctuated seasonally, but it would appear that at least some people remained in residence throughout the year, as was probably true of all the ethnographic Makah "winter villages" (Huelsbeck and Wessen 1995).

The remarkably complete material record at Ozette and the extensive nature of the excavations, which exposed entire house floors, have resulted in insights into the social realm, both within and between houses. Analysis of floor deposits within each house has indicated individual family spaces and various activity areas (Samuels 1989, 1994). Even the living areas of individual basket weavers can be discerned when the distributions of minor variations in style are examined (Croes and Davis 1977). The differential distribution of artifacts and faunal remains across the house floors provides evidence of status distinctions within the houses, particularly in House 1 (Huelsbeck 1989; Samuels 1989). Uncommon items such as decorative shells, including a string of dentalium beads, were concentrated in one rear corner of the house, correspondeding to the ethnographic location of high-status residential areas.

Various lines of evidence suggest that the occupants of House 1, the structure closest to the beach, held higher status than did those of the other two households in the excavated area (Huelsbeck 1989, 1994a; Samuels 1989, 1994; Wessen 1988, 1994a). This was the only house to contain carved wall panels, decorated bench planks, and a central hearth. It also contained the largest number of decorative shells and whaling gear. Differences in the overall pattern of faunal remains also suggest differential access to resources between households. House 1 had considerably more salmon and halibut bones, suggesting control of the restricted areas in which these species could be taken, while the occupants of House 5 had to exploit more widely available fish species (Huelsbeck 1988a, 1989). Analysis of shellfish also indicates that House 5 exploited a different set of beaches than did the other two houses (Wessen 1988, 1994a). Huelsbeck (1989:166) concludes: "Houses 1 and 2 exploited similar resource territories but more of the preferred foods were consumed in House 1 than in House 2. These two households probably were members of the same local group, with House 1 ranked higher than House 2. House 5 exploited a different suite of territories and almost certainly belonged to a different local group."

The preserved house deposits at Ozette allow us to develop a remarkably complete picture of late precontact lifeways. They provide unique insights into all aspects of a functioning community, including the social realm. Ozette serves as an invaluable reference point in interpreting the more poorly preserved archaeological remains from shell midden sites, which provide most of the evidence on which our understanding of Nuu-chah-nulth, Ditidaht, and Makah culture history is based. As the main excavated area at Ozette is protohistoric, however, dating only to the period immediately preceding European contact, this site yields little evidence concerning either the origin or the development of the cultural traits evident.

Hoko River

Two excavated sites lie close together near the mouth of the Hoko River, on the Strait of Juan de Fuca approximately 30 km from the northwest tip of the Olympic Peninsula at Cape Flattery. The Hoko River was considered the ethnographic boundary between the Makah and the Clallam, a Straits Salish-speaking group to the east. Both groups apparently maintained seasonal fishing stations along the lower river. A number of Makah families moved from Neah Bay each summer and fall to fish along the Hoko River, a practice that continued well into this century (Colson 1953:44; Virden and Brinck-Lund 1980).

The oldest of the two sites is the Hoko River wet/dry site (45CA213), which is located on the river about half a kilometre from its mouth (Figure 24). The "wet" portion of the site was formed in a lagoon or estuary setting, where vegetal materials, such as twigs and pine cones, became waterlogged and sank in the still waters (Blinman 1980; Croes 1995). The organic mats that were formed in this way also include numerous artifacts of plant fibre that were lost or discarded in the estuary and also sank to the bottom. Over the following centuries, the deposits were uplifted by tectonic activity and exposed by the changing course of the river, although most remain within the range of tidal fluctuations and can only be examined during low tides. The "dry" portion of the site, consisting of the sands and gravels above the wet deposits, represents the original bank on which the fishing camps were located. An initial test of the waterlogged deposits in 1967 employed what is thought to have been the first developed hydraulic excavation techniques employed on any Northwest Coast site (Croes 1976:209). A later test excavation in 1973 was followed by more extensive fieldwork from 1977 to 1987 (Croes and Blinman 1980; Howes 1982; Croes 1995).

This site contains the oldest perishable materials in the study area. Radiocarbon dates from both the wet riverbank deposits and the dry campsite range between about 2800 BP and 2200 BP (Croes 1995). An additional date, taken from a hearth in an excavation unit further downriver, towards the Late Period rockshelter near the mouth of the Hoko, is 1700 BP. This suggests that the lower Hoko area as a whole may have been used seasonally throughout most of the last 3,000 years. See Table 9 for all radiocarbon dates from the Hoko River sites.

Numerous plant fibre artifacts are encased in the layers of vegetal fibre that characterize the waterlogged deposits (Figures 25 and 26). Cordage is by far the most common artifact class, comprising about 61 percent of the

24   Hydraulic excavation in the intertidal zone at the Hoko River wet site, 1978. The tires along the bank are to protect the workers from falling gravel. *Photo courtesy of Dale Croes*

total, with most representing parts of fishing lines or leaders (Ayers 1980; Croes 1980c, 1993, 1995). Basketry artifacts, including baskets, mats, and hats in several distinct styles, are also abundant. Many of the baskets are open-weave pack baskets of the type used for carrying fish. Over 400 wooden fishhooks recovered from the riverbank indicate the major activity carried out at this site (Croes 1988, 1995; Croes and Hackenberger 1988). These fishhooks are of two types: V-shaped composite hooks with bone barbs, which are thought to have been used mainly for flatfish, and U-shaped bentwood hooks that are thought to have been used mainly for Pacific cod (Hoff 1980; Croes 1988). Several hafted microliths, still held in their cedar splint handles with spruce root or cedar bark bindings, are believed, as a result of replicative analysis and experimental use, to have been fish processing knives (Flenniken 1980, 1981; Croes 1988:136). Wooden wedges, floats, and small points were also found, as were a number of large unilaterally barbed points, some of which are elaborately decorated (Croes 1992a, 1995; Ayers 1980). A finely carved wooden sculpture depicting two birds (possibly kingfishers or pileated woodpeckers) shown beak-to-beak came from the earliest levels at this site and may be the oldest known artwork in wood on the Northwest Coast (Croes 1988:137; 1995:175).

The dry campsite area lacks any preservation of organic materials but does contain stone tools and such features as slab-lined hearths, concentrations of fire-cracked rock, and manufacturing areas for vein quartz microliths

25 Composite fishhook, with wooden shanks, bone barb, and spruce-root wrapping, along with its cordage leader, in situ in the waterlogged deposits at Hoko River. *Photo courtesy of Dale Croes*

26 Large fragment of open-weave carrying basket in situ in the waterlogged deposits at Hoko River. *Photo courtesy of Dale Croes*

(Flenniken 1981; Howes 1982; Croes and Hackenberger 1988; Croes 1995). The stone tools include chipped basalt and chalcedony projectile points, large ground slate projectile points, small rectangular celts, quartz crystal microblades, and vein quartz microliths. Small post moulds suggest that a cluster of temporary mat-covered dwellings, similar to those used in ethnographic summer fishing camps, once provided shelter at this location (Howes 1982; Croes 1988, 1995).

At the mouth of the Hoko River is the second excavated site, the Hoko River Rockshelter (45CA21). Shell midden deposits, reaching a maximum depth of 3.3 m, fill a large natural rockshelter. Forty-three 1 m × 1 m units were excavated between 1979 and 1985, resulting in a large sample of faunal remains and over 1,600 artifacts (Wigen and Stucki 1988). The most common of the latter were small bone bipoints and harpoon arming points, along with mussel shell knives and abrasive stones. Chipped stone implements, however, including cores, cobble tools, cortex flakes, and scrapers, were also fairly common. Numerous features, including hearths and refuse dumps, identify living surfaces and activity areas within the rockshelter (Miller 1984; Croes and Hackenberger 1988:21). This site represents a considerably later occupation than does the nearby wet/dry site, spanning the period from about 900 BP to 100 BP (Miller 1984:174; Wigen and Stucki 1988:90; Croes 1989:107).

Table 9

Radiocarbon dates from Hoko River sites

^{14}C age	Lab no.	Comments

Hoko River wet/dry site (45CA213)

^{14}C age	Lab no.	Comments
2210 ± 70	WSU-1442	wet site
2530 ± 60	WSU-2014	wet site
2570 ± 70	WSU-2201	wet site
2580 ± 80	WSU-2016	wet site
2610 ± 100	WSU-2015	wet site
2750 ± 90	WSU-1443	wet site
2750 ± 90	WSU-2200	wet site
2520 ± 90	WSU-2203	dry campsite
2770 ± 90	WSU-2202	dry campsite
1700 ± 65	WSU-2656	from hearth, downriver from main site

Hoko River rockshelter (45CA21)

^{14}C age	Lab no.	Comments
150 ± 60	WSU-2872	near surface
185 ± 85	WSU-2344	
175 ± 70	WSU-2873	
225 ± 120	WSU-2308	3 m depth
720 ± 95	WSU-2307	
920 ± 50	WSU-2343	

Sources: Wet/dry site: Croes and Blinman 1980:89; Flenniken 1981:34; Croes 1995. Rockshelter: Croes, pers. comm. 1995

Fishing appears to have been the primary activity carried out at Hoko River over the past 3,000 years. Flatfish such as halibut dominate the faunal remains from the wet site, followed by rockfish, cod, salmon, and dogfish (Huelsbeck 1980:105; Croes 1992b:346). At the later rockshelter site, most of the fishbones represent locally available rocky-bottom fish, such as greenling and rockfish, followed by salmon; halibut and other flatfish are relatively rare (Wigen and Stucki 1988:90-91). Bones of a variety of bird and mammal species, the latter dominated by northern fur seal, are also preserved in the rockshelter's shell midden deposits. Seasonality assessment based on shellfish suggests high collection levels for late spring through summer, followed by a drop in fall and probable abandonment of the site in the winter (Miller 1984). Fish remains from the wet site also suggest a summer and probable fall occupation (Huelsbeck 1980:108).

In a series of articles based on the Hoko River research, Croes (1987, 1988, 1989, 1992a, 1992b) and Croes and Hackenberger (1988) have argued that the well established "phases" or "culture types" for the southern coast are better understood as economic plateaus. Based on such lithic artifact types as thick ground slate points, chipped contracting stem points, and quartz crystal microblades, the Hoko River wet/dry site has been placed in the Locarno Beach culture type established for the Strait of Georgia (Mitchell 1990). The later deposits of the rockshelter, dominated by small bone points, are placed within the late precontact Strait of Georgia culture type. Such shifts in economic adaptation and technology, in this argument, characterize a broad region and have no direct bearing on ethnicity. Perishables such as basketry and cordage are believed to be far more sensitive indicators of ethnicity than are implements of stone and bone (Bernick 1987; Croes 1987, 1989). In this regard, Hoko basketry and cordage styles show the closest resemblance to those at the much later Ozette site, while differing markedly from basketry at temporally equivalent waterlogged sites, such as Musqueam Northeast, in the Strait of Georgia. In this argument, then, technological similarities with the Locarno Beach and Strait of Georgia culture types are viewed as reflecting similar economic adaptations, while the ethnic identity of the Hoko River people is linked with Ozette and the Makah.

Other Makah Area Sites

Two of the five Makah "winter villages" listed by Swan (1870:6) were located at Neah Bay on the Strait of Juan de Fuca near Cape Flattery. The inhabitants of Bihada (*Bi7id7a*), at the eastern end of the bay, moved in the mid-nineteenth century to join the residents of Diah (*Diiyaa*), often rendered as Neah, near the western end. The modern Makah community of Neah Bay sits on disturbed shell midden deposits, designated site 45CA22, dating to the late Prehistoric and early Historic Periods.

Two small-scale archaeological projects have taken place at this site. While testing several ethnographic Makah sites to place the Ozette research in a broader context, Friedman (1976) excavated two 1.5 m × 1.5 m test pits and one 1 m × 2 m unit in the midden deposits near the beach. Two radiocarbon determinations provided "modern" results, despite deposits that reached depths of nearly 2 m, although neither date came from the lowest stratum. In 1988, Wessen (1991) excavated a 1 m × 2 m test unit at a location further back from the modern beach, obtaining two radiocarbon dates indicating that this site was occupied over two millennia ago. The meagre collection of artifacts from both excavations (a total of sixteen objects of Aboriginal manufacture from Friedman's work and nine from Wessen's) are dominated by small bone points (Wessen 1991:12, 24). Faunal remains are much more numerous, indicating use of a wide range of marine and terrestrial resources. Bones of fur seal were the most common vertebrate remains recovered by Friedman, while fish, particularly greenling and rockfish, dominate the fauna in Wessen's sample.

Three sites around Cape Flattery were identified as Makah summer villages by Swan (1870:6). Tatoosh Island (45CA207) lies immediately off the cape, Warmhouse (or Kiddekubbut) (45CA204) is at the entrance to the

Strait of Juan de Fuca, and Archawat (45CA206) lies on the open Pacific. All three were tested by Friedman (1976). Only "sparse midden deposits" were encountered at Archawat, where two excavated units yielded only a few artifacts and a small quantity of faunal remains, with fur seal and deer being the most common mammals. Two excavated units at Warmhouse reached depths of over a metre but again yielded few artifacts or faunal remains, although it appears that the ubiquitous rockfish was a major economic resource for residents at this site. Tatoosh Island, ethnographically a vital Makah halibut fishing location, has deeper and more concentrated, although disturbed, deposits. Two excavated units reached depths of 1.3 m and 1.4 m, while a third unit was discontinued when human skeletal elements were encountered. In addition to abundant fish remains, bones of sea mammals were common, with fur seal comprising more than 90 percent of the total. Artifacts were primarily small bone points, although bone harpoon valves and stone fishhook shanks were also found. Radiocarbon dates for Archawat and Warmhouse show occupation only within the last several hundred years, while use of Tatoosh Island dates back at least a millennium. In addition, an unexcavated site at Cape Flattery (45CA2) has yielded a date of approximately 2,000 BP, based on charcoal taken from an exposed midden face (Wessen, pers. comm. 1995). Table 10 lists all known radiocarbon dates for Makah-area sites.

Wayatch (*Wa7ach'*; 45CA1), on the open Pacific side of the Olympic Peninsula, is another of the major winter villages identified by Swan. Eleven 1.2 m × 1.2 m units, forming two trenches, were excavated at this site in 1955 (Taylor 1974). No radiocarbon samples were taken and little specific information has been reported, except that clams, mussels, and sea mammals, particularly whales, made up much of the diet. In 1991 Wessen (1993:18) excavated a 1 m × 2 m unit at this site, obtaining two radiocarbon dates within the last 200 years. Much greater time depth, however, is indicated by a road cut through a ridge back from and above the excavated unit and the modern beach. A profile cleared at this location revealed about 1.6 m of midden deposit and yielded radiocarbon age estimates of 1790 BP from the uppermost stratum and 3810 BP from near the bottom of this exposure (Wessen 1992, pers. com. 1995). The latter date makes this the earliest dated site on the ocean coast of Washington. Faunal remains, consisting largely of sea mammals and deep water fish, suggest a fully maritime economy from earliest occupation. Faunal remains also indicate that, despite the ethnographic classification as winter village, this site was probably occupied year-round (Wessen 1993:19; Huelsbeck and Wessen 1995).

Further south, about halfway between Cape Flattery and Ozette, is the ethnographic winter village of Tsoo-yess, or Sooes (*Ts'uuyas*; 45CA25). Friedman (1976) excavated two 1 m × 2 m units and one 2 m × 2 m unit at this site, in deposits that reached 3 m in depth. Radiocarbon samples from near the base of the deposit in two different units yielded age estimates of approximately 1,000 and 1,100 BP. The small artifact assemblage consists largely of bone points, but harpoon valves, several stone fishhook shanks, and a decorated bone comb were also found. As at the other open-ocean Makah sites, a maritime economy is indicated in the faunal remains by a variety of fish species and a mammalian assemblage heavily dominated by northern fur seal.

Two excavated sites lie a short distance south of Ozette in an area that may have been used by both the Makah and the Quileute (Renker and Gunther 1990; Powell 1990). The most northerly, and the first to be excavated, is the White Rock Village site (45CA30). Initial test excavations in 1955 were followed by a larger project in 1961 (Guinn 1963). Twenty-nine 1.5 m x 1.5 m squares were excavated, forming several long trenches, into deposits reaching 1.7 m depth. A total of 248 artifacts was collected, of which 69 (27.8 percent) are wedges, primarily of whalebone. Other artifact types include bone points, harpoon valves, abrasive stones, and stone sinkers. Sea mammal hunting, fishing, and shellfish collecting were the basis of the economy. Guinn's (1963:13) assessment of late age for the site was borne out by one radiocarbon determination of less than 400 years.

A short distance south of White Rock is the Sand Point site (45CA201), located on what appears to be an old marine terrace a considerable distance back from the modern beach. It was first tested by Daugherty and the Ozette crew in 1966, during the initial examination of the Cape Alava area (Wessen 1984:3; 1993:19-20). Unfortunately, no field notes or other documentation from this early work are available, although a radiocarbon age of over 6,000 years was apparently obtained (Daugherty and Fryxell n.d.:4, 13; Wessen 1993:20). As the exact circumstances and provenience of this date are unknown, and as it was not substantiated by later fieldwork, this date must be considered suspect.

This suggestion of an early age prompted Wessen to do further work at this site. In 1979 he excavated a 1 m x 2 m unit near the location of the original test (Wessen 1984), returning in 1991 to excavate a 0.5 m x 2 m extension to this unit (Wessen 1993). Radiocarbon dates, taken from the uppermost and lowermost cultural strata in the 1.8 m deep exposure, indicate that this site was occupied between about 1,600 and 2,300 years ago. The eighty-two artifacts recovered from the combined three field projects differ from those at other open-ocean Makah sites in that chipped stone implements comprise the majority. Most are debitage, showing evidence of both simple and bipolar percussion techniques, but retouched spall tools and several biface fragments were also found. Bone implements are dominated by small bone points and bipoints but also include unilaterally barbed points and a fishhook shank. Fish, primarily halibut, rockfish, and lingcod, were the most abundant faunal remains. Fur seal bones were also numerous, comprising over 80 percent of all mammal remains. Faunal studies suggest a multi-season, possibly year-round, occupation at this site (Wessen 1993:60).

An unexcavated shell midden site (45CA423) is on the lower terrace near Sand Point, directly below 45CA201. This was examined as part of the 1991 fieldwork in an attempt to understand the timing of terrace formation. Whalebone eroding from the beach face of the midden yielded a radiocarbon age of 650 BP, while charcoal from the inland edge of the midden gave a date of 1550 BP (Wessen 1993:38), indicating occupation following abandonment of the upper terrace site. Probing at another unexcavated site at Cedar Creek (45CA29), a short distance south of Sand Point and also associated with modern sea levels, provided a date of over 1,100 BP (Wessen, pers. comm. 1995).

Table 10

Radiocarbon dates from other Makah-area sites

^{14}C age	Lab no.	Comments	Reference
Neah Bay (45CA22)			
"modern"	WSU-1607	83 cm depth	Friedman 1976:80
"modern"	WSU-1608	150 cm depth	Friedman 1976:80
2170 ± 60	Beta-28734	probably disturbed	Wessen 1991:22
2070 ± 70	Beta-28735	near base	Wessen 1991:22
Archawat (45CA206)			
150 ± 60	WSU-1604	near base (122 cm depth)	Friedman 1976:85
Warmhouse (45CA204)			
200 ± 60	WSU-1603	near base (96 cm depth)	Friedman 1976:82
Tatoosh Island (45CA207)			
960 ± 70	WSU-1606		Friedman 1976:87
Cape Flattery (45CA2)			
1970 ± 80	Beta-58385	from exposure face	Wessen 1995
Wayatch (45CA1)			
110 ± 60	Beta-47545	from test pit	Wessen 1995
180 ± 70	Beta-47546	from test pit	Wessen 1995
1790 ± 70	Beta-47547	from road cut (top)	Wessen 1995
3810 ± 60	Beta-47548	from road cut (bottom)	Wessen 1992, 1995

▶

◀ *Table 10*

¹⁴C age	Lab no.	Comments	Reference
Upper Wayatch (45CA400)			
2690 ± 60	Beta-80923	raised terrace inland	Wessen 1995
Tsoo-yess (45CA25)			
980 ± 60	WSU-1611	at base (2.88 m depth)	Friedman 1976:91
1110 ± 60	WSU-1612	near base (2.52 m depth)	Friedman 1976:93
White Rock (45CA30)			
387 ± 42	not given	lowermost level	Guinn 1963:13
Sand Point (45CA201)			
1600 ± 75	SI-4366	uppermost deposit	Wessen 1984:15
2270 ± 75	SI-4367	lowermost deposit	Wessen 1984:15
6065 ± 250	WSU-498	date not accepted	Wessen 1993:20
Sand Point, lower terrace site (45CA423)			
650 ± 60	Beta-57136	beach erosion, whalebone	Wessen 1993:38
1550 ± 80	Beta-57566	back of midden	Wessen 1993:38
Cedar Creek (45CA29)			
1120 ± 70	Beta-55630		Wessen 1995
Norwegian Memorial (45CA252)			
1070 ± 50	Beta-68682	raised terrace	Wessen 1995

Note: All Wessen 1995 references are personal communications.

Although Sand Point is the only raised terrace site in the area to have been excavated, several others have been recorded. Upper Wayatch (45CA400), located several kilometres inland from Wayatch, yielded a radiocarbon date of 2690 BP from charcoal recovered under an uprooted tree. This is only slightly older than Sand Point and considerably younger than the oldest date from Wayatch. At Norwegian Memorial (45CA252), south of Sand Point, charcoal from a pothunter's hole provided an age estimate of just over 1000 BP, a date that Wessen (pers. comm. 1995) considers unrealistically late for this elevated site context.

Although several of the ethnographic sites yielded only very recent dates, evidence for earlier occupation is also apparent. The area historically occupied by the Makah seems to have been first settled at least 3,800 years ago, based on the earliest date from Wayatch. There is no evidence of continuous occupation, however, from that date to the Late Period Makah settlement at Wayatch. Sites with dates in the 2,000- to 3,000-year range consist of Hoko River, Sand Point, and Upper Wayatch, with Neah Bay and Ozette being first occupied by the end of this time range. The latter two continued to be inhabited villages into historic times, and most investigators have emphasized cultural continuity to the historic occupants. If Wakashan-speaking peoples arrived on the Olympic Peninsula in relatively recent times, as linguistic evidence suggests (see Chapter 2), then evidence of initial occupation at these large sites sometime around 2000 BP may roughly date that arrival. In that case, the distinctive artifact assemblages, including abundant chipped-stone tools, found at Sand Point and Hoko River may reflect the activities of an earlier population.

4

The Emergence of the West Coast Culture Type

Cultural Antecedents

Archaeological Evidence

No excavated sites in the study area date to the Early Period of Northwest Coast prehistory, generally considered to predate 5000 BP (Borden 1975; Carlson 1979, 1990, 1996a; Fladmark 1982, 1986; Matson and Coupland 1995). Yuquot, with a date of about 4200 BP for Zone I deposits, is the oldest dated site in Nuu-chah-nulth territory. Similarly, the date of about 3800 BP from Wayatch is the earliest from Makah territory. Evidence of much earlier human presence in surrounding regions, however, suggests that the archaeological traces of this area's first occupants have not yet been recovered.

The date of initial human arrival on the coasts of southern British Columbia and adjacent Washington is uncertain. The archaeological record in this area currently extends back nearly 9,000 years, but few would argue that this dates the earliest occupation. If the initial entry into the Americas was by a southward movement along the west coast at a time when large areas of coastal shelf were exposed by lowered sea levels, as is argued by Fladmark (1979), then any trace of this passing would now lie below the waters off the outer coast. Evidence that large areas of now submerged land would have been available to early human migrants along the coast was obtained in a geological core sample taken from the ocean bottom north of Vancouver Island at a depth of 95 m. The core contained a paleosol with in situ rooted plant remains that were radiocarbon dated to 10,500 BP, indicating that this was dry land at that time (Luternauer et al. 1989).

A controversial claim for archaeological evidence of human presence around 12,000 BP comes from the Manis Mastodon site (45CA218) on the northern Olympic Peninsula. Excavation at this site exposed a largely complete mastodon skeleton, which was interpreted by the investigators as evidence of human hunting and butchering practices (Gustafson, Gilbow, and Daugherty 1979). Support for this view came primarily from what was thought to be a bone "projectile point" embedded in a rib of this animal. As this pointed bone is not indisputably of human manufacture, however, the claim that people were hunting elephants in this region at this early period remains unsubstantiated.

More definite evidence for human presence in southern coastal British Columbia and adjacent Washington is evident at about 9000 BP. This early stage is marked by the presence of unifacial pebble choppers and leaf-shaped bifaces. The predominance of crudely flaked pebble (or cobble) tools in such assemblages led Carlson (1979, 1983a, 1983b, 1990, 1996a) to term this the Pebble Tool tradition. Although pebble tools served as general purpose implements, appearing in a number of different cultural contexts, their abundance in this early stage becomes a defining characteristic. Matson (1976) and Matson and Coupland (1995) use the term "Old Cordilleran Culture" to refer to the same stage, while Mitchell (1971) places this within his Lithic culture type. More than just terminological preferences are involved here, however, as "Old Cordilleran" implies a generalized culture of the interior mountains, which only later moved to the coast, while Carlson (1990:66; 1991:113; 1996a:8) argues that this was initially a coastal adaptation, which later followed the salmon up the rivers to the interior. Dates as early as 9700 BP for similar materials from the lowest levels at the Namu site, on the central British Columbia coast, lend support to this view (Carlson 1996b).

Much of our information on this early stage comes from the oldest component at the Glenrose Cannery site located on the lower Fraser River (Matson 1976, 1996). The earliest radiocarbon date from this deep, multi-component site is 8150 ± 250 BP, although this was obtained about 1 m from the base of cultural deposits. Matson and Coupland (1995:70) date the Old Cordilleran (or Pebble Tool) component at Glenrose to between about 8500 and 5000 BP. Cobble tools dominate the artifact assemblage, comprising about 44 percent of the total, while bifacial leaf-shaped points are present in small numbers. A barbed antler point and several antler wedges also occur in this assemblage. Bones of elk (wapiti) and deer, followed by seal, are the most abundant faunal elements, although these primarily date to the later part of this component. Fish remains include salmon, flatfish, eulachon, and stickleback. Substantial lenses of concentrated shell occurred at considerable depths, indicating that shellfish gathering was part of the economy throughout this component. A seasonal encampment of generalized hunters, fishers, and gatherers is indicated for this early occupation.

A similar picture comes from Bear Cove, an early Pebble Tool tradition site located on northeastern Vancouver Island (C. Carlson 1979). A radiocarbon date of 8020 ± 110 BP was obtained from near the base of deposits underlying a shell midden. As at Glenrose, the upper levels of this component are undated but are older than about 4500 BP. Similar, but undated, material from non-shell deposits at the base of the nearby O'Conner site

(Chapman 1982) may also belong to this period. The artifacts from Bear Cove closely resemble those from Glenrose, with a small number of bifacial leaf-shaped points and knives and abundant pebble tools, the latter comprising 48 percent of the total.

Despite the similarities in age and artifact forms, the faunal remains from Bear Cove differ significantly from those at Glenrose (C. Carlson 1979; Matson 1996; Matson and Coupland 1995:76-77). Mammal bones, which are twice as numerous as are those of fish, are dominated by several species of sea mammals. Fully 80 percent of sea mammal remains from Bear Cove were identified as *Delphinidae* (porpoise), with northern fur seal and Stellar sea lion making up most of the rest. Fish remains were dominated by rockfish, with salmon a distant second. The numerous porpoise, fur seal, and rockfish elements provide evidence that a developed maritime economy existed at this early period. Intensive hunting of sea mammals such as porpoises would have required watercraft and probably harpoons with bone or antler heads. However, all faunal remains at Bear Cove came from the upper levels of this component and cannot demonstrate that the earliest arrivals at this location brought with them a fully developed maritime economy.

Only a short distance from Bear Cove across Vancouver Island is Quatsino Sound, immediately north of ethnographic Nuu-chah-nulth territory. During a survey in Quatsino Sound in 1973, Carlson and Hobler (1976:126) recorded six locations where stone tools produced by simple percussion flaking were found on intertidal beaches, in two cases without any above-tide midden present. Several hundred pebble tools, pebble cores, flakes, and several leaf-shaped bifaces are among the chipped stone artifacts collected (Carlson and Hobler 1976; Apland 1982). Carlson and Hobler place these in their Early Period, estimated at 9000 BP to 4000 BP. These objects were considered to be "essentially identical" to those recovered from the early component at Bear Cove (C. Carlson 1979:190). In a detailed study of the chipped stone artifacts from intertidal sites in Quatsino Sound and the central coast, Apland (1982) described the Quatsino assemblage as based on a pebble-spall technology closely affiliated with the Pebble Tool tradition. He argued that the Quatsino Sound chipped stone objects are not only distinct from the intertidal lithics of the central coast but are likely to be earlier, probably predating 5000 BP.

A number of undated surface discoveries of chipped stone tools in Nuu-chah-nulth territory have raised the question of the cultural relationships of the earliest occupants. A series of elevated sites along the Somass River in the Alberni Valley (McMillan 1981, 1996b; McMillan and St. Claire 1982) may cast some light on this issue. Lithic artifacts of a well developed microblade industry are found with bifacial leaf-shaped points, retouched cortex spalls, and other large flake tools (Figure 27); pebble tools and cores occur but are relatively rare. Microblade technology has a north-to-south temporal gradient on the Northwest Coast. In southeastern Alaska microblades first appear between about 9200 BP and 8900 BP (Ackerman 1992; Davis 1990; Carlson 1990). In the Gwaii Haanas region of the southern Queen Charlotte Islands microblade cores are found at several intertidal locations dated as early as between 9400 BP and 9000 BP (Fedje et al. 1996). By about 8500 BP microblade technology appears on the central coast, where it is added to the Pebble Tool tradition assemblage at Namu (Carlson 1996b). The Somass River sites may similarly represent an interface where technologies based on pebble tools and bifaces merge with those based on microblades. Borden (1975, 1979) had earlier speculated that bearers of these two early cultural traditions met somewhere in the vicinity of northern Vancouver Island, with their merger providing the basis for subsequent development of Northwest Coast cultures. Artifact typology and the elevated nature of the Somass River sites argue for their placement within the Pebble Tool tradition, although the presence of microblades would suggest that they date towards the later end of that tradition, perhaps in the 7000 BP to 5000 BP range (Carlson 1990:67; McMillan 1996b:214). They certainly predate the excavated Shoemaker Bay site, with a basal date of 4000 BP, which is associated with modern sea levels (McMillan and St. Claire 1982).

Surface discoveries of chipped stone artifacts have also been made on the outer coast of Nuu-chah-nulth territory in undated intertidal contexts

27 Surface collected lithic artifacts from DhSf 31, an elevated site in the Alberni Valley (upper left, chipped bifaces; upper right, retouched cortex spall tool; lower row, microblade cores)

(Figure 28). In Nootka Sound, Marshall (1992a, 1992b, 1993) reports beach discoveries of leaf-shaped bifaces, cores, and flakes. Most implements were produced by a pebble-spall flaking technology and closely resemble the beach discoveries from Quatsino Sound (Marshall 1993:80). Similar discoveries have also been made in Barkley Sound, including a large leaf-shaped biface similar in style and material to Nootka Sound specimens (McMillan and St. Claire 1991:69). A basalt core with three long narrow flake scars, found on a beach in Nootka Sound, indicates the former presence of the blade technology (Arcas Consulting Archeologists 1993). These implements may have been used in the intertidal zone and have been lost or discarded directly onto these beaches, or they may have eroded out from midden deposits behind the beaches. However, as chipped stone artifacts were extremely rare in the 4,200-year sequence established for Yuquot, another explanation for the intertidal materials in Nootka Sound would be that they predate the earliest deposits at Yuquot and represent the remains of sites that

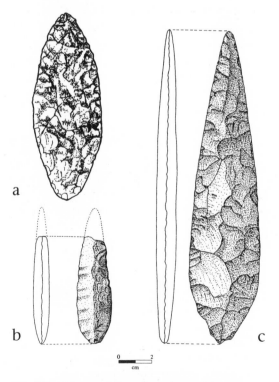

28 Chipped stone bifaces from intertidal contexts in Barkley and Nootka Sounds (*a,* from DfSi 72, near Toquart Bay, Barkley Sound; *b,* from DkSo 6, Nootka Sound; *c,* from DjSo 8, Muchalat Inlet, Nootka Sound) (*b* and *c,* from Marshall 1992:109; 1993:75)

were occupied when sea levels were lower. If these intertidal lithics are re-lated to the Pebble Tool tradition, then this would provide a logical cultural antecedent for the West Coast culture type. It would also link the Early Period in Nuu-chah-nulth territory with surrounding areas and raise the possibility that historic Wakashan and Salishan populations shared a distant common ancestor, as was argued earlier by Carlson (1983a, 1983b, 1990, 1991).

It must be stressed, however, that no site in Nuu-chah-nulth, Ditidaht, or Makah territory has been shown to be older than 4,200 years. Furthermore, few sites predate about 2500 BP. This situation is at least in part attributable to the fact that most archaeological fieldwork has concentrated on sites associated with modern sea levels. Archaeologists must also consider geo-logical factors that may have affected site visibility and accessibility on the west coast.

Geological Factors
During the climax of Wisconsinan glaciation much of the study area as it now exists would have been rendered uninhabitable, with only the Brooks Peninsula and the end of the Hesquiat Peninsula spared from glacial ice (Clague, Armstrong, and Mathews 1980). Valley glaciers from the central Vancouver Island mountains reached the outer coast through what are to-day the major inlets. In Barkley Sound, several local glaciers met and co-alesced, extending in two lobes out onto the continental shelf (Carter 1973:443). A radiocarbon age of 16700 ± 150 BP, obtained from a wood sample found at the top of glaciofluvial sediments overlain by till of the last glaciation, provides an estimate for the onset of the final glacial advance in the Clayoquot Sound area (Clague, Armstrong, and Mathews 1980). Glacial retreat had apparently freed the outer coast by about 13000 BP, based on radiocarbon dates from post-glacial marine deposits in Hesquiat Harbour and Clayoquot Sound (Friele 1991:79; Clague et al. 1982; Howes, in Haggarty 1982:37).

Shortly after deglaciation, the sea rose rapidly relative to the land along western Vancouver Island. Marine inundation reached 32 m to 34 m above present sea level at Hesquiat Harbour (Clague et al. 1982:611). Elevation of post-glacial marine deposits above modern sea levels increases with distance inland along the inlets, presumably due to the greater weight of ice inland, reaching about 45 m near the head of Espinosa Inlet, between Nootka Sound and Kyuquot Sound (Howes, in Haggarty 1982:37). In the Alberni Valley, at the end of the long Alberni Inlet, the marine limit reached about 90 m above modern levels (Fyles 1963:90; Holland 1964:117; Mathews, Fyles, and Nasmith 1970:692, 693).

Relative sea levels dropped rapidly following these early post-glacial highs. Radiocarbon dates on in situ stumps in the intertidal mud near Tofino in

Clayoquot Sound indicate that the sea was about 3 m below present levels between 7000 BP and 8000 BP (Bobrowsky and Clague 1992; Friele 1991:80). Based on fieldwork on Vargas Island, Friele (1991:78) has prepared a sea level curve that he believes is generally applicable to the west coast of Vancouver Island from Nootka Sound to Barkley Sound, an assumption supported by recent research in Barkley Sound (Friele and Hutchinson 1993:839). Friele proposes that sea levels rose gradually from the Early Holocene lows, attaining a height of about 3 m above the present level by 5100 BP. Relative sea levels then remained stable for over a thousand years, a period Friele has termed the Ahous Bay Stillstand. After 4000 BP sea levels began to drop, reaching another stillstand around 2200 BP, at which time mean sea level stood about 2 m higher than it does today. The land has gradually emerged relative to the sea over the past several millennia along the west coast of Vancouver Island, in a process which is still continuing (Friele 1991; Hebda and Rouse 1979; Clague et al. 1982:612). This is in contrast to the inner coast, on the east side of Vancouver Island, where the sea is presently rising relative to the land. Late Holocene emergence on the outer Olympic Peninsula also appears to be still in progress (Wessen 1993:8).

Tectonic uplift is generally considered to be the driving force behind Middle and Late Holocene emergence of the land along the outer coast of Vancouver Island (Clague et al. 1982:616; Muller 1980:9; Hebda and Rouse 1979:129; Friele 1991:92; Friele and Hutchinson 1993:840). Late Holocene uplift appears to have been largely continuous and gradual, although there is some evidence of subsidence from megathrust earthquakes (Clague and Bobrowsky 1990; Bobrowsky and Clague 1991). Both geological and archaeological evidence suggest that major earthquakes affected human occupation of the outer coast on a number of occasions during the Late Holocene (Hutchinson and McMillan 1997).

Associated with massive earthquakes are tsunamis, which can often affect areas far from the quake centre. The huge 1964 earthquake in Alaska, for example, resulted in a tsunami that caused extensive damage along the west coast of Vancouver Island, particularly to communities (such as Port Alberni) that lie at the ends of long inlets. Clague, Bobrowsky, and Hamilton (1994) identify a widespread sand sheet just below the marsh surface at the end of Alberni Inlet as having been deposited by the 1964 event, and they argue by analogy that similar sand sheets at lower levels in the same location identify the presence of prehistoric tsunamis. Similarly, sand sheets overlying peaty soil have been identified at several tidal marsh locations on the outer coast near Tofino and Ucluelet. Clague and Bobrowsky (1994a, 1994b) interpret these deposits as former marsh surfaces that subsided suddenly during a large earthquake and were covered with sand from the ensuing tsunami. They suggest that several such quakes may have occurred in the last 500 to 800 years and that they could have been more powerful than the 1964 event (Clague and Bobrowsky 1994a). A thick sand layer near the base of midden deposits at the Ittatsoo North site near Ucluelet may be archaeological evidence of a tsunami which struck the village about 2300 BP (Arcas Consulting Archeologists 1998). Similarly, Wessen (1991:21) identifies several thin sand layers in shell midden deposits well back from the modern beach at Neah Bay as possible evidence of past tsunamis affecting the Makah.

Nuu-chah-nulth oral traditions provide additional evidence of these past catastrophic events. A Huu-ay-aht story tells how a huge wave following an earthquake destroyed a village at Pachena Bay, just to the east of Barkley Sound, killing many of the inhabitants (Clamhouse et al. 1991:230-231). Similarly, stories of a great ebb of the sea followed by a massive flood may reflect ancient tsunamis. Sproat (1868:183-185) recorded such a tradition for Barkley Sound, recounting how the Toquaht and Tseshaht survived the great flood. Swan (1870:57) was told a similar flood story by a Makah chief, in a version that also accounts for the close relationship between the Makah and Vancouver Island groups.

> A long time ago, but not at a very remote period, the water of the Pacific flowed through what is now the swamp and prairie between Waatch village and Neeah Bay, making an island of Cape Flattery. The water suddenly receded, leaving Neeah Bay perfectly dry. It was four days reaching its lowest ebb, and then rose again without any waves or breakers, till it had submerged the Cape, and in fact the whole country, excepting the tops of the mountains at Clyoquot. The water on its rise became very warm, and as it came up to the houses, those who had canoes put their effects into them, and floated off with the current which set very strongly to the north. Some drifted one way, some another; and when the waters assumed their accustomed level, a portion of the tribe found themselves beyond Nootka, where their descendants now reside.

Informants among the Quileute and Chemakum related to Swan the same tradition, which was seen as an explanation for the separation of these two related peoples.

These geological data have major archaeological implications. If Friele's sea level curve is accurate, then evidence of occupation prior to about 6000 BP may lie below modern tides, eroded and largely inaccessible. Any cultural deposits later than this time, but prior to the advent of the Ahous Bay Stillstand at about 5100 BP, would have been eroded by both rising and falling sea levels. Intertidal lithic artifacts found along the coast may represent such eroded sites. In addition, earthquake-induced coastal subsidence may have affected portions of the west coast of Vancouver Island on several different occasions. Tsunamis may also have played a role in reshaping foreshores, although the extent of damage to archaeological sites is unknown.

The earliest known intact and dated archaeological remains occur late in the Ahous Bay Stillstand. At Yuquot, artifacts and faunal remains from the lowest levels are water-rolled and are interpreted as having been deposited on a low-lying sand and gravel spit that was subject to periodic wave action (Dewhirst 1980:43). Today, these deposits are about 5 m above the high tide line. The lowest levels at Ch'uumat'a, in Barkley Sound, also contained waterworn artifacts and faunal remains apparently deposited on an old beach that was later uplifted. At Little Beach, near Ucluelet, waterworn fire-cracked rock and sandy layers interbedded with midden show that the lowest deposits, now about 6 m above sea level, were just above wave action when the site was first occupied (Arcas Consulting Archeologists 1991:5; Friele and Hutchinson 1993:838). In all three cases, extensive midden deposits did not begin to accumulate until roughly 4,000 years ago, corresponding to the onset of lowered sea levels, when these low-lying areas became more suitable for human habitation. Areas occupied during the height of the Ahous Bay Stillstand, which would have been abandoned as uplift exposed new land and moved the former surface further from the beach, should now be sought on raised terraces above the level of the Late Holocene shell midden sites. Several archaeological tests at elevated terrace sites in Makah territory (see Chapter 3), however, failed to yield evidence of such an age.

In summary, although data are scarce and inconclusive, the surface lithic discoveries in Nuu-chah-nulth territory suggest early ties to the widespread Pebble Tool tradition. Changing sea levels have rendered inaccessible much of the evidence for earlier stages in the human occupation of Nuu-chah-nulth territory. The oldest archaeological evidence for the West Coast culture type is associated with the 4200 BP date at Yuquot. This chapter examines what is known of the human presence in Nuu-chah-nulth territory prior to 2000 BP.

Continuity and Variation in West Coast Sites to 2000 BP

Even at this relatively late stage of Northwest Coast prehistory there are few known sites in Nuu-chah-nulth, Ditidaht, and Makah territory. Only six offer dates in the 4,200- to 3,000-year range. The fullest information comes from Yuquot and Ch'uumat'a, which provide lengthy sequences extending into the Historic Period. Midden deposits at Little Beach are encompassed entirely within the time span between 4000 to 3000 BP, although some cultural materials may come from the overlying dark layer, making them as late as about 2500 BP. The final three sites offer little cultural information of this age. Shoemaker Bay has an initial date of roughly 4,000 years, but this refers only to a few waterworn artifacts on the old beach surface prior to accumulation of the major midden deposits. Site DdSc 12, near Port Renfrew, has a basal date of about 4100 BP, but this came from a single small excavation unit with a limited sample of cultural remains. The 3,800-year date for the Makah site of Wayatch came from the bottom of a road cut exposure and does not date any of the excavated materials, which belong to a much later time.

The lowest component at Shoemaker Bay and the Hoko River wet/dry site join Yuquot and Ch'uumat'a in covering the 3000 BP to 2000 BP period. However, both contain large numbers of chipped stone artifacts and do not fall within the West Coast culture type as it is presently characterized. Near the end of this temporal span we also have dates from two sites on Nitinat Lake, the Ittatsoo North midden, and from Sand Point on the Olympic Peninsula. All three, however, are known only from very limited test excavations, and the Sand Point materials also seem to lie outside present definitions of the West Coast culture type. Finally, at about 2000 BP, we have evidence of initial occupation at Ozette and Neah Bay. The beginning of major midden deposits at these sites is argued to mark the period of more intensive occupation discussed in the next chapter.

Claims of cultural continuity throughout this time have been most strongly made for Yuquot, where the pre-2000 BP period encompasses all of Zone I and lower and middle portions of Zone II. Dewhirst (1980:337) notes that almost all artifact classes from the earliest levels also occur in later deposits and concludes that "the basic cultural patterns of later periods" were already established. By Zone II deposits, Dewhirst (1980:338) maintains that artifacts "reflect basic cultural patterns that are known ethnographically." Faunal remains are poorly preserved in the early strata, hindering attempts to assess changes in economic adaptation.

Despite this evidence for cultural continuity, there are changes over time in the artifact forms at Yuquot. Narrow, round-polled celts, for example, are restricted to Zone I and the lower levels of Zone II, eventually being supplanted by flat-polled and broad celts in a process that Dewhirst considers to be stylistic evolution rather than functional change. Small flaked pebbles, classified as "wedges" by Dewhirst, are also restricted to Zone I and the base of Zone II. Their apparent "early" classification, however, is called into question by the presence of similar chipped pebbles at Kupti, a much later site in Nootka Sound (McMillan 1969). Important absences from the pre-2000 BP artifact inventory at Yuquot include stone fishhook shanks, bone fishhook shanks with rectangular bases, and mussel shell tools. Changes also occurred in the form of composite toggling harpoon heads; slotted valves and channelled valves with biconical arming points are restricted to later time periods, leaving only simple and self-arming valves in the earlier stages.

Recent evidence from Barkley Sound seems strikingly different from the picture that has emerged from Yuquot. Instead of cultural continuity to the historic Nuu-chah-nulth, sites such as Shoemaker Bay and Little Beach display traits that link them with cultural stages in the Strait of Georgia region.

Shoemaker Bay I exhibits such distinctive traits as chipped, stemmed, and leaf-shaped projectile points, chipped schist and phyllite knives, quartz crystal microblades, large-faceted ground slate points, a labret, and a cairn burial. Little Beach, despite limited excavation and a small artifact sample, has also yielded cairn burials, a leaf-shaped chipped stone projectile point, a thick ground slate point fragment, and a possible large labret fragment. These are all considered characteristic traits of the Locarno Beach culture type, generally dated to about 3300 BP to 2400 BP in the Strait of Georgia (Mitchell 1990; Matson and Coupland 1995). Initial dates of 4000 BP for both Little Beach and Shoemaker Bay, however, indicate that if these are Locarno Beach components, then this culture type has its earliest known manifestations on the west coast of Vancouver Island. Locarno Beach affinities for Shoemaker Bay I seemed understandable considering this site's proximity to the east coast of Vancouver Island, its continuing cultural ties to the Strait of Georgia in the later component, and the ethnographic evidence of historic Salishan occupation in the Alberni Valley. The discovery of similar materials at Little Beach, on the outer coast at the entrance to Barkley Sound, however, posed a challenge to established views.

The Toquaht Project excavations at Ch'uumat'a, only a short distance from Little Beach at the western entrance to Barkley Sound, offered another opportunity to assess the cultural affiliations of the earlier occupants of this region. This site, which also has an initial occupation date of about 4000 BP, was used into early historic times. Although no sharp cultural break is evident, the sequence at Ch'uumat'a can be divided at about 2000 BP. The earliest stage encompasses almost all the deposits from the deep trench dug at the back of the site, along with the lowest levels of the two deepest units in the front portion of the site (see Chapter 3). Of the site total of 750 artifacts, 340 can be assigned to the earliest stage (McMillan and St. Claire 1996; McMillan 1998). Several distinctive artifact types, including all chipped stone objects, are restricted to this period. Conversely, certain artifacts characteristic of the West Coast culture type, such as stone and bone fishhook shanks, occur only in the later deposits at Ch'uumat'a.

Chipped stone artifacts are relatively abundant in the earlier Ch'uumat'a deposits (Figure 29). Two large bifacial projectile points, one leaf-shaped and one stemmed, came from the trench excavation. Their place in the stratigraphy suggests an age of between 3000 BP and 3500 BP. Two small pebbles showing bipolar flaking, classified as pièces esquillées, came from even deeper in the trench stratigraphy, dating to around 3500 BP. Several chipped schist tools include a complete, roughly circular knife, crudely chipped around its circumference, which came from a layer in the trench dated to about 2500 BP. The remaining items in this category are debitage from flaking activities. Those from the trench excavation consist of one broken and battered pebble of vein quartz and twelve flakes (two of vein

29 Chipped stone artifacts from Ch'uumat'a (upper row: projectile points, schist knife, pièces esquillées; lower row: andesite and chert debitage; the example on the far right has been reworked as a possible piercer)

quartz, two of quartzite, two of chert, and six larger flakes of andesite or basalt). All date to between about 2500 BP and 3500 BP. In addition, eighteen flakes, all of green chert, came from several layers near the base of two units in the front portion of the site, dating between 2000 BP and 2300 BP. Several of these chert flakes show evidence of edge retouch, in one case resulting in a sharp projection that probably served as a piercer. Including detritus, chipped stone makes up 10.6 percent of the artifact total from deposits predating 2000 BP at Ch'uumat'a. Although this figure is low compared to Locarno Beach sites in the Strait of Georgia region (Matson and Coupland 1995: Table 6-2), it is significant considering the virtual absence of chipped stone from Yuquot. The projectile points and schist knife have close parallels among the Shoemaker Bay I artifacts as well as among those from Locarno Beach sites along the Strait of Georgia.

Some of the ground stone artifacts suggest similar ties. Several fragmentary ground slate implements include the tip of a thick faceted projectile point, one of the diagnostic artifacts of the Locarno Beach culture type (Mitchell 1990:341; Matson and Coupland 1995:156). Celts from this period tend to be small to medium in size, rectangular in cross-section, extensively shaped, and flat-polled, similar to those described for Locarno Beach contexts (Mitchell 1990:341) and dissimilar to the round-polled "pebble celts" that are most common in the earlier stages at Yuquot (Dewhirst 1980).

30 Ch'uumat'a ground stone and bone objects resembling Gulf Islands complex artifacts (*a,* argillite; *b* and *c,* limestone; *d,* bone)

One of the early Ch'uumat'a celts, however, is of the round-polled "pebble celt" variety. One small bit fragment of nephrite also suggests ties to the Strait of Georgia, as the closest major source area for this material is in the coastal mountains along the Fraser River.

Also from this time period are several carefully shaped ground stone and bone objects of unknown function (Figure 30). They have a general similarity to artifacts from the Strait of Georgia region that are collectively termed Gulf Islands complex items (or "whatzits") that comprise a distinctive feature of Locarno Beach assemblages at some sites. Dahm (1994) argues that these are items of personal adornment, worn in, or suspended from, holes in the lips, ears, and nose. The Ch'uumat'a examples, however, are not made of the characteristic soapstone for that complex and do not closely match specific types established for the Strait of Georgia. One complete specimen,

of black argillite, has flaring sides, parallel top and bottom, and one con-
cave face, closely resembling a soapstone example from a Gulf Island site
illustrated by Duff (1975:34-35). Another is a white limestone "plug," circular in cross-section, with converging sides and a flat base and top. An additional white limestone artifact, broken at its base, is a thin flattened curving
object with a squared projection, or "tab," on its upper surface. A fourth
object, of dense highly polished bone, is characterized by pronounced flattened flanges at its ends, although much of one has broken away. A channel,
or groove, runs the length of the object, making it somewhat similar to the
"slide" category of Gulf Island Complex artifacts illustrated by Dahm (1994).
All came from the trench excavation, from a stratum dated to about 2500 BP,
making them contemporaneous with late Locarno Beach examples.

In addition, a flat polished and incised object of greenish-grey schist was
excavated from the base of the Ch'uumat'a trench deposits (Figure 31). One
face of this large fragment is incised with a design, following the shape of its
scalloped decorative edge, which may be interpreted as a feather pattern.
One small, biconically drilled hole remains. This object was found in situ
on an area of heavily burned shell and ash, with a small amount of charcoal
that yielded a radiocarbon age of 4000 ± 140 years BP. Somewhat similar
fragments of schist and shale, with incised designs associated with decorative indented edges, came from equivalent time periods at the Glenrose site
on the Fraser River (Matson 1976).

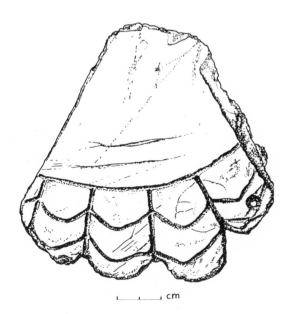

31   Decorated schist object from the base of deposits at Ch'uumat'a

The presence of cairn burials, another characteristic of the Locarno Beach stage in the Strait of Georgia (Matson and Coupland 1995:161), also links the earlier deposits at Ch'uumat'a with Little Beach and Shoemaker Bay I. Two excavated cairn burials, along with a third exposed in the excavation wall, came from the trench deposits at the back of Ch'uumat'a. The three burials were clustered together in shallow pits, with concentrations of rounded cobbles covering the skeletal remains and extending above the pit surface (McMillan and St. Claire 1996). The Ch'uumat'a examples appear to be identical to those reported from Little Beach. Two charcoal samples immediately adjacent to the burials yielded radiocarbon dates of 2510 ± 110 BP and 2560 ± 70 BP, respectively.

It would appear, then, that the occupations of Shoemaker Bay I, Little Beach, and the lower levels at Ch'uumat'a are closely related. All three appear to show greater ties to the Locarno Beach culture type in the Strait of Georgia than to the West Coast culture type (as known from Yuquot). The Ch'uumat'a assemblage, however, lacks such typical Locarno Beach traits as quartz crystal microblades, labrets and earspools, and cobble and boulder spall implements. In addition, the most common artifacts in the early Ch'uumat'a deposits, making up 35.6 percent of the total, are the small bone points and bipoints that dominate West Coast culture type assemblages, including the later Toquaht materials. In all, bone artifacts comprise 74.1 percent of the pre-2000 BP artifact total, compared to 42.6 percent of the assemblage at Little Beach. Much of Little Beach's apparent distinctiveness, however, may be attributable to its small artifact sample and its unique status as a burial site.

Additional evidence for long-standing ties to the Strait of Georgia region comes from several unexcavated and undated sites in Barkley Sound and environs. Surface collections from such sites feature abundant chipped stone and other artifacts closely resembling those known from the Strait of Georgia. An undated private collection from a site in Huu-ay-aht territory near Bamfield (DeSg 10) includes chipped leaf-shaped and stemmed projectile points, chipped pebbles, and rectangular celts. A review by Mackie (1992), based on collections and records of the Royal British Columbia Museum, identified numerous artifacts found in Nuu-chah-nulth territory that seem out of place in West Coast culture history as it is understood from Yuquot. These anomalous items include chipped obsidian leaf-shaped projectile points from Clayoquot Sound and the head of Ucluelet Inlet, a quartz "whatzit" (Gulf Islands complex artifact) from Tofino, and a zoomorphic carved stone bowl from Meares Island in Clayoquot Sound.

To the south of Barkley Sound, in the ethnographic territories of the Ditidaht and the Makah, similar materials have been obtained from several excavated sites. The Hoko River wet/dry site, across Juan de Fuca Strait on the Olympic Peninsula, provides the most extensive parallels. A series of radiocarbon dates places occupation at this site between about 2800 BP and 2200 BP (Croes 1995), overlapping in time with the early Ch'uumat'a deposits. Although bone and antler artifacts have not been preserved, such lithic implements as chipped leaf-shaped and stemmed projectile points, chipped schist knives, faceted ground slate points, quartz crystal microblades, and vein quartz chipping detritus link Hoko River with the early periods at Shoemaker Bay and Ch'uumat'a as well as with the Locarno Beach culture type. Hierarchical cluster analysis, using lithic artifact variables only, links Hoko River most closely with Montague Harbour I and Georgeson Bay I, two Locarno Beach components in the Gulf Islands, as well as with Shoemaker Bay I (Croes 1992b:344, 1995:227). Chipped stone tools also dominate the small artifact samples from Sand Point (on the Olympic Peninsula south of Ozette) and DdSc 12 (near Port Renfrew on Vancouver Island), both of which overlap in time with the early Ch'uumat'a materials.

Small numbers of chipped stone artifacts, however, do occur in sites of the West Coast culture type, even in quite late times. A jasper projectile point fragment, quartz crystal microblade, several cores, and a pebble tool came from Hesquiat Village (Haggarty 1982). A number of small chipped pebbles and a cobble tool were excavated at Kupti (McMillan 1969), and several of the Toquaht sites have yielded flake tools (McMillan and St. Claire 1992). Pebble tools, cortex spall tools, pièces esquillées, and heavy ground slate knives are also reported for the Ozette midden in an assemblage interpreted as ancestral to the historic Ozette people (McKenzie 1974). Chipped stone points are also reported for the Late Period Hoko River rockshelter (Wigen and Stucki 1988:90). The requirement for absence or near-absence of chipped stone in West Coast culture type sites may be misleading.

The fact that the three excavated Barkley Sound sites with deposits that predate 2000 BP show greater similarities to the Locarno Beach stage than to the lower levels at Yuquot suggests that these areas were culturally distinct at that time. Linguistic evidence, reviewed in Chapter 2, suggests that Nuu-chah-nulth origins were on northwestern Vancouver Island, with their movement south along the coast leaving a chain of dialects from Kyuquot Sound to Barkley Sound. Prior to this Nuu-chah-nulth expansion, Barkley Sound may have been occupied by populations culturally linked to the Strait of Georgia. The Toquaht, at the western end of Barkley Sound, historically hold the territory that would have been first occupied by any such Nuu-chah-nulth movement into the sound. If these initial arrivals settled in this area, only later expanding to the rest of the sound, then this may explain Sproat's (1868:19) interesting early observation that the other Barkley Sound groups considered the Toquaht to be the original population, "the tribe from which the others sprung." Continued southward movement later gave rise to the southernmost Wakashans – the Ditidaht and the Makah. The

Locarno Beach association for the Hoko River wet/dry site may reflect the cultural ties of the population prior to the relatively late arrival of the Makah.

The whole question of ethnic identification in the past, however, raises major concerns for archaeologists. Whether distinct ethnolinguistic groups can be detected in the archaeological record is a moot point, and many researchers have questioned any direct correlation of such units with specific sets of material culture items. Croes and Hackenberger (1988) argue that "culture types," defined primarily on the basis of stone and bone artifacts, should be understood as broad plateaus in economic adaptation, offering little insight into cultural affiliation or ethnicity. At sites such as Hoko River, where water-saturated deposits have preserved plant fibre artifacts, basketry and cordage styles are thought to provide the most compelling insights into cultural affiliation (Bernick 1987; Croes 1987, 1989, 1993). Such comparisons link Hoko River perishables with those at the much later Ozette site and with historic Makah basketry, while Strait of Georgia basketry of the same age as Hoko is markedly different. This identification of the Hoko River perishables as ethnically Makah, however, places the Makah on the Olympic Peninsula earlier than the linguistic or other archaeological data suggest. One possibility is that the expanding southern Wakashan population that gave rise to the Makah leap-frogged over a still-Salish coast from about Barkley Sound south to settle on the Olympic Peninsula. Somewhat later, in this view, the Nuu-chah-nulth arrived in Barkley Sound and the ancestral Ditidaht split from the Makah to take over the southern portions of the west coast. Another possibility is that the basketry and cordage at Hoko River actually represent the handiwork of the Chemakuan peoples, who, according to Powell (1993), are distantly related to the Wakashans.

Despite the problems with ethnic identification, the culture history of some historic ethnolinguistic groups can be extended, with caution, a considerable distance into the past through demonstrated continuity in the archaeological record. Dewhirst (1978, 1980) makes a convincing case for Yuquot, leading Mitchell (1990) to characterize the West Coast culture type as the material record of Nuu-chah-nulth culture history. Such ethnic continuity is not necessarily the case in the Strait of Georgia, however, where greater change over time is evident in the archaeological record. While Mitchell (1971, 1990), Carlson (1983b, 1990), and Carlson and Hobler (1993) stress lengthy cultural continuity, Burley and Beattie (1987) have argued that a population replacement took place around 2400 BP, at the end of the Locarno Beach period. Shoemaker Bay I and Little Beach may be linked culturally with the Strait of Georgia, but they are not necessarily Salishan.

Despite this suggestion of population replacement in Barkley Sound, some continuity is also likely. The Nuu-chah-nulth spread seems to have been accomplished by "linguistic capture" or cultural assimilation of earlier residents. Ethnographic traditions, as discussed in Chapter 2, confirm that at least two of the modern groups, the Hupacasath of the Alberni Valley and the Pacheedaht around Port Renfrew, were originally Salishan but were acculturated during a late stage of Nuu-chah-nulth and Ditidaht expansion. Even if a linguistic shift has taken place, the modern Nuu-chah-nulth, Ditidaht, and Makah can still claim the archaeological remains discussed here as those of their ancestors.

Emergence of the Ethnographic Pattern

Even for the earliest deposits at Yuquot, Dewhirst (1980) and Mitchell (1990) maintain that the Nuu-chah-nulth ethnographic pattern was in place. Although some changes in artifact forms occurred over time, Dewhirst argues that this only reinforces the picture of cultural continuity, as more complex forms emerged from simpler early versions. Large, rock-rimmed firepits, found in lower and middle Zone II levels, were frequently superimposed, suggesting that their spatial location was constrained (as would occur if they had been built inside a permanent structure). Dewhirst (1980) and Folan (1972) interpret this as evidence of a large multi-family house similar to those known historically. Presumably this structure had a permanent framework, which was clad with split cedar planks in the ethnographic fashion. The location of the excavation trench within the centre of this presumed house area would explain why no large post moulds were encountered. Small stake holes around several of the firepits and concentrations of small fire-cracked beach stones in the pits suggest the historic cooking practices of roasting food over the fire and boiling it in wooden containers, using rocks from the fire to heat the water. Shoemaker Bay also provides evidence, in the form of rock-lined firepits and a row of three very large post moulds in the early component, for the existence of large permanent house structures at this time (McMillan and St. Claire 1982).

Even from this earliest period, the economy of these West Coast peoples was strongly maritime. With the exception of Shoemaker Bay, all of the earliest sites (Yuquot, Little Beach, Ch'uumat'a, Wayatch) are on the open ocean. Few faunal remains are preserved from Zone I at Yuquot, but Zone II was dominated by a variety of fish species as well as by such open-ocean fauna as northern fur seal and albatross. Fish elements also dominate the faunal remains from Little Beach and Ch'uumat'a. Whalebone was found in considerable quantities in these sites but is not necessarily evidence for active whaling, as artifacts clearly associated with whaling do not appear until later. The abundance of whalebone in archaeological deposits, however, suggests that whales were important in the economy, and the use of whalebone to cap burials at Little Beach suggests that this importance might have extended into the symbolic realm. Unfortunately, little else can be said for this early period. Faunal analysis for Yuquot remains incomplete, particularly for fish and mammals. Only a preliminary analysis exists for

Little Beach fauna (Arcas Consulting Archeologists 1991), while faunal analysis at Ch'uumat'a is only in initial stages (Monks 1992). The early date from Wayatch is from a road cut and is not associated with any excavated data. By the end of this period, at around 2000 BP, the great numbers of fur seal elements at Sand Point and in the lowest levels at Ozette confirm the highly maritime nature of early occupants in the Makah area.

Procurement technology for sea mammals consisted of harpoons with bilaterally barbed whalebone heads. Three such implements came from the middle portion of Zone II at Yuquot, from near a firepit dated around 2000 BP (Dewhirst 1980:290, 341). A similar example came from Ch'uumat'a, although from somewhat later deposits. Composite toggling harpoon heads, with self-armed valves or simple valves with wedge-based arming points, were also in use. These appear to be too small for larger sea mammals and may have been primarily for salmon. Other fish were taken on hooks, with bone or wooden shanks and bone barbs. Many of the numerous small bone points in collections from all sites in this area functioned in such a fashion. The large quantity of wooden fishhooks preserved in the waterlogged deposits at Hoko River, however, show that not all fishhooks had bone barbs (Hoff 1980; Croes 1992a). Ethnographically, slender bipoints, also numerous in these sites, were baited and used as gorges for taking diving ducks as well as fish (Drucker 1951:34).

Despite the very maritime nature of adaptation at West Coast sites from earliest times, some use was made of inland resources. Coast deer make up a substantial portion of the faunal remains from all time periods at Yuquot (Dewhirst 1979). Recent evidence for hunting marmot (*Marmota vancouverensis*), a creature of the alpine and upper sub-alpine meadows that rarely descends to lower elevations, shows human use of the Vancouver Island mountains at this early period. Although Shoemaker Bay is the only excavated village site on Vancouver Island with marmot remains, several high-altitude caves inland in Nuu-chah-nulth territory have been discovered with clusters of marmot bones showing apparent cut marks. Radiocarbon dates of 2490 ± 50 BP and 2630 ± 50 BP have been obtained on cut marmot bones from a cave on the Clayoquot Plateau, at an elevation of 1,220 m asl, in the mountains behind Clayoquot Sound (Nagorsen, Keddie, and Luszcz 1996).

The period beginning around 3300 BP, corresponding to the Locarno Beach culture type in the Strait of Georgia, has been seen by a number of recent researchers as crucial to the development of the ethnographic pattern on the Northwest Coast (Croes and Hackenberger 1988; Croes 1992b; Matson 1992; Matson and Coupland 1995). In computer simulation modelling based on Hoko River data, Croes and Hackenberger (1988) project that population growth in the preceding St. Mungo stage reached the area's carrying capacity. The development of storage techniques then allowed continued population growth and marked the beginning of the next economic plateau, the Locarno Beach stage (Croes 1992b, 1995). At Hoko River the major resource for intensification and production of a stored surplus was flatfish (particularly halibut and petrale sole). In this argument, previous researchers may have accorded salmon too large a role in the growth of more complex cultures, and the intensification of the salmon fishery occurred only after the storage technology was already in place.

Based on his work at Crescent Beach in the Strait of Georgia, Matson (1992) also argues for the development of large-scale storage techniques at the beginning of the Locarno Beach period. Salmon was the dominant resource at this site from Locarno Beach times on; no evidence of a pre-salmon flatfish storage period was detected (Matson 1992:422; Matson and Coupland 1995:245). This may simply represent intensification based on suitable local species in two different environmental settings, or it may indicate that flatfish were being processed in a way that did not leave a discernible archaeological trace. Evidence for salmon storage in the Locarno Beach and Marpole stages at Crescent Beach comes from under-representation of salmon cranial elements, indicating that these fish were procured and processed elsewhere and brought to this site as dried food. Older deposits at Crescent Beach have fewer salmon remains, and these include cranial elements. Matson (1992:423) confidently concludes that "we appear to be on the verge of being able to say with certainty that the Northwest Coast salmon-storage economy came into being during the 3500-3000 BP period." Not all researchers would accept this relatively late date, however. Cannon (1991:61, 64), for example, maintains on more tenuous evidence that salmon storage was a feature of the economy at Namu since at least about 7000 BP.

A storage-based economy is thought to have allowed higher population levels and the development of the full Northwest Coast ethnographic pattern. Considerable agreement exists that social stratification emerged only after salmon specialization and storage techniques were in place (Croes and Hackenberger 1988; Matson 1992; Matson and Coupland 1995), although these may have continued to be "mutually reinforcing" (Ames 1981:798). Archaeological indicators of social distinctions include labrets and the enigmatic "Gulf Islands complex artifacts," which adorned the face and conveyed messages regarding the personal status of the wearer (Dahm 1994). Marked social distinctions may have characterized the Strait of Georgia region as early as about 4000 BP (Carlson and Hobler 1993:45; Dahm 1994:107). Status indicators, however, do not necessarily mark the full Northwest Coast pattern of hierarchical ranking based on birth, something that may not have been achieved in the Strait of Georgia until Marpole times (Burley 1980; Burley and Knusel 1989).

Possible evidence of distinctions in social status at Hoko River comes from the presence of preserved hats, some with small knobbed tops, in the waterlogged deposits (Croes 1995). Knob-topped hats historically identified members of the upper class among the Nuu-chah-nulth, Ditidaht, and Makah. If, by analogy, the hat styles at Hoko River can be interpreted as demonstrating similar social distinctions, then individuals who owned and managed resources and territories on behalf of extended family units were a feature of west coast life almost 3,000 years ago. Zoomorphic carvings in wood, such as appear on a number of barbed wooden projectile points from Hoko, might also, more speculatively, reflect early social distinctions, as emerging elites manipulated symbols to demonstrate ties to the supernatural world. Such a process, termed "ritual promotion," is a common phenomenon in the emergence of ranked societies (Ames 1981:800; 1994:212).

Little evidence of social distinctions can be found in sites of the West Coast culture type. Decay of wooden and basketry objects has removed much of the evidence, and the general unimportance of stone in the technology means that many of the key artifact types in the Strait of Georgia region do not occur here. Several fragments of whalebone clubs, tentatively identified at Little Beach and from lower Zone II at Yuquot, may possibly have status implications. A handle fragment from Yuquot with a carved zoomorphic image is one of the few decorated artifacts found at this site. Among the historic Nuu-chah-nulth, a carved whalebone club was the badge of office of the war chief (Drucker 1951:335).

The models of intensification and storage presented for Hoko River and Crescent Beach cannot be fully evaluated at West Coast sites. Detailed faunal analyses are essential to detecting such processes in the archaeological record, and none has been completed on West Coast sites of this age. The models that have been derived from nearby regions, however, were intended to have some application to the entire Northwest Coast, although the extent and tempo of change would vary at the local and regional level. The people of the West Coast culture type should not be seen as living in an isolated and marginal environment, contrary to the views of some early anthropologists (see Chapter 2), but as being participants in broad economic developments that occurred along the coast. Salmon may not have played the vital role that it did in the Strait of Georgia region, as good salmon rivers were scarce and valued commodities, providing much of the incentive for later intergroup hostilities (Swadesh 1948). Maritime resources seem to have been sufficient, however, to allow the degree of sedentism suggested at Yuquot, where superimposed hearth features and other indications of house deposits suggest the presence of large permanent structures as early as about 3000 BP. The continuity seen at Yuquot suggests to Dewhirst (1978, 1980) and others (Folan 1972; Mitchell 1990) that the ethnographic pattern of resource use was in place early in the archaeological record for western Vancouver Island.

As discussed above, few West Coast sites significantly predate 2000 BP. Evidence for increased population in Nuu-chah-nulth and Makah territories comes from a number of additional sites that were first occupied around this date and that continued in use into historic times. The more complete archaeological record available from these later sites gives fuller evidence of the evolution of the ethnographic pattern, as is outlined in the next chapter.

5
The Late West Coast Culture Type

A larger number of sites and fuller range of data allow a more complete understanding of West Coast life in the final two millennia prior to contact with Europeans. With this more extensive information, archaeological reconstructions can approach "ethnographies of the past," including social and ideological dimensions. The humanistic nature of "holistic archaeology" promotes the investigation of past belief systems and other symbolic aspects of culture. Ethnographic accounts of the Nuu-chah-nulth and their relatives are used as a framework against which to assess archaeological data, allowing the recent past to be evaluated in terms of evolving Nuu-chah-nulth culture, consistent with the "direct historic approach" advocated by Trigger.

By around 2000 BP the initial occupants had settled at Ozette and Neah Bay, two Makah villages that persisted into modern times. Benson Island in Barkley Sound, Ittatsoo North at Ucluelet, and two Ditidaht sites on lower Nitinat Lake were first occupied a few centuries earlier. Shortly following 2000 BP there is evidence of initial occupation at Macoah in Barkley Sound, at First Radar Beach and Esowista in the Clayoquot Sound area, and at a habitation cave (DiSo 9) in Hesquiat Harbour. Settlement at Chesterman Beach followed by about 1500 BP. An expansion in the number of dated settlements occurs around 1200 BP, with the earliest dates from Kupti, Hesquiat Village, T'ukw'aa, and Aguilar Point, followed soon after by Tsoo-yes and Tatoosh Island. Once established, all continued as occupied villages into historic times. In addition, the earlier sites of Yuquot and Ch'uumat'a, discussed in the previous chapter, continued as occupied villages throughout this period. See Chapter 3 for site locations and details of radiocarbon dates.

This chapter examines evidence of the West Coast culture type from roughly 2000 BP to 200 BP, terminating with the initial contact between indigenous West Coast peoples and the European explorers and traders of the late eighteenth century. All the defining traits of the West Coast culture type as outlined by Mitchell (1990) were characteristic of this period, although not all date to its inception. Throughout the area, the archaeological remains reflect the culture history of the Nuu-chah-nulth people and their relatives.

Subsistence and Settlement

Settlement Patterns
The considerable increase in the number of dated sites in Nuu-chah-nulth and Makah territories indicates population increase and expansion after 2000 BP, with the pace becoming more rapid after about 1500 BP. The location of these sites on the outer coast and in the major sounds suggests that maritime-adapted populations were expanding along the outer coast. Excavated data also indicate increased efficiency of adaptation to open-ocean resources at this time. Dewhirst (1980) notes this as a general feature of his Late Period, corresponding to Zone III deposits at Yuquot, which is dated to after about 1200 BP. The key technological indicators he uses to argue for greater maritime adaptation include large toggling valves for composite harpoon heads, which would have been armed with points of ground mussel shell and used in whaling, and stone shanks for composite fishhooks, of the type used ethnographically for open-ocean salmon trolling. Although such stone fishhook shanks occur late in the Late Period at Yuquot, they are found at all four Toquaht sites, dating to about 1200 BP at Ch'uumat'a. Based primarily on the Nootka Sound data, Marshall (1993:40) has argued for widespread changes in settlement pattern along the outer coast between about 1500 BP and 1000 BP. The small number of sites excavated and dated, however, renders the nature and timing of such a shift somewhat speculative. Recent radiocarbon dates suggest that this shift was well under way somewhat earlier than this estimate and was largely in place by about 1200 BP.

Whaling may have been the key adaptation that allowed this relatively late population expansion along the outer coast. According to traditions reported by Drucker (1951:49), whaling originated among two outer coast groups in northern Nuu-chah-nulth territory on the outside of Nootka Island and outside Esperanza Inlet. Both groups were year-round occupants of the outer coast and lacked access to salmon streams, instead adopting whaling as an economic mainstay. The lengthy continuity evident in the archaeological record at Yuquot, plus evidence of an increasing adaptation to maritime resources over time, supports the ethnographic tradition that reliable whale hunting techniques developed in situ in the general region of Nootka Sound. Once established in northern Nuu-chah-nulth territory, such whaling techniques would have allowed greater population concentrations on the outer coast and fostered the spread of Nuu-chah-nulth people along the coast to the south. Marshall (1993:138, 143) argues for such a Nuu-chah-nulth expansion south along the outer coast and islands, which would have been lightly populated prior to that development, and for population replacement in Barkley Sound. Similarly, Arima (1988:23; Arima et al. 1991:289) attributes the Ditidaht and Makah occupation of their historic homelands to their mastery of effective whaling techniques and consequent shifts in their settlement pattern. The importance of whaling in the evolution of Nuu-chah-nulth culture is explored further in the next section.

Sites on the outer coast are frequently large, with deep midden deposits suggesting fairly continuous occupation from the initial settlement. Yuquot is the largest of the excavated Nuu-chah-nulth sites, but even larger villages, such as the Tla-o-qui-aht community of Opitsat (DhSl 11) in Clayoquot Sound, are known. T'ukw'aa is also impressive in the extent and depth of its deposits. In Makah territory, the huge site of Ozette is by far the largest. Excavated data are highly biased towards these large outer coast sites. Of the twenty-five excavated sites with dates between 2000 BP and 600 BP, sixteen are on or near the open-ocean coast. An additional six are in the upper sounds or harbours, two are on lower Nitinat Lake, and only one, the Shoemaker Bay site, is on an inlet, although this site appears to be unrelated to Nuu-chah-nulth culture history. Regional surveys show that the inlets have a very different site pattern, consisting of numerous small and medium settlements, often with quite shallow deposits (Marshall 1993:114, 137; McMillan 1981:91). These tend to be located in proximity to specific resources, such as salmon streams, and reflect seasonal economic activities. The outer coast sites, by contrast, show a more generalized resource base, and their locations are primarily determined by ease of access and shelter from rough water and storms.

The antiquity of the ethnographic settlement pattern has been a subject of contention among researchers in this area. The widespread Nuu-chah-nulth pattern documented in the ethnographies involved seasonal movement between outer locations, providing access to such important open-ocean resources as whales, sea lions, fur seals, and halibut, and inner settlements, usually near salmon rivers and streams. Warfare, alliance, and confederation were the ethnographic strategies used to obtain rights to locations in both environmental settings. Dewhirst (1980:15) maintains that groups that occupied only one type of environment would have been subject to extreme hardships and that the historic pattern of seasonal movement between inner and outer locations was a long-established one in Nootka Sound.

Other researchers (Calvert 1980; Haggarty 1982; Inglis and Haggarty 1986; St. Claire 1991), however, trace the ubiquitous nature of this settlement pattern among the Nuu-chah-nulth to the depopulation caused by early historic epidemics, which forced political amalgamations of surviving groups and the emergence of the seasonal round as a consequence of holding a much larger consolidated territory. Calvert's (1980) detailed faunal analysis of three sites in Hesquiat Harbour documents year-round occupation and indicates that access to different local habitats accounts for most of the assemblage variation between sites. The numerous large shell midden sites recorded by intensive survey in the Broken Group Islands of Barkley Sound (Inglis and Haggarty 1986) also suggest the former presence of many separate polities resident in year-round villages exploiting local resources within socially constrained territories. A similar pattern is emerging in Makah territory, where faunal analyses indicate that the seasonal winter villages described by Swan (1870) were actually occupied for much or all of the year (Huelsbeck and Wessen 1995). Some people undoubtedly left temporarily for seasonal camps associated with specific economic resources, but a relatively permanent resident population seems to have been characteristic of the larger communities.

The development of political confederacies brought a change in settlement pattern to the northern groups sometime just prior to or immediately following European contact. Confederated polities maintained their distinct tribal identities, with separate winter villages and seasonal resource sites, but aggregated in large populations at outer coast villages such as Yuquot during the summer months (Drucker 1951; Mitchell 1983). Morgan (1980) has pointed out that these confederated polities developed in areas where the availability of salmon was limited, suggesting that confederation was a strategy to obtain access to a wider range of resource territories. Whaling also may have played a role, facilitating the distribution of large quantities of meat and blubber to an assembled population at outer coast locations during the summer (Mitchell 1983:104-106). Groups to the south of Nootka Sound, with access to more abundant salmon resources, never developed confederated polities, retaining the winter villages as the largest population aggregates.

Marshall (1993:131) maintains that a distinctive West Coast settlement pattern can be distinguished in the archaeological landscape. Much of her argument is based on her survey and mapping fieldwork in Nootka Sound (Marshall 1992a), but comparisons are made to the results of surveys in southern Clayoquot Sound (Arcas Associates 1988; Mackie 1983) and Pacific Rim National Park (Inglis and Haggarty 1986). She divides recorded habitation sites into five classes, from Very Small to Very Large. Small and Medium sites are characteristically the most numerous. Large sites are relatively rare and Very Large sites even more so. Large and Very Large sites, characteristically exhibiting platforms, ridges, and other surface features marking the former presence of large house structures, tend to be on or near the outer coast, while Very Small sites, representing specific economic activity locations, are most common on islands in the sounds. An exception to the general pattern occurs in Hesquiat Harbour, where Very Small sites, many in rockshelters, comprise 65 percent of the total (Marshall 1993:126, 127).

Results of the Toquaht Project survey can be compared to these findings. The long exposed coastline of western Barkley Sound that makes up most of Toquaht territory provides few protected locations for settlement. Only fifty-one sites were recorded in the survey area, of which fourteen (27.5 percent) are habitation sites. This contrasts markedly with the nearby Broken Group Islands in central Barkley Sound, where numerous sheltered locations contained a total of 163 sites, of which eighty (49 percent) are habitation sites (Inglis and Haggarty 1986:242-243). Three of the Toquaht habitation sites have been largely destroyed and their former dimensions are unknown, leaving only eleven to be classified. T'ukw'aa, at roughly 12,000 m², is the largest site in Toquaht territory, although it does not qualify with Yuquot (at 24,000 m²) for Marshall's Very Large category. Table 11 compares settlement size distributions for southern Clayoquot Sound, Long Beach and the Broken Group Islands (two sections of Pacific Rim National Park, on each side of the Toquaht), and Toquaht territory. The size classes used follow those established by Marshall (1993:126). Although site numbers are very small, the Toquaht data fit the general pattern characteristic of other Nuu-chah-nulth regions. The exposed coastline has resulted in a much smaller total number of sites, but the proportions of size classes are roughly the same.

Table 11

Settlement size distributions: Clayoquot Sound, Long Beach, Broken Group Islands, and Toquaht territory

Class	Length, range	Clayoquot Sound*		Long Beach*		Broken Group*		Toquaht territory	
Very Small	<20 m	35	28%	9	26%	20	25%	2	18%
Small	21-60 m	46	37%	16	47%	34	42%	3	27%
Medium	61-200 m	28	23%	7	21%	23	29%	4	36%
Large	201-350 m	13	10%	2	6%	3	4%	2	8%
Very Large	>350 m	3	2%	–	–	–	–	–	–
Site totals		125		34		80		11	

* Data from Marshall 1993:126

Whaling

As discussed in Chapter 2, the whaling practices of the Nuu-chah-nulth, Ditidaht, and Makah posed a fascinating problem for early researchers. The limited distribution of whaling on the Northwest Coast and the numerous similarities with Eskimo-Aleut groups in Alaska led to proposed models of an early broad coastal continuum, later broken by arrival of the more northerly Northwest Coast groups (Lantis 1938; Borden 1951; Drucker 1955a). In this view, the Nuu-chah-nulth people became isolated and marginal survivors of an earlier way of life, retaining whaling as part of a much earlier coastal adaptation. As such diffusionist explanations gradually lost their hold on anthropological thought, whaling came to be seen as an ingenious innovation, developed indigenously by these open-ocean peoples. The timing of this development, however, still causes some debate.

In the ethnographic traditions, whaling emerged among the "outside" people of Nootka Island and Esperanza Inlet in response to food shortages. Whaling then provided a secure food supply similar to salmon for the "inside" groups (Drucker 1951:49). This view gives temporal priority to an inside, salmon-based economy. Dewhirst (1977, 1978, 1980) reinforces this view in his interpretations based on Yuquot. Whaling is seen as a late development, occurring as part of a general trend towards a more maritime adaptation. Other researchers, however, have questioned this picture. In a review of Nuu-chah-nulth site distribution, Haggarty and Inglis (1983:16) conclude: "The pattern that emerges is one of emphasis on the outside with scheduling to exploit the inside on a seasonal basis." In the Broken Group Islands of Barkley Sound, for example, numerous large shell middens suggest lengthy year-round occupation, while the small shallow sites that dominate the inlets and other inner locations reflect relatively recent and limited seasonal use (Inglis and Haggarty 1986; McMillan and St. Claire 1982). It now appears that, prior to early historic disruptions in political structure and settlement pattern, most of the large outside settlements were occupied for much or all of the year. Reliable access to whales would have been a key aspect in effective occupation of the outer coast.

Some use of whale products characterizes the entire archaeological record in Nuu-chah-nulth territory. Whalebone was recovered from all zones at Yuquot, although it was not abundant (Dewhirst 1977; 1979:6). Whalebone artifacts and fragments occur "in significant quantities" at Yuquot at least as early as 3000 BP (Dewhirst 1978:5). The presence in Zone II deposits at Yuquot of a whale barnacle (*Coronula reginae*) that occurs on the skin of the humpback whale indicates that such whales were being consumed by about 2200 BP (Dewhirst 1977:15; Dewhirst and Fournier 1980:100). Whalebone also came from the deepest deposits at Ch'uumat'a and from Little Beach, where its association with cairn burials argues for its considerable importance in the culture, placing use of whales as early as nearly 4000 BP. Concentrations of whalebone occurred throughout the Ozette midden trench (McKenzie 1974) in deposits spanning roughly the last 1,500 years. Whalebone also occurred frequently at T'ukw'aa and makes up a major portion of the faunal remains from Hesquiat Village, both occupied over the last 1,200 years. In fact, whalebone is found in almost all excavated faunal assemblages of any size in the study area, including at the end of the long Alberni Inlet at the Shoemaker Bay site (McMillan and St. Claire 1982). Whalebone was so abundant in the Late Period Ozette house deposits that Huelsbeck (1988b) refers to whales as "the most important food resource of the Ozettes."

The whales represented by the bones in the Ozette house deposits had clearly been hunted by harpoon, with large toggling harpoon heads being used in the ethnographic fashion. The thin lines of mussel shell evident on a number of the whalebones are the still-embedded remnants of the harpoon cutting blades (Huelsbeck 1994:281; Fisken 1994:367). Complete harpoon heads with mussel shell cutting blades, still in their protective sheaths or pouches, along with harpoon shafts and line, were found with other items that were inside the excavated Ozette houses when the mudslide struck (Kirk and Daugherty 1974:128-129; Huelsbeck 1994:280). Huelsbeck (1994:302) concludes that the "pattern of [whale] procurement was essentially unchanged throughout the last 2000 years." The basis for this claim is not clear, however, as all the unambiguous evidence for whaling comes from the Late Period house deposits.

Several of the whale remains from T'ukw'aa also show evidence of harpooning. Broken tips of mussel shell blades are still embedded in a scapula and an unidentified whalebone fragment from this site (G. Monks, pers. comm. 1997). As these were found in late precontact deposits, however, they provide little additional information about the antiquity of the practice. Of more potential significance in this regard is the scapula of a humpback whale from Ch'uumat'a, which exhibits a long, deep linear gouge on its surface. This element was found stratigraphically between radiocarbon dates of about 2500 BP and 3000 BP. If this deep gouge can be demonstrated to be a harpoon wound, then this would date the practice of whaling in Barkley Sound to at least that time.

Dead whales that floated ashore, commonly known as "drift whales," were important sources of meat and oil for the historic Nuu-chah-nulth, Ditidaht, and Makah. Chiefs jealously guarded their drift rights to anything that washed up on the beaches of their territories (Drucker 1951:39; Arima 1983:23), and bitter intertribal disputes over dead whales occasionally ensued (Sproat 1868:228; Clamhouse et al. 1991:297). Rituals held to cause drift whales to wash ashore involved secluded whalers' shrines, use of human corpses, and occasional sacrifice of slaves (Drucker 1951:171-173; Arima 1983:24; Webster 1983:52). All of the whalebone from earlier midden deposits at Ozette could have come from drift whales, as is also true for whalebone at early levels at Yuquot, Ch'uumat'a, and other sites. The ethnographic importance of drift whales, however, is linked to the active pursuit of whales. Many of the drift whales that washed up on beaches were animals that had been struck during active whaling, subsequently dying of their wounds and washing ashore. Jewitt's account of Mowachaht whaling indicates that whales struck and lost greatly exceeded those taken. Thus even unsuccessful whaling increased the chances of acquiring whales, and chiefs could benefit from the activities of whalers in neighbouring communities. Prior to the development of whale hunting techniques, drift whales would not have been as numerous as they were historically, and occasional good fortune in finding a beached whale may not be sufficient to account for the considerable number of whalebones in early midden deposits.

Dewhirst (1977, 1978, 1980) argues that development of the full ethnographic whale hunting technology did not occur until the Late Period at Yuquot (after 1200 BP), when large composite toggling harpoon valves first appeared. Most of the Yuquot valves, however, are too fragmentary to classify, too small to have been used in whaling, or lack provenience; only one example, incised with the punctate zigzag motif often seen on ethnographic specimens, seems definitely to be a whaling harpoon (Figure 32). No such large valves were found at Kupti in the upper sound (McMillan 1969). Although toggling harpoon valves were relatively common at Hesquiat Village and the upper component of DiSo 9 in Hesquiat Harbour (Calvert 1980:135; Haggarty 1982:181), both dating to after 1200 BP, only a few were the large slotted valves meant to take the broad cutting blade used for whaling. Six valves from T'ukw'aa, which also dates to after 1200 BP, were judged to be of a size and type consistent with identification as whaling gear, as were two from Ch'uumat'a, from levels dating within the last 1,000 years. Slotted harpoon valves, some large enough to have been used in whaling, were also found in the middle and upper portions of the Ozette midden trench (McKenzie 1974).

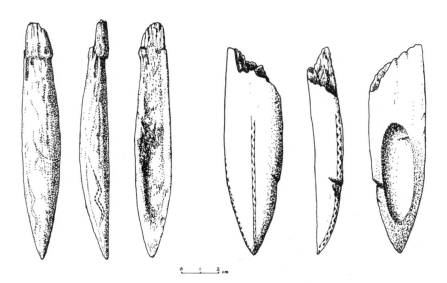

0   1   2 cm

32 Valves from whaling harpoon heads, decorated with incised designs (left, surface discovery from DgSh 9, near Toquart Bay, Barkley Sound; right, from Yuquot, Zone III, redrawn from Dewhirst 1980)

The small number of definite whaling harpoon heads recovered from these sites indicates the difficulty in dating the advent of whaling by use of such evidence. These artifacts are rare even in late precontact and early historic deposits, when whaling was known to have been practised. The harpoon heads were carefully treated and stored, with their effectiveness ritually enhanced through incised designs representing the Lightning Serpent (*hiy'itl'iik*), associated in myth with the whaling activities of the Thunderbird (Sapir 1922:314). Such valued implements would rarely be discarded in archaeological contexts and would be abundant only in such unusual circumstances as the Ozette house floor. Also, it is possible that other types of harpoons were used in earlier times, at least occasionally, to take whales. Dewhirst (1980) reports unilaterally and bilaterally barbed harpoon heads, several of which are very large, from as early as about 2000 BP. Although these would probably be less efficient than the later large toggling harpoon heads, it is possible that whaling technology evolved over time and that whales were occasionally being taken well before development of the technology used ethnographically.

A major problem in assessing this issue is that the quantity of whalebone in archaeological sites does not directly reflect the number of whales taken. Whales were hauled onto the beaches, where they were butchered. Meat and blubber were brought up to the village, as was the saddle area from the back of the whale, which was taken to the whaler's house and ritually honoured (Swan 1870:21-22; Drucker 1951:178-180; Waterman 1920:46; Arima 1983:43). No special treatment was accorded the bones, which were discarded on the beach (Waterman 1920:47).

The presence of these bones in the site reflects cultural activities not directly related to the food quest. Many were selected as raw material for tool manufacture; large pieces of whalebone with tool "blanks" removed were found at Ozette (Huelsbeck 1994b:284, 288; Fisken 1994:369) and T'ukw'aa. Virtually all excavated sites contain artifacts of whalebone, which number over 1,000 at Ozette (Huelsbeck 1988b:7, 1994b:271). In addition, whalebones were hauled up to the village area to be used in various structural features. At Ozette, whalebones were stacked up as retaining walls and were used with wooden planks to line trenches for diverting water away from the houses (Huelsbeck 1994b:289; Samuels 1991:187; Mauger 1991:93). At T'ukw'aa, whalebone had been dragged up to the top of the defensive site, where a complete whale scapula was used to brace a small post in the shallow deposits above bedrock, and several large whalebone alignments were found in the village area of the site (McMillan and St. Claire 1992:135-136). In addition, some whalebone in the village sites may represent trophies of the successful hunt, as is likely for several whale skulls stacked to the side of House 1 at Ozette. Ethnographically, whalers attempted to accumulate such memorials of their successes, beaching the whales in front of the village to add their bones to those of previous kills (Drucker 1951:55; Arima 1983:43). Several Barkley Sound whalers even attempted such feats as filling the passes between islands with the bones of their kills as monuments to their whaling prowess (St. Claire 1991:140, 157).

While the whalebone in an archaeological site gives only a limited view into the importance of whales in the diet, the actual meat and blubber taken into the village leaves almost no archaeological trace. The only indication of their presence comes from the occurrence of barnacles that live exclusively on the skin of cetaceans, primarily humpback whales. Their presence within the house deposits at Ozette indicates that whale products were being consumed in the houses. Whale barnacles have also been identified at Yuquot (Fournier and Dewhirst 1980), Hesquiat Village (Calvert 1980:192), and Ch'uumat'a. They give little indication of the total quantity of meat and blubber consumed, however.

As most whalebone found in archaeological sites has been fragmented or made into tools, relatively few elements can be identified to species. Only at Ozette and the Toquaht sites of T'ukw'aa and Ch'uumat'a has whalebone identification been made to the species level. At Ozette, the identifiable whalebone was almost equally divided between California grey whales (50.5 percent) and humpback (46.5 percent), with a small number of right (2.3 percent) and finback (0.7 percent) whales (Huelsbeck 1994b:271). The latter two species were likely obtained as opportunistic kills or as drift whales.

Humpbacks are clearly the dominant cetacean species at the Toquaht sites, although the number of identified elements is comparatively low (nineteen at T'ukw'aa and sixteen at Ch'uumat'a) (G. Monks, pers. comm. 1997). Humpbacks are strongly represented at T'ukw'aa, making up 78.9 percent of the identified whale remains. Only a few elements were found of grey whale (10.5 percent), right whale (5.3 percent), and killer whale (5.3 percent). At Ch'uumat'a, humpbacks comprise 50 percent of the whale remains, while greys account for 31.3 percent. A few elements from right whales (12.5 percent) and minke whales (6.3 percent) have also been identified. Humpback and grey whale remains were found throughout the site deposits at Ch'uumat'a, with the earliest identified element, a partially charred humpback caudal vertebra, associated with a radiocarbon date of approximately 3500 BP. As at Ozette, the minor species probably represent opportunistic kills or drift whales.

Ethnographically, Swan (1870:19) and Waterman (1920:42) list seven whale species known to the Makah, as does Drucker (1951:48-49) for the Nuu-chah-nulth. Not all whales, however, were hunted. The California grey was the species most commonly associated with Nuu-chah-nulth and Makah whaling (Swan 1870:16; Waterman 1920; Swanson 1956; Curtis 1916:18; Arima 1983:38). It appears seasonally, migrating along the coast each spring. According to Drucker (1951:48), it was "thought to be running, just like salmon." Similarly, Sapir (1924:80) states in a story of two Ditidaht whalers that "when winter was over, the California whales began to run." Although their migration takes them close to shore, the greys tend to stay on the outside coast, rarely entering the sounds (Banfield 1974:271). Sapir's (1910-1914) ethnographic work with Nuu-chah-nulth informants documents their movements for Barkley Sound. The whales crossed from Cape Beale through the outer Deer Group Islands in Huu-ay-aht territory to the outer islands of the Broken Group in the central sound, then up the Ucluelet coast, not entering western Barkley Sound or Ucluelet Inlet. T'ukw'aa and the sites on the George Fraser Islands were well situated to intercept this migration, but the Toquaht villages further into Barkley Sound were not.

Although often considered secondary to the grey, the humpback is also identified as a major prey species in the ethnographic literature. It was hunted during the summer when the seas were calm and most of the California greys were gone (Sapir 1924; Drucker 1951:48). Their high oil content would make them a more attractive resource than the greys, which were arriving on the west coast after a prolonged period of fasting. This species is "rather docile and ... easily approached" and "one of the slower whales" (Banfield 1974:279). Unlike the greys, the humpbacks frequently entered the bays and sounds to feed on small fish, with some staying in Barkley Sound throughout the summer months (Banfield 1974; Kool 1982; Cavanagh 1983). Dewhirst (1978:6) initially speculated that humpbacks may have been the more common prey in earlier times, at least for the more northerly Nuu-chah-nulth, a position that Kool (1982) has further documented. Depletion of humpback stocks by commercial whaling in the nineteenth and early twentieth centuries may have left so few humpbacks that only the grey whales were remembered at the time most ethnographic data were collected. When the Sechart whaling station opened in upper Barkley Sound early in this century, it quickly and drastically reduced whale populations, with humpbacks comprising the vast majority of the animals killed (Webb 1988).

In areas such as Barkley Sound, humpbacks may have provided a year-round resource, as some individuals are known to remain through the winter (Cowan and Guiguet 1965:270). One of Sapir's Tseshaht informants, Frank Williams, stated that the humpbacks went up the inlets feeding on herring in the winter months. Specific accounts place the humpbacks in Alberni Inlet in November, Uchucklesit Inlet in December, and Effingham Inlet in January and February (Sapir 1910-1914). The whales were so numerous that Williams describes tapping the canoe thwarts to frighten them away while raking for herring in Alberni and Effingham Inlets. Similarly, an early non-Native settler described his fears that the numerous whales in Effingham Inlet might capsize his canoe (Kool 1982:34). Sapir (1910-1914) also noted that the Uchucklesaht were whalers but that their hunt was restricted to Alberni Inlet and took place only in winter, as they held no outside territory for summer whaling. The waters of these protected bays and inlets are much calmer than are outer coast waters during the winter months, and whaling in these narrow confines likely had a higher rate of success than it did on the outer coast.

As a result of these facts, archaeological evidence of whaling in Barkley Sound cannot be assumed to represent spring and summer activities, as is implied by the ethnographic record. Whales appear to have been available within the sound for much or all of the year. Kool's (1982:43) hypothesis that a major excavation in Barkley Sound would provide evidence that humpbacks were the primary species exploited in precontact whaling is supported by the Toquaht data. In contrast, Ozette is in a different environmental setting, on the outer coast far from any major bays or inlets. Humpbacks and greys would both have been available during their coastal migrations, and the two species are found in roughly equal numbers in the site. In these circumstances, whaling would have been primarily a spring and summer activity. As Ozette was a year-round village, however, and as small numbers of whales were present during much of the year, whaling could have occurred occasionally during the winter as well. Also, drift whales were most likely to wash up on the beaches during winter storms (Drucker 1951:39). Simple occurrence of whalebone in the site cannot be used as evidence for seasonality.

Drucker (1951:49) maintains that whaling was primarily a prestige activity and that successful hunts were relatively rare events. Based on the limited number of whalebones excavated at Yuquot, Dewhirst (1978:5-6) also concludes that the role of whaling in the economy has been exaggerated. He also recognizes, however, that the location of the excavated trench, well above the beach and in a possible house area, is unlikely to yield much trace of activities that took place on the beach (1979:6; 1980:33-34). Despite the limitations of the archaeological record, whales clearly played a significant role in the economy for many groups. This is particularly evident at Ozette, where whalebones were very numerous, with over 3,400 complete enough to be identified (Huelsbeck 1988b, 1994b). A minimum of sixty-seven individual whales is represented by the bones in the house floor deposits, which accumulated over a relatively short period of time. Huelsbeck (1994b:267) estimates that whales could account for between 70 percent and 85 percent of all meat and oil available to the inhabitants of the excavated Ozette houses, assuming all whalebone in the site represents animals fully utilized for food. Whalebone was also abundant at Hesquiat Village, where whales are estimated to account for 86 percent of the total food potential in the excavated faunal remains (Huelsbeck 1988a:160). This vast amount of meat and oil suggests that trade in whale products was an important part of the precontact economy for these groups (Cavanagh 1983; Huelsbeck 1988a, 1988b, 1994b).

33 Ceremonies, including ritual bathing, were an essential part of Nuu-chah-nulth whaling. These were carried out by the whaler and his wife, as is shown in this staged photograph by E.S. Curtis, taken circa 1915. *National Archives of Canada C22611*

Some ethnographic and ethnohistoric evidence suggests that whaling was of considerably greater importance to the central and southern groups than it was to those groups in Nootka Sound and other northern areas. Meares (1790:125) noted in 1788 that Wickaninish's people from Clayoquot Sound had a "more thriving appearance," which he attributed to being from an area "where whales were in greater plenty." Similarly, in 1789 Haswell was of the opinion that the people of Clayoquot Sound placed more emphasis on whaling than did any other group on the west coast of Vancouver Island (Howay 1941:70). In 1785, Walker (1982:47) noted eleven skeletons of recently killed whales on the beach in front of a village in Hesquiaht or Ahousaht territory. Banfield (1858) observed whaling among the southern groups, stating that "the Netineth [Ditidaht], as well as the Macaws [Makah], kill a great many in a season." Swan (1870:19) described whales and halibut as the "principal subsistence of the Makahs" in the nineteenth century. These observations are consistent with the archaeological evidence of greater emphasis on whaling south of Nootka Sound, and they help to reconcile the views of Drucker and Dewhirst with the excavated data from Hesquiat Village, T'ukw'aa, and Ozette.

Whaling was essential to chiefly power and authority. Hunting whales was a chiefly prerogative, a demonstration of the chief's prowess and ability to draw on supernatural power. As befitting an event of such importance, the whale hunt was preceded by ritual bathing and other ceremonies carried out by the whaler and his wife (Figure 33) (Curtis 1916:16; Sapir 1924; Gunther 1942; Jewitt 1967:110-111; Densmore 1939:47; Koppert 1930:56-57; Drucker 1951:169-170; Singh 1966:44-45). The killing of the first whale of the season required a ceremony at which a slave might be sacrificed, an event noted by several late eighteenth-century observers (Howay 1941:77-78; Wagner 1933:161). A chief's prestige was enhanced by the distribution of the great quantity of meat and oil from a successful hunt or from a whale beached on his lands. It was a demonstration of his personal, political, and ritual power.

Whaling also provided an incentive for population movements and dislocations. Although Nuu-chah-nulth oral traditions are filled with accounts of outside groups conquering inside territories for their productive salmon streams, there are also accounts of conquests of outer coast territories for access to whaling. Several of the Kennedy Lake groups, for example, successfully waged war against the people living on the outer coasts of Clayoquot Sound, beginning a period of Tla-o-qui-aht expansion (Drucker 1951:240). These events, according to Drucker, took place early in the Historic Period. Centuries earlier, whaling may have provided the economic base for southern Nuu-chah-nulth, Ditidaht, and Makah movement into what became their historic territories. As argued earlier in this chapter, this seems to have taken place between about 2000 BP and 1200 BP.

Other Economic Aspects
The Nuu-chah-nulth, Ditidaht, and Makah demonstrated ingenious adaptations to a wide range of open-ocean resources. Sea mammals, fish, and aquatic birds, many of them taken far from shore, were important aspects of the diet. Many of these resources required levels of technological sophistication and ritual preparation that were similar to those required in whaling. Although whaling has captured much of the public interest and anthropological attention, it was only part of a range of subsistence activities that demonstrated mastery of the maritime environment.

Fur seals are migratory and pelagic, with only young animals straying into littoral waters along the British Columbia coast (Cowan and Guiguet 1965:346-347; Banfield 1974:360). Drucker (1951:46) maintains that fur seals were not hunted prior to the sealing-schooner trade in the late nineteenth century. Singh (1966:21), noting that fur seals were hard to hunt, also claims that they became economically important only in historic times. Archaeological data clearly show that these opinions are in error, reaffirming that ethnographic data should be evaluated through the archaeological record.

Fur seal bones heavily dominate the vertebrate faunal remains from the Ozette trench, showing that fur seal was a major economic resource throughout the entire time represented by the midden deposits (Gustafson 1968). In all excavated open-ocean Makah-area sites, from Tatoosh Island to Sand Point, fur seal is the most abundant of the mammalian remains and often dominates the entire faunal assemblage. The Makah were in the most favourable location for taking fur seals, as the spring migration brought the animals in close to the rocks around Cape Flattery, but fur seal bones are also numerous in such excavated Nuu-chah-nulth sites as Yuquot, Hesquiat Village, Chesterman Beach, Ittatsoo North, and Aguilar Point. Faunal remains have not yet been fully analyzed for the Toquaht sites, but fur seal almost certainly played an important role in the economy of this area as well.

Other seals and sea lions played a vital role in the economies of all Nuu-chah-nulth, Ditidaht, and Makah groups. Their bones are found in virtually all excavated sites. Such animals were easier to take than were fur seals, as they could be harpooned in coastal waters close to the villages or clubbed where they gathered on rocky islets (Drucker 1951; Singh 1966). Porpoises, which are fast, agile, and can only be taken from watercraft, posed much more of a challenge to the Aboriginal hunter. Although their flesh was prized, they were only occasionally taken, with the same type of harpoon as was employed for seals and sea lions (Swan 1870:30; Koppert 1930:67; Drucker 1951:26, 36). Their bones, however, occur in many excavated sites. They were relatively common at T'ukw'aa and dominated the mammalian remains at DgSl 61, one of the Chesterman Beach sites (Wilson 1991).

In general, sea mammals made up a large portion of the Aboriginal diet, as is evident from both the archaeological record and ethnographic accounts. A good example comes from the Hesquiat Harbour sites. Excavated data provided by Calvert (1980) were used by Huelsbeck (1988a:160) to calculate the percentage contribution by meat weight of each major faunal category to the total food available. At DiSo 9 in the upper harbour, the faunal remains indicate that sea mammals made up almost half the food consumed. At DiSo 1, the Hesquiat Village site near the outer coast, the abundance of whalebones in the deposit reduces all other taxa to minor levels. Whales are estimated to account for over 86 percent of all available food, with the total sea mammal contribution reaching a whopping 96 percent. A nearly identical situation prevails at Ozette, where whales make up almost 88 percent of the food represented by faunal remains, with the total contribution from all sea mammals again estimated at 96 percent (Huelsbeck 1988a:154).

The maritime adaptation of the ethnographic groups is also evident in several species of fish taken. Halibut were second only to whales in the economy of the Makah (Swan 1870:22; Singh 1966:48), and dried halibut was a winter staple (Figure 34). Although chum salmon outweighed halibut

34 Cleaning halibut on the beach at Neah Bay, circa 1915. *Photo by E.S. Curtis, National Archives of Canada C34793*

in importance among the Nuu-chah-nulth, halibut was a significant resource and some outer coast groups, such as the Kyuquot, relied on it extensively (Drucker 1951:36). Halibut hooks showed great ingenuity and required skill in use. Although some halibut were taken close to shore, the major fishery for large halibut was on the offshore banks. Sproat (1868:223) states that the best halibut grounds were twelve miles off land. Sapir and Swadesh (1955:41) report that Nuu-chah-nulth men would set out from villages in Barkley Sound when it got dark and paddle all night to reach the halibut banks by dawn. Similarly, the Ditidaht set off around midnight for their favoured halibut banks, about fifteen to twenty-five miles offshore, arriving in the early morning (Clamhouse et al. 1991:295). Singh (1966:32) estimates that the Makah halibut banks were eight to ten miles offshore, while Swan (1870:22-23) places them fifteen to twenty miles from land. Tatoosh Island, off Cape Flattery, was a major summer residence for many Makah while they were intensively fishing for halibut (Figure 35).

Despite the ethnographic importance of halibut, it is not well represented in the excavated sites. Although halibut bones occur in all but the lowermost deposits at Yuquot, the relatively small quantities led Dewhirst (1979:7) to conclude that halibut "does not seem to have been a major food species" and to suggest that its importance has been exaggerated due to Nuu-chah-nulth participation in the late commercial halibut fishery. Halibut remains are very rare in all excavated Hesquiat Harbour sites (Calvert 1980) and are

35   Tatoosh Island continued to be an important seasonal fishing location even after the construction of a lighthouse on its upper surface. Makah plank houses are visible below the lighthouse in this 1912 picture taken by Asahel Curtis. *Washington State Historical Society 23795*

absent at Kupti (Marshall 1990:109). Although halibut elements occur in some quantity in the Late Period house deposits at Ozette, this fish ranks well behind lingcod, rockfish, greenling, sculpin, and salmon in importance (Huelsbeck 1994a:71-73). This anomaly is at least in part attributable to taphonomic factors, as ethnographically halibut were cleaned and processed on the beach (Swan 1870:23) and many of their bones may have been discarded there. However, Swan's description of how halibut were prepared indicates that the heads, the tails, and the vertebrae (with adhering flesh) were all dried and packed away for later consumption, which suggests that the technique of processing cannot fully explain the low representation of halibut in the excavated sites.

Nuu-chah-nulth mastery of the exploitation of marine resources is also evident in the presence of bluefin tuna elements at almost all excavated sites. This is a large and powerful fish, up to 3 m in length, that entered British Columbia waters during warm weather conditions (McMillan 1979; Crockford 1994, 1997). No ethnographies describe the taking of these huge fish, and there are only a few brief ethnohistoric references to the consumption of tuna (e.g., the mention of a tuna and porpoise stew served during Vancouver's visit to Nootka Sound in 1792 [Newcombe 1923:120]). Despite this lack of ethnographic attention, tuna was clearly an important resource in the precontact economy. Tuna elements are found at Yuquot, Kupti, Hesquiat Village, the Toquaht sites (T'ukw'aa, Ch'uumat'a, and Macoah), Shoemaker Bay, and Ozette (Crockford 1994), and they are also tentatively identified at Chesterman Beach (Wilson 1994:15). They occur in all four zones at Yuquot, covering the entire known span of Nuu-chah-nulth culture history (McMillan 1979). While most sites have only a few tuna elements, they are relatively common in the Toquaht sites, with cut marks and burning on some of the vertebrae suggesting butchering and cooking practices (Crockford 1994:165). Bluefin tuna travel on the warmer surface water and enter the sounds and inlets to feed. Recent research with Mowachaht informants indicates that tuna were harpooned at night as they fed at the surface of shallow water well inside Nootka Sound (Crockford 1994). In terms of equipment and skill required, such activities resembled those involved in whaling.

As would be expected, the degree of dependence on open-ocean resources varied with local conditions. Substantial differences are evident in the excavated faunal remains. At Yuquot, the bones of coast deer were the most numerous of the identified mammalian remains (Dewhirst 1979). This contrasts with a much more maritime economy evident in the identified mammals at Ozette, which are dominated by whales and fur seals, with deer and elk playing very minor roles.

Some argument has been made that pelagic resources became important only within the last millennium (Matson and Coupland 1995:272). Matson (1983:131) has used Calvert's (1980) data from Hesquiat Harbour to argue for intensification of pelagic sealing in relatively recent times. As success in hunting fur seals led to improved technology and greater commitment to pelagic sealing, greater emphasis would simultaneously have been placed on hunting sea mammals of all types while use of other resources would have declined. This argument fits well with Dewhirst's (1977) model of late development of effective whaling techniques. Only one of the excavated Hesquiat sites predates 1200 BP, however, and it is located in the upper portion of the sound. Certainly the great abundance of fur seal bones throughout the midden trench at Ozette (Gustafson 1968) and substantial numbers of fur seal elements in Zones II to IV at Yuquot (Dewhirst 1979) argue for a longer period of emphasis on such open-ocean resources.

Social Relations

Warfare
In the ethnographic literature warfare appears to have permeated all aspects of Nuu-chah-nulth life. All such sources document the well developed military complex among these people, and the texts collected by Sapir from Barkley Sound groups are filled with accounts of specific hostilities, told

from a Native perspective. Swadesh (1948:76), in reviewing the motivations underlying Nuu-chah-nulth warfare, noted that "the entire social structure of band and tribe, kinship and caste, as well as economy and social philosophy, are illuminated against the war background."

War chiefs, often younger brothers of the main chiefs, led the military campaigns (Swadesh 1948:93; Drucker 1951:270). As was required for any activity of great importance, such leaders prepared for war through ritual bathing and other ceremonial activity (Drucker 1951:170; Koppert 1930:105). A favoured tactic was a night or dawn raid on a sleeping village, with specific members of the attacking party assigned to each house of the target village (Drucker 1951:337; Curtis 1916:54; Ferguson 1984:272). Aggressor groups might launch prolonged campaigns of attrition against their enemies or those whose resource territories they desired. At the culmination of a successful attack, heads of all the slain were taken as trophies, captured women and children were taken as slaves, and the houses were plundered and burned. According to a number of traditions, treachery was also a tactic successfully employed, as sometimes a group would feign peace offers and invite their foes to a feast, only to strike out against their guests at a prearranged signal from the war chief (Drucker 1951:338). Slave-raiding expeditions were also part of Nuu-chah-nulth hostilities, with war parties setting out to pick off small groups of individuals engaged in tasks away from their villages. Slaves and booty provided important economic motivations for hostilities, as numerous slaves enhanced a chief's wealth and prestige (Ferguson 1984; Mitchell 1984; Donald 1983).

The underlying motivations behind Northwest Coast warfare have been the subject of considerable theoretical debate (Ferguson 1983, 1984; Coupland 1989; Langdon 1976). On a broader level, Yesner (1980) maintains that the relatively high population densities and semi-sedentism characteristic of maritime hunter-gatherers promote a greater degree of territoriality and higher levels of endemic warfare than exists among hunter-gatherers in other environmental settings. An ecological-functional perspective views both warfare and the potlatch on the Northwest Coast as mechanisms for balancing population levels and distributions with resources (Vayda 1968; Langdon 1976; Ferguson 1983). Warfare is linked to feasting and potlatching, as redistribution of food supplies and other goods neutralized potential enemies and bound them as allies.

Virtually all ethnographic sources on the Nuu-chah-nulth emphasize the economic basis of warfare. The oral traditions are replete with accounts of outside groups seeking to acquire inside resources, particularly productive salmon streams (Swadesh 1948; Sapir and Swadesh 1955; St. Claire 1991). Slaves, booty, and ceremonial privileges were additional incentives for war. Revenge was frequently mentioned as a motivation for warfare by Nuu-chah-nulth informants, but this may have been a convenient rationalization

(Swadesh 1948:91; Drucker 1951:333; Ferguson 1984:308). In varying circumstances, insults or other grievances could be forgotten or serve as rallying points, even long after the events, and were often merely justifications for wars of territorial expansion or for slave raiding.

Individual motivation, however, should not be dismissed as a frequent source of hostilities. War chiefs, in particular, stood to gain prestige in successful military ventures. Warriors who had taken many heads were feared and respected. Relatives of someone killed in war could demand revenge, requiring a war chief to mount a retaliatory expedition. Warfare also provided ambitious chiefs with an opportunity for self-aggrandizement through the use of military might to increase territorial holdings, slaves, and prestige.

Weapons, designed for combat in close quarters, consisted of wooden spears with fire-hardened tips, clubs, and daggers (Drucker 1951:335; Koppert 1930:104; Mills 1955:59; Arima 1983:105). Drucker's informants also told him that slings were used in warfare prior to the introduction of firearms. Only the war chiefs wore armour, made from several thicknesses of elkhide (Cook 1784:307-308; Drucker 1951:335; Koppert 1930:105); wooden rod armour was also described to Drucker by a Hesquiaht informant. Military leaders carried clubs of stone or whalebone, often finely carved and referred to by ritual names or euphemisms such as "orphan maker" (Drucker 1951:335). Whalebone clubs with handles carved in the stylized image of the Thunderbird suggest the importance of supernatural power in military endeavours. Finely carved stone and whalebone clubs are well represented in ethnographic collections made among the Nuu-chah-nulth in the late eighteenth century (Gunther 1960; 1972; King 1981; Kaeppler 1978; Boas 1907) before they were replaced by firearms as high-status weapons.

Few archaeological traces remain in Nuu-chah-nulth sites to gauge the antiquity of these practices or their extent in precontact times. This is in contrast to the archaeological record on the northern British Columbia coast, which indicates that warfare was well established prior to 2000 BP (Fladmark, Ames, and Sutherland 1990:234). The evidence comes primarily from a series of midden interments in the Prince Rupert Harbour area, where male skeletons show unusually high levels of trauma, including parry fractures of the forearm and depressed skull fractures (Cybulski 1990:58), and are associated with grave goods that include decorated bone and stone clubs. No such evidence comes from Nuu-chah-nulth territory, where midden interment is almost unknown in the archaeological record of this period.[1]

---

1 The only known midden interments for the late West Coast culture type (2000 BP to historic contact) are one articulated human skeleton partially visible in the wall of a unit at the Toquaht site of Ch'uumat'a, several interments encountered during excavation at Tatoosh Island (Friedman 1976), and a number of burials disturbed during house construction at Hesquiat Village (R. Inglis, pers. comm. 1995). All were left in place and reburied; no detailed reports are available.

Occasionally, however, weapons have been discovered in archaeological contexts. Three fragments of whalebone clubs in the distinct Nuu-chah-nulth style were found at Yuquot, in deposits dating to about 2000 BP (Dewhirst 1980:327-329). Two are blade fragments while one is a slender decorated handle, carved with a zoomorphic image with a downturned beak-like mouth and feather-like projections (Figure 36, upper left). It resembles a simplified version of the stylized zoomorphic handles known from late eighteenth-century collections. Another decorated handle fragment, with the stylized Thunderbird characteristic of historic Nuu-chah-nulth examples, came from the Toquaht site of Macoah (Figure 36, upper right). Unfortunately, it was not recovered as part of the controlled excavation and cannot be

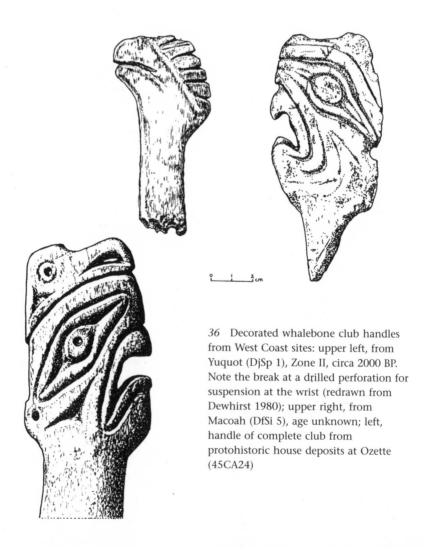

36   Decorated whalebone club handles from West Coast sites: upper left, from Yuquot (DjSp 1), Zone II, circa 2000 BP. Note the break at a drilled perforation for suspension at the wrist (redrawn from Dewhirst 1980); upper right, from Macoah (DfSi 5), age unknown; left, handle of complete club from protohistoric house deposits at Ozette (45CA24)

assigned any age estimate; it may belong to the historic component at that site. Several similar whalebone clubs, in both incomplete and fully finished forms, came from the late precontact house deposits at Ozette (Huelsbeck 1994b:286; Fisken 1994:364; Daugherty and Friedman 1983: Fig. 10:11).

The major evidence for precontact Nuu-chah-nulth warfare comes from site locations that were clearly selected for defence. These are usually situated on rocky headlands or steep-sided islets, reached only by a steep climb or, in some cases, by ladders. Access was difficult and living in such conditions would have been inconvenient, yet such sites offered good vantage spots from which to watch for enemies and were highly defensible locations. Many had their defensive capabilities enhanced with construction of stockades or log ramparts. Known variously as "forts," "defensive sites," and "refuges," such sites are distributed along the north Pacific shores from the outer Aleutian Islands to the Oregon coast (Moss and Erlandson 1992:76).

At least thirty-three such sites are recorded for Nuu-chah-nulth territory, along with one (the well-known fortified village of Whyac) in Ditidaht territory (Map 9).[2] Three more are found among the Makah. Such sites are likely to be underrepresented in the archaeological record, as other examples are known through ethnographic and ethnohistoric sources.[3] Also, other types of defensive locations are not included in this category. Stockades are known to have been erected around a number of historic villages (Sproat 1868:196; Swan 1870:51; Drucker 1951:338), including Macoah. The category of "defensive site" here refers only to elevated rocky headlands, islets, sea stacks, or similar locations that are today draped with relatively shallow midden deposits. Some of these sites, however, may have served primarily as lookouts for migratory sea mammals.

With the exception of several examples along the inlets of Nootka Sound, all known defensive sites are on the outer coast. They tend to be located where they could control the access to major sounds and inlets. Clusters of such sites guard the entrances to Kyuquot Sound and Barkley Sound, in particular. Movements of people along the coast could have been monitored and controlled from fortified settlements in such strategic locations as Yuquot, Cape Beale (at the eastern entrance to Barkley Sound), and Cape Flattery.

2 A computer search of the British Columbia site records by the Archaeology Branch, Victoria, located most sites identified here as "defensive," "refuge," or "fortification." Several others were added upon examination of regional survey reports (Haggarty and Inglis 1985; Inglis and Haggarty 1986; Marshall 1992).

3 For example, in 1789 Haswell noted a "fortification bluff" as he entered the harbour near modern Tofino (Howay 1941:68). Several of the war texts collected by Sapir for Barkley Sound also contain references to defensive locations. Before their defeat by the Ucluelet and Tla-o-qui-aht, the people of Effingham Inlet retreated to their "hill village," which was equipped with log rollers (Sapir and Swadesh 1955:374). As such sites have not been archaeologically located and recorded, they are not included here.

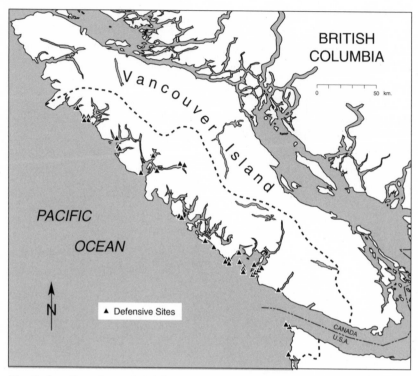

Map 9 Location of recorded defensive sites or lookouts in Nuu-chah-nulth, Ditidaht, and Makah territories. Only four of the eight recorded defensive sites near the entrance to Kyuquot Sound are shown.

Many of the most impressive defensive sites are in immediate association with large villages, either as part of one continuous site or in close proximity, such as on an offshore islet. T'ukw'aa (DfSj 23), the largest Toquaht village, is a good example, with midden deposits from the main village area extending to the top of an immediately adjacent steep-sided headland. Similarly, the Tseshaht village of *Hutsatswilh* (DfSh 31), on Dicebox Island in the Broken Group, is located beside a high flat-topped defensive area (DfSh 79) with steep cliffs in all directions except for immediately over the village (Figure 37). A very similar situation prevails in Huu-ay-aht territory near Bamfield, where a steep-sided defensive area (DeSh 2) towers over the major village of *Kiix7in* (DeSh 1) (Figure 38). In all three cases, the village and defensive area are so closely associated that it is logical to assume that the presence of a suitable flat elevated area for defence was a major criterion in selecting the village location.

In Ditidaht territory, the only recorded defensive site is at the major village of Whyac (*Waayaa7ak*), strategically located on the rocks at the entrance to Nitinat Narrows (Figure 39). Explorer Robert Brown discussed the

37 The defensive site (DfSh 79) on Dicebox Island, Broken Group, Barkley Sound. The Tseshaht villages *Hutsatswilh* (DfSh 31) is to the left of this picture. *Photo by author*

38 The Huu-ay-aht village site of *Kiix7in* (DeSh 1) is in the trees in the centre of this picture. Its defensive site (DeSh 2), known locally as "Execution Rock," is atop the steep-sided bluff to the right. *Photo by author*

defensive features of Whyac in 1864: "Most of the Nettinaht villages were fortified with wooden pickets to prevent any night attack, and from its situation, Whyack, the principal one (built on a cliff, stockaded on the seaward side, and reached only by a narrow entrance where the surf breaks continuously), is impregnable to hostile canoemen" (Bouchard and Kennedy 1991:26).

Among the Makah, Swan (1870:51) notes "stockade forts at Tatoosh Island, and on one of the rocky islets composing Flattery Rocks." As the latter are immediately offshore from Ozette, Swan is likely referring to Tskawahyah (also known as Cannonball) Island. This impressive, steep-sided islet, surmounted by relatively extensive midden deposits, is joined to the Ozette village site at low tides and would have provided a convenient lookout for sea mammals as well as a refuge in times of war.

Oral traditions tell of prolonged residence in such locations during times of danger. House platforms are evident on the surface of many defensive sites. Other features relate to defensive measures. Stockades were erected at some sites, traps and warning devices were set along trails, and logs were stacked along the cliff edge to roll down on attackers. Informants described the defensive strategy of pegging in large logs along the upper lip of the defensive site bluff at *Hutsatswilh* (Dicebox Island) to be released against ascending attackers – a technique apparently successfully employed by the

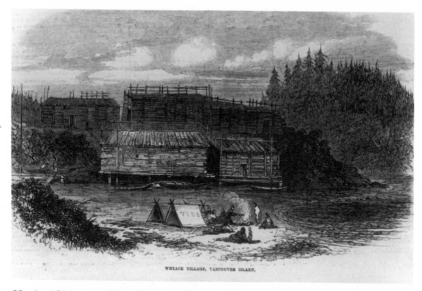

39 An 1864 view of the Ditidaht village of Whyac at Nitinat Narrows is shown in this engraving from the *London Illustrated News* of 1866. The houses along the edge of the beach were erected on short pilings. The defensive palisade at this village is not visible in this view. *Royal BC Museum PN15522*

Tseshaht against the Ahousaht (McMillan and St. Claire 1982:30; St. Claire 1991:146). Similarly, ethnographic accounts describe a large log roller at the top of the *Kiix7in* fort, meant to be used against Clallum raiders (Clamhouse et al. 1991:224-225; Scott 1972:255). Among the Makah, Swan (1870:51) describes "stockades of poles and brush" around houses and identifies several "stockade forts" on islands. The only fort in existence at the time of his observations, however, was among the Quileute, to the south of Ozette. He describes a "precipitous rock," with a single difficult trail to the summit, from which "great logs" could be rolled down on an attacking force. Curtis (1913:143), referring to the same site, describes "rolling bowlders [sic]" down on the enemy.

The Aguilar Point defensive site (DfSg 3), on a rocky headland in eastern Barkley Sound near the entrance to Bamfield Inlet, overlooks the ethnographic Huu-ay-aht village of *7O:ts'o:7a* (DfSg 2). To protect the landward side of this defensive site a trench was dug across the headland, with the earthen embankment on the inside of the trench probably originally supporting a palisade. This defensive earthwork is unique among West Coast sites, although such features are relatively common in the Strait of Georgia region. Except for the defensive earthwork, however, this site and its associated village are typically Nuu-chah-nulth. A Huu-ay-aht legend refers to Aguilar Point as the "fort" of a "bear man" and his family, who constructed a rampart on the landward side of the point to protect their home but eventually were destroyed by their enemies (Scott 1972:260-262).

Radiocarbon dates from several excavated defensive sites give some idea of the antiquity of intensive warfare among the Nuu-chah-nulth and Makah. The earliest date for the defensive portion of T'ukw'aa is about 800 years; however, as the village area was occupied as early as about 1,200 years ago, occasional use of the adjacent headland that forms the defensive site likely also dates to that time. At Aguilar Point, the trench embankment appears to have been constructed about 700 years ago (Buxton 1969); another radiocarbon date, however, indicates that people were living out on this headland, presumably for defensive purposes, about 1,200 years ago. In Makah territory, rocky Tatoosh Island was inhabited by about 1,000 years ago. Although this was ethnographically a major halibut fishing and processing location, the steep sides of this island would have also made it an admirable defensive area. Swan describes a "stockade fort" there. At Ozette, radiocarbon dates for deposits atop Tskawahyah Island are 980 ± 180 BP and 2010 ± 190 BP (Table 8), the latter providing the oldest date at Ozette and possibly the oldest date for a defensive site on the Northwest Coast (Moss and Erlandson 1992:84). Another date of about 2000 BP comes from an exposure face at an unexcavated site (45CA2) high atop a bluff at Cape Flattery. Such dates closely correspond to what appears to be the beginning of intensive settlement in this area.

Such elevated locations served as lookout points for migrating sea mammals and vantage points from which sentinels could watch for enemies, as well as being places of refuge during hostilities. Racks for drying fish may have stood on some sites, as they offered better exposure to the winds than did the sheltered villages (Buxton 1969:41; Moss and Erlandson 1992:76). Some not directly associated with villages were only sporadically used, primarily as lookouts. Others, particularly those on elevated points adjacent to major villages, were occupied on a fairly sustained basis. This would be the case, for example, at Whyac, at T'ukw'aa, and at the defensive site (DjSp 32) associated with Yuquot (Marshall 1993:122). Excavated defensive sites contain ordinary domestic refuse that is indistinguishable from materials obtained at the village sites. At T'ukw'aa, for example, the same types of artifacts and faunal remains occur across the site, including the top of the defensive area. This situation has also been noted for excavated defensive sites in other coastal regions, such as at the Rebecca Spit trench embankment in the Strait of Georgia (Mitchell 1968), three defensive islets in Kwakwa̱ka'wakw territory (Mitchell 1981), and a number of Tlingit "forts" (Moss and Erlandson 1992:76). While these elevated locations offered defensive capabilities in times of warfare, most of the activities that took place there were common domestic ones.

Although archaeological evidence is limited, the distribution and ethnographic importance of these steep-sided defensive locations, plus the prominence of war accounts in the recorded oral histories, attest to the importance of warfare in shaping Nuu-chah-nulth life. The appearance of defensive sites on the Olympic Peninsula by about 2000 BP and in Barkley Sound by at least 1200 BP corresponds closely with the period earlier suggested for the expansion of southern Wakashan peoples into their historic territories. As populations increased and territorial tensions became more prevalent, these highly visible sites became public statements of the group's military power. Ethnographically, chiefs enhanced their power and prestige through expansion of territory, control of trade, and possession of wealth (which included slaves). Heavily defended sites enabled chiefs to maintain control of their territory and all trade that passed by, and raids on weaker or hostile neighbours allowed them to acquire additional slaves and booty. Evidence of heightened hostilities seen in the defensive sites suggests the presence of social hierarchies and the control of territory and wealth.

Trade

The transfer of goods and services between individuals or groups is the central feature of all exchange systems. The extent of trade and types of exchange systems provide some insight into the level of complexity of the society. On the Northwest Coast, powerful chiefs controlled the trade routes, maintaining exclusive access to important resources within their territories.

Such commodities might be traded for economic gain to neighbouring groups or might be publicly redistributed in status-enhancing events such as the potlatch. Archaeologists, however, deal only with the tangible and durable products of trade, usually recoverable as artifacts of exotic raw materials or remains of non-local fauna. Such intangibles as names, songs, and ritual prerogatives, which were publicly transferred during historic potlatches, are not recoverable archaeologically, and only rarely do archaeologists get insight into such major trade commodities as dried salmon and halibut, eulachon oil, clover roots, furs and hides, and slaves. Intragroup exchange in local commodities may also elude archaeological attention; most archaeological evidence consists of exotic items indicating long-distance trade.

Ethnographically, most Nuu-chah-nulth trade was with other Nuu-chah-nulth groups. Although the Chicklisaht and Kyuquot in the north had some contact along the coast with the Kwakwaka'wakw of Quatsino Sound, the most important arteries of commerce with the Kwakwaka'wakw were the overland trails that led across Vancouver Island from the heads of Kyuquot and Nootka Sounds to the Nimpkish River (Drucker 1951: Map 1).[4] Trails also led from the ends of Muchalat and Alberni Inlets across Vancouver Island to the Comox, Pentlatch, and other Salish groups. The Ditidaht traded extensively with the Makah, although commerce was also transacted with the neighbouring Sooke Salish. In the south, the Makah were strategically situated for coastal commerce, trading goods received from the Nuu-chah-nulth and Ditidaht south as far as the Chinook of the lower Columbia River. The importance of this activity was evident to Swan (1870:30), who described the Makah as "emphatically a trading, as well as a producing people."

A first-hand account of Nuu-chah-nulth trade early in the historic period comes from the observations of John R. Jewitt, who was held as a captive among the Mowachaht from 1803 to 1805. His journal notes the arrival in Nootka Sound of various Nuu-chah-nulth groups, the Makah, and the Kwakwaka'wakw from the Nimpkish River (who had arrived via the overland trail).

The trade of most of the other tribes with Nootka [the Mowachaht] was principally train oil [whale oil], seal or whale's blubber, fish fresh or dried, herring or salmon spawn, clams, and muscles [sic], and the *yama* [salal berries], a species of fruit which is pressed and dried, cloth, sea otter skins, and slaves. From the Aitizzarts [Ehattisaht], and the Cayuquets [Kyuquot], particularly the former, the best I-whaw [dentalium shells] and in the greatest quantities was obtained. The Eshquates [Hesquiaht] furnished us with wild

---

4 The importance of these trails is shown in the names of the villages where they began. Both locations, in Kyuquot Sound and in Nootka Sound, were known as Tahsis (or Tacis), meaning "doorway" (Drucker 1951:224, 228).

ducks and geese, particularly the latter. The Wickinninish [Tla-o-qui-aht] and Kla-iz-zarts [Makah] brought to market many slaves, the best sea otter skins, great quantities of oil, whale sinew, and cakes of the *yama*, highly ornamented canoes, some I-whaw, red ochre and pelpelth [black mica] of an inferior quality to that obtained from the Newchemass [Kwakwaka'wakw of the Nimpkish River], but particularly the so much valued *Metamelth* [elk hide], and an excellent root called by the Kla-iz-zarts *Quawnoose* [camas] ... the size of a small onion ... of a most agreeable flavour. From the Kla-iz-zarts was also received, though in no great quantity, a cloth manufactured by them from the fur already spoken of, which feels like wool and is of a grey colour [probably dog hair]. (Jewitt 1967:78-79)

Sproat (1868:79) also notes that the Nuu-chah-nulth traded dried hali-but, herring, and cedar bark baskets to the Salish tribes of southern Vancou-ver Island in exchange for camas bulbs and swamp rushes for making mats. The southernmost Ditidaht – the Pacheedaht – were famed as slave traders, primarily to the Clallum and Sooke, and they also traded canoes, although few were made by them (Clamhouse et al. 1991:296). Swan (1870:31) notes that the Makah traded dried halibut as well as whale oil and blubber to the Nuu-chah-nulth, receiving in turn dried salmon, cedar bark, dentalium shells, canoes, and slaves. These commodities were then traded south to such groups as the Quileute and Chinook.

With the exception of dentalium shells, virtually none of these commodi-ties would be preserved in the archaeological record. Archaeological claims for prehistoric trade networks usually rely on the occurrence of such pre-served non-local raw materials as obsidian, chert, catlinite, nephrite, and other types of stone used in tool production. Obsidian is particularly useful for such analysis, as it has excellent flaking and cutting properties, was traded widely from a limited number of source locations, and can be attributed to source through several non-destructive techniques. With the use of x-ray fluorescence obsidian artifacts from archaeological sites can be matched with known source locations through the study of the distinctive pattern of trace elements characteristic of each obsidian flow (Nelson et al. 1975; Carlson 1994).

The only excavated site reporting obsidian artifacts in the ethnographic Nuu-chah-nulth area, however, is Shoemaker Bay. Obsidian flakes were fairly common in the early component, Shoemaker Bay I, which was clearly linked to contemporaneous cultures in the Strait of Georgia region. Most of the analyzed obsidian came from two unlocated sources on the south-central coast of British Columbia, although two specimens were traced to known flows in central Oregon (McMillan and St. Claire 1982:70), indicating at least sporadic contacts far to the south. No such items came from sites of the West Coast culture type, although a fragment of a chipped projectile point made of jasper came from Hesquiat Village. Its unique form and material for West Coast sites led Haggarty (1982:120) to conclude that it "was likely obtained in trade." In the Toquaht sites, a small bit fragment of a nephrite celt was found at Ch'uumat'a, from a level dating to about 2300 BP, and a reworked greenstone celt came from a level at T'ukw'aa dating to about 900 BP. The main source location for nephrite is thought to be the Fraser River Canyon, while a major quarry for greenstone is found in the Bella Coola Valley (Carlson 1994). While non-local lithic materials are often used in archaeological analyses as indicators of extensive exchange networks, their paucity in West Coast sites likely reflects only the general unimportance of stone in Nuu-chah-nulth material culture.

Less direct evidence may also be used to understand the extent of exchange systems in late precontact times. Huelsbeck (1988a, 1988b) argues, based on the huge amount of oil and blubber represented by the whalebones in the protohistoric house deposits at Ozette, that whale products would have dominated all other food sources at this site and would have provided a surplus that served as a major trade commodity. The faunal remains from Hesquiat Village yielded a similar pattern, leading Huelsbeck (1988a) to suggest that the Ozette and Hesquiat economies were specialized, with whaling providing a surplus that could be exchanged for non-local necessities. Yuquot, with its relative paucity of whalebone, lacked evidence for such specialization. This is consistent with the ethnographic importance of trade in whale products among the Ditidaht and Makah (Clamhouse et al. 1991:297; Swan 1870:32; Singh 1966:82), who received in exchange such products as cedar canoes and house planks (Swan 1870:31; Huelsbeck 1988a:171). The northern Nuu-chah-nulth appear to have been the recipients of whale products in such trade. Although John Jewitt noted few whales being taken by the Mowachaht during his two and a half years of captivity in Nootka Sound, he frequently made references to the consumption of whale oil and blubber. Despite Jewitt's aversion to such food, it was a year-round staple, traded in by other groups, often over some distance (Cavanagh 1983:56, 134). Jewitt noted fifteen occasions when whale oil or blubber was brought to Nootka Sound; almost half of these involved the Tla-o-qui-aht, while the remaining trading expeditions came from the Ehattesaht, Hesquiaht, and Makah (Marshall 1989b:267; 1993:251).

In extraregional trade, the Nuu-chah-nulth were famed as the suppliers of dentalium shells (_ḥiixwa_), a wealth good valued far inland. These were procured and traded by the peoples of western Vancouver Island, including the Kwakwa̱ka'wakw of Quatsino Sound and Cape Scott as well as the Nuu-chah-nulth. Major dentalium beds have been noted in the territories of the northern Nuu-chah-nulth: the Chicklisaht, Kyuquot, and Ehattesaht (Drucker 1951; Barton 1994). One of the most important beds was in the waters of Ehattesaht territory, although chiefs of the Kyuquot, Chicklisaht, and Nuchatlaht also owned dentalium-fishing rights there (Drucker 1951:111, 256). Drucker also mentions an important dentalium bed in Barkley Sound, although he does not give a specific location. More recently, dentalium sources have been noted in Clayoquot Sound and Hesquiat Harbour (Bouchard and Kennedy 1990). Elaborate devices were developed to procure dentalium in fairly deep offshore waters (Drucker 1951:112-113; Jewitt 1967:63; Ellis and Swan 1981:73; Andrews 1989:96-109; Barton 1994:57-93). Dentalium shells were also known to wash ashore in locations such as Long Beach (Drucker 1951:112; Ellis and Swan 1981:73), but this was only a minor source of supply. In Nootka Sound, the Mowachaht seem to have relied on trade with neighbouring groups. According to Jewitt, in 18 transactions in which Maquinna received dentalium, the Ehattesaht were the suppliers in 14 cases, the Nuchatlaht in 2, the Chicklisaht in 1, and an unknown group to the south (possibly the Hesquiaht) in 1 (Barton 1994:108, 111). To the south, the Makah traded with the Nuu-chah-nulth for dentalium (Swan 1870:31; Singh 1966:83), which they traded further south. In the mid-nineteenth century, however, the artist Paul Kane noted that dentalium occurred in abundance at Cape Flattery, and he described the technique by which it was taken (Kane 1968:165).

Dentalium shells, in summary, were highly sought after, were traded between Nuu-chah-nulth groups, and had important uses and meaning in Nuu-chah-nulth society. Drucker (1951:139-140) describes (and illustrates) long hair ornaments, covered in dentalium, that were worn by pubescent girls of high status; these required the holding of a major potlatch or public feast before they could be removed. Swan (1870:13, 16) also describes and illustrates dentalium shell headdresses and pendants worn by Makah girls at puberty. Bracelets and necklaces consisting of a number of strings of dentalia were worn by the nobility (Jewitt 1967:62). Jewitt observed these shells used in ceremonial contexts by the Mowachaht, describing on two occasions the burial of high status individuals with considerable quantities of dentalium (1967:105, 111; 1988:57); he also noted the transfer of large strings of dentalium to Maquinna during a marriage ceremony (1988:112).

Dentalium was also a valuable commodity in the early maritime fur trade. Aware of the high regard in which this shell was held by the Native peoples of the coast, some European traders purchased quantities from the Nuu-chah-nulth to use in exchange with other groups. In 1793-94 the captain of the *Jefferson* purchased "160 fathoms" (about 300 m) of strung dentalium from the Nuu-chah-nulth of Clayoquot and Barkley Sounds (Magee 1794; Gibson 1992:229).

In archaeological contexts, dentalium shells are found as far inland as the Plains and Western Subarctic. They are found in small quantities at several Northwest Coast sites as early as about 4400 BP (Andrews 1989:141). By

2500 BP, dentalia are found in greater numbers, both on the southern coast and in the interior plateau (Barton 1994:2). In the Strait of Georgia region, dentalia are frequently found in burial contexts dating to the Marpole period (Burley 1980; 1981; Burley and Knusel 1989; Mitchell 1971; 1990). Certainly the origin of most dentalium shells found in Strait of Georgia sites was on the west coast of Vancouver Island, although other origin possibilities exist.

Despite the ethnographic importance of dentalium among the Nuu-chah-nulth, known patterns of trade in dentalium between Nuu-chah-nulth groups, and the occurrence of dentalium from the Pacific coast in archaeological sites far inland, almost no evidence of this trade exists in West Coast sites. Only two fragmentary dentalium shells were excavated at Yuquot, and both came from historic levels (Clarke and Clarke 1980:46). Similarly, a single dentalium shell came from T'ukw'aa, again from historic deposits. At Ch'uumat'a, one dentalium shell came from a level dated at over 1000 BP, while a second, decorated with an incised design, came from a level dated at 2000 BP. Another incised dentalium shell came from DeSf 9, one of the Ditidaht sites on lower Nitinat Lake (Eldridge and Fisher 1997). At Shoemaker Bay, which is well situated to have been a vital link in the dentalium trade between the west coast and the Strait of Georgia, only a single dentalium shell, with an incised encircling line, was found in the upper component (McMillan and St. Claire 1982:111). Despite the great quantities of dentalia from the Strait of Georgia and the Plateau attributed to Nuu-chah-nulth sources, these seven shells are all that are reported from West Coast sites. The difference is almost certainly attributable to the lack of midden interments in sites of the West Coast culture type, resulting in a near absence of wealth items in archaeological contexts. Only in the unique circumstance at Ozette do we find dentalium shells in some quantity. The protohistoric house deposits at that site contained 256 dentalium shells, almost entirely from the high-status House 1 (Wessen 1994b:353). The only other Makah area site with reported dentalium is Tatoosh Island (E. Friedman 1976:156).

Highly valued metal objects were also important late precontact or protohistoric trade items. The late house deposits at Ozette contained small numbers of woodworking tools and knives with iron cutting blades as well as pendants of copper (Wessen 1990:416). Pérez noted small quantities of copper and iron among the Natives who came out to his ship near the entrance to Nootka Sound in 1774 (Beals 1989:89; Moser 1926:163; Mills 1955:71). Four years later, Cook (1784:267) noted the abundance of iron chisels and knives among the Natives of Nootka Sound, stating that they seemed "perfectly acquainted with the use of that metal." In trying to determine the source of metal implements, Cook discounted the Spanish, who had preceded him by only a few years, considering iron "too common, in too many hands and too well known for them [the Nuu-chah-nulth] to have had the first knowledge of it so late" (Cook in Beaglehole 1967:321). Instead, Cook (1784:332) speculated that these objects were traded along Aboriginal trade networks from more distant European sources. Mills (1955:71-72), on the other hand, argues that iron might ultimately have come from the Bering Sea region of Alaska, where it is found in archaeological contexts dating back several millennia. The late date of metal artifacts in Nuu-chah-nulth sites, however, supports Cook's contention that they were of European origin, reaching areas such as Nootka Sound prior to direct European contact through rapid distribution along Native trade routes. Control of vital trade routes, such as the overland trails across Vancouver Island, would have greatly enhanced the power and prestige of chiefs.

While exchange systems at some level characterize virtually all human societies, the social context in which exchange occurs varies. The evolution of social hierarchies has been linked to the development of centralized redistribution systems, where chiefs controlled access to valued resources (Earle 1994). Earle, however, distinguishes between trade in the subsistence economy and exchange in prestige goods, maintaining that only the latter was a significant element in the development of complex societies. The West Coast dentalium trade would clearly be an example of this, as, ethnographically, access to dentalium procurement areas and control of the trade in dentalium were the jealously guarded prerogatives of high-status individuals. The ethnographic importance of trade among the Nuu-chah-nulth, however, is poorly reflected in the archaeological record.

Status Distinctions

Mortuary data provide one of the most productive avenues to the detection of social inequalities that the archaeological record has to offer. Among other indicators, differential treatment in burial form and associated materials may reflect social differences during life. Burial of wealth items with certain individuals, including subadults and both sexes, suggests the presence of ascribed rather than achieved ranking. Such data have been used to argue that ascribed ranking characterized the Strait of Georgia region by Marpole times (Burley and Knusel 1989; Matson and Coupland 1995:209-210).

The lack of midden interments in West Coast sites, however, frustrates such analysis. Burials have been excavated at Shoemaker Bay and Little Beach, but both sites are early and neither can be encompassed within the West Coast culture type. No midden burials have been excavated and reported for late West Coast sites predating European contact.[5] Most human remains

5 As indicated previously, however, this does not mean that no such burials exist. Midden interments dating to this time were exposed, but not removed or analyzed, at Hesquiat Village, Ch'uumat'a, and Tatoosh Island.

analyzed from Nuu-chah-nulth territory date to the Historic Period and involve above-ground disposal of the body in caves, rockshelters, or trees (Cybulski 1978; McPhatter 1986; Schulting and McMillan 1995), although human remains were also found in the upper midden deposit at Yuquot (Cybulski 1980) and an apparently historic burial was excavated at Bamfield (McLeod and Skinner 1987). Artificial cranial deformation was noted on individuals from Yuquot, Hesquiat Harbour, and Bamfield. Although this trait has frequently been advanced as evidence for status distinctions in the Marpole period in the Strait of Georgia (Mitchell 1971:54; 1990:346; Matson and Coupland 1995:209), its frequent occurrence in Nuu-chah-nulth skeletal remains, along with ethnographic claims for the universality of this practice (Drucker 1951:122), prohibit any such assumptions in this area.

Although little direct evidence for status distinctions exists in the archaeological record, some interpretations can be derived through ethnographic analogy. The continuity demonstrated at many of these Late Period sites supports the utility of such an approach. Status distinctions featured prominently in Nuu-chah-nulth life. Hereditary chiefs (*hawilh*) controlled access to all valued economic resources, coordinated group economic and ceremonial activities, distributed food and goods at feasts and potlatches, managed the supernatural realm through inherited secret knowledge, and were ultimately responsible for group prosperity and security. They were distinguished from other members of the society through the occupation of particular high-status areas of the houses and through the wearing of more elaborate clothing and ornamentation, at least on public occasions. Such traits are potentially recognizable in the archaeological record, and there are a few indications that such status distinctions are characteristic of the late West Coast culture type.

Drucker (1951:244) specifically mentions "ornaments of abalone shell and dentalia" as part of the more ornate costume that marked chiefly status. The limited occurrence of dentalia in West Coast sites, largely attributable to the absence of excavated mortuary contexts, has already been mentioned. Two abalone pendants, for suspension from the ears or nose, were found in late precontact or early contact period deposits at a Toquaht site (DfSj 30) on the George Fraser Islands (McMillan and St. Claire 1994), and a preform for a large ornament of rock scallop came from one of the Nitinat Lake sites (Eldridge and Fisher 1997). A number of small bone pendants and combs from various West Coast sites may have served the same type of ornamental function. Several fragments of decorated whalebone clubs from Yuquot, dating to about 2000 BP, led Dewhirst (1980:341) to suggest that "status and ranking" was present that early.

More complete and convincing evidence comes from the waterlogged house deposits at Ozette. The abundance of carved and decorated items preserved at this unique site suggests chiefly patronage and control of inherited crest images. Particularly revealing is the occurrence of a large decorated wooden replica of a whale saddle (the area around the dorsal fin), suggesting chiefly rituals associated with whaling, as were known ethnographically. Differences in faunal assemblages between the houses at Ozette have been related to differing access to resources, reflecting status distinctions between the social groups occupying them (Huelsbeck 1989, 1994a; Samuels 1989, 1994; Wessen 1988, 1994a; see also Chapter 3). Within House 1, which shows evidence of being the most highly ranked, a concentration of dentalium shells and other wealth items occurred in one rear corner, ethnographically corresponding to the domestic space of the highest ranked individual. The spatial patterning of food remains in this house even led Huelsbeck (1989:166) to infer that feasts were being hosted by high-status individuals. Although these data relate only to the period immediately prior to European contact, they likely reflect social systems that had been achieved considerably earlier. Status distinctions are likely to have characterized much or all of the two millennia that make up the late West Coast culture type.

Ideology/Cosmology

Glimpses into how people in the past perceived their relationship with the supernatural world may be found in the images they created. These include carved bone and stone objects occasionally found in West Coast sites, abundant wooden artworks recovered from the waterlogged house deposits at Ozette, and the painted or carved images left on the rocks at a number of locations in Nuu-chah-nulth, Ditidaht, and Makah territories. With some caution, several archaeological sites can also be considered ritual places that reflect ancient belief systems.

An underlying theme in Nuu-chah-nulth life is the ritual necessity of preparing and purifying the body prior to any important undertaking. This included fasting, sexual continence, and ceremonial bathing, often scrubbing the flesh with hemlock boughs until it bled. Whaling was one of the most supernaturally charged activities and required the most elaborate ritual preparation. The whaler might retire to an isolated location, where rituals could be carried out in secret (Curtis 1916; Gunther 1942; Drucker 1951). Human corpses or skeletal elements and carved wooden representations of humans and whales were used in the rituals performed at such locations. The Mowachaht whalers' "shrine," or "washing house" (Figure 40), located on a small island in a lake near Yuquot, is the most famous example of such a structure (Boas 1930:261-269; Drucker 1951:171-172). In 1904, in a move that still causes controversy and resentment, the entire shrine, including the wooden structure, over sixty carved figures, and a number of human skulls, was disassembled and taken to the American Museum of Natural History in New York (Jonaitis 1988:183-185). The former location of this

40 Inside the whaling shrine near Yuquot, showing a row of carved wooden human figures, along with two wooden whales near the centre of the picture. Note also the human skulls arranged on the ground. Photo by George Hunt, probably taken in 1903, shortly before the structure and its contents were removed. *Canadian Museum of Civilization 76-4310*

shrine has been archaeologically detected and recorded (as site DjSp 6), although little is left but several post remnants and an area where the rocks were removed to allow canoe access (Inglis and Haggarty 1984; Marshall 1992a:83-84). Ethnographically, Folan (1972:56) mentions another whaling shrine on Crawfish Lake, also on Nootka Island, and Brabant (1977:50) describes a whaling shrine with human skeletons that once existed at Hesquiat. Similarly, Drucker (1951:172-174) refers to whaling shrines among the Hesquiaht and Ahousaht as well as to a Muchalaht shrine used in rituals to ensure abundant salmon.

In addition to the ritual preparation prior to whaling, there was the ceremonial treatment of the whale following a successful hunt. Mention has already been made to the ritual welcoming of the whale and the removal of the whale's saddle to the home of the whaling chief. The presence of a carved wooden effigy of a whale saddle in the house deposits at Ozette shows that this practice extends back into precontact times (Daugherty and Friedman 1983:184). Sea otter teeth inset into the side of the wooden effigy outline the image of the Thunderbird (*tuta* or *tutuut-sh*) with the Lightning Serpent (*ḥiy'itl'iik*) (Figure 41). In Nuu-chah-nulth mythology, Thunderbirds preyed on whales, hurling the Lightning Serpents as their harpoons (Sapir

41   Richard Daugherty, director of the Ozette excavation project, poses at Ozette in 1970 with a carved wooden effigy of a whale dorsal fin. The object is inlaid with approximately 700 sea-otter teeth, some of which are arranged to form outline images of the Thunderbird and Serpent. *Photo courtesy Makah Cultural and Research Center, Neah Bay*

1922:314; Drucker 1951:153). The frequent association of Thunderbird, Whale, and Lightning Serpent is a prominent feature of ethnographic Nuu-chah-nulth and Makah art, symbolically reflecting the cultural importance placed on whaling.

More modest welcoming rituals extended to certain other animals hunted. When a bear was killed it was set up in the house, sprinkled with eagle down in welcoming, and offered provisions (Jewitt 1967:96; Drucker 1951:180-181). After the bear was butchered and cooked, a feast was held. Although not mentioned in the ethnographies, special disposal of the bones may be associated with such treatment. A burial cave in Nootka Sound was found to contain about twenty-two bear skulls, along with other bones, perhaps representing the ritual treatment of this animal (McMillan 1969:46-49). Similarly, a cave located in inner Clayoquot Sound near Kennedy River, containing seven bear skulls thought to have been deliberately placed, has been interpreted as being a ritual space (Arcas Consulting Archaeologists and Archeotech Associates 1994:58).

Depictions on artworks recovered archaeologically may also reflect such ritualistic practices. Small carvings in stone, bone, or antler, however, are rare in West Coast sites. The decorated handles of whalebone clubs from Yuquot and Macoah, the former with a simple bird-like head and the latter with the stylized Thunderbird characteristic of historic Nuu-chah-nulth examples, have already been mentioned. Such images reflect the importance of supernatural power in military endeavours. A small stone carving of a whale was recovered from late precontact deposits at T'ukw'aa, as was a small zoomorphic bone pendant (possibly representing the Thunderbird), a bone fragment with an incised eye design, and a bone cut-out figure possibly representing a stylized whale's tail (McMillan and St. Claire 1992). An incised zoomorphic antler figure, possibly the handle of a comb, came from Late Period deposits at Ch'uumat'a (McMillan and St. Claire 1994). A cut-out bone figure of the Thunderbird, in typical Nuu-chah-nulth style, was excavated in historic levels at Yuquot (Dewhirst 1980:334-335). Among several decorated objects from the Ozette midden trench was a bone comb with an incised human face (McKenzie 1974:73). The relative paucity of such artworks reflects factors of preservation, as most artistic production was in wood.

The waterlogged deposits at Ozette clearly demonstrate the wealth of decorated objects that were part of Makah households in late precontact times. Boxes, bowls, clubs, tool handles, and other implements were embellished with fine carving, in a style characteristic of historic Nuu-chah-nulth and Makah art (Daugherty and Friedman 1983). Thunderbirds and wolves are depicted on a large incised and painted plank panel, while the outline image of a whale covers another. Thunderbirds and whales reflect the importance of whaling, while Wolf was the dominant supernatural figure in the most important Nuu-chah-nulth and Makah ceremonial (Ernst 1952; Moogk 1980; Drucker 1951; Curtis 1916; Arima 1983). Owls, dreaded by the Makah as transformed spirits of the dead (Ernst 1952:23), are carved on both ends of a slender wooden club. As this shows no evidence of actual use, it may have been a ceremonial object. Human figures are also well represented in the artwork at Ozette.

One of the most enigmatic of archaeological site types, and one which holds the promise of casting light on past belief systems, is the category of "rock art." At twenty-nine locations in the study area, images have been left on prominent rock surfaces (Map 10). In twelve cases, these were painted in red ochre (pictographs), while at the remaining seventeen sites they were carved or pecked into the rock surface (petroglyphs). Individual sites range from single depictions on a rock surface to large clusters of carved or painted images. At the Wedding Rocks site (45CA31) just south of Ozette, for example, over forty carved images can be seen on a cluster of boulders extending for a considerable distance along the beach.

Several patterns are clearly evident in rock art distribution in this area. Pictographs are located along protected inner waterways, while petroglyphs are found in exposed outer coast locations. The only exceptions are two petroglyph sites in the Alberni Valley, at Sproat and Great Central Lakes, and these may have been executed prior to the relatively late acquisition of this area by Nuu-chah-nulth peoples. Pictographs are concentrated in northern Nuu-chah-nulth territory, particularly in the inlets of Nootka Sound,

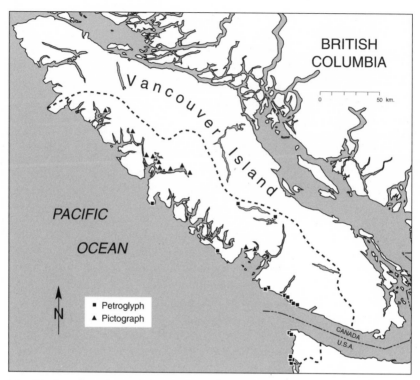

Map 10   Location of recorded rock art sites in Nuu-chah-nulth, Ditidaht and Makah territories.

where they are the only recorded rock art type. The only other pictograph sites are two locations in the inlets of upper Barkley Sound. Aside from the two Alberni Valley examples, the only petroglyphs recorded in Nuu-chah-nulth territory are outside Hesquiat Harbour and at Quisitis Point, in outer coast Ucluelet territory. The Ditidaht have seven recorded sites, all petroglyphs, with two near Pacheena Point and five near the major ethnographic village of Clo-oose. Makah territory has six petroglyph sites, with two near the village of Archawat and four clustered near Ozette. All of the latter consist only of one or two images, with the exception of the major concentration at the Wedding Rocks site.

   Typical images are those that characterize historic Nuu-chah-nulth, Ditidaht, and Makah art. Whales are prominent depictions at such large and important sites as Clo-oose Hill and Wedding Rocks. The Thunderbird, with its distinctive downturned beak, is carved into the rocks at both the Blowhole and Hill sites near Clo-oose (Hill and Hill 1974) and painted in several Nootka Sound pictographs (Figure 42). Fish are also featured at such petroglyph sites as Wedding Rocks and Quisitis Point as well as in the pictographs at Effingham Inlet in Barkley Sound. Anthropomorphs are common,

42 Red ochre pictograph of Thunderbird (DkSp 8), Hisnit Inlet, Nootka Sound. *Photo by Yvonne Marshall*

shown as heads or full figures (Figures 43 and 44), the latter often engaged in activities. A full-bodied human appears to be holding a trophy head at the Clo-oose Hill site (Hill and Hill 1974:79), while at Wedding Rocks one human holds a whale and another uses what appears to be a fish spear or dip net (Ellison 1977:29,32). Rays emanating from the head of one anthropomorph with upraised arms may indicate shamanic power, although Ellison (1977:70) interprets these to be a headdress used in whaling rituals. Sexual imagery is also common in Ditidaht and Makah petroglyphs. Among the other images carved into the sandstone bedrock at Clo-oose Hill is a copulating couple (Hill and Hill 1974:79), and vulvic depiction on anthropomorphs occurs at the Clo-oose sites, Carmanah Point, and Wedding Rocks (Figures 43 and 44). An isolated bisected oval, interpreted as vulvic imagery, is one of the most common elements of the rock art at Wedding Rocks (Figure 46) and also occurs at several other Makah and Ditidaht sites.

Some rock art images may reflect specific myths or traditions. Marshall (1992a:79-80; 1992b), for example, interprets a pictograph site (DkSp 31) in Hisnit Inlet, Nootka Sound, in such a manner. The site consists of two anthropomorphic faces with radiating lines, suggesting sun figures. These may relate to the story of Umiq, the founding ancestor of the local group that occupied Hisnit Inlet. In this story, as originally recorded by Curtis (1916:183-186), Umiq was impregnated by a supernatural being and gave birth to four children, including a boy whose "face was of dazzling brilliance." The location and nature of this pictograph strongly suggest that it depicts an element of Umiq's story.

43　Anthropomorphs and whales, Clo-oose Hill petroglyph site (DdSe 14). *Photo from rubbing by Beth Hill, courtesy Royal BC Museum*

44　Petroglyphs on boulders at the Wedding Rocks site (45CA31) south of Ozette: left, anthropomorphic faces and whales; right, anthropomorphic figures with vulvic imagry. *Photos by author*

45   Detail of the Sproat Lake petroglyphs (DhSf 1), showing mythical marine creatures. *Photo by author*

The two inland petroglyphs, located on lakes in the Alberni Valley, differ from other rock art in the study area. At Sproat Lake, a group of mythical marine creatures, with x-ray vision showing internal details, give the illusion of movement across a vertical rock face at the edge of the water (Figure 45). Stylistically, they closely resemble images at sites on the east side of Vancouver Island, such as the famous Nanaimo petroglyphs. Although Newcombe (1907) interpreted them as being representations of the Nuu-chah-nulth *ḥiy'itl'iik* (Lightning Serpent), these finned creatures with sinuous bodies lack any counterparts in Nuu-chah-nulth rock art but are closely paralleled in the Nanaimo images (see Hill and Hill 1974:102). They provide yet another cultural link to the Strait of Georgia and likely predate Nuu-chah-nulth arrival in the Alberni Valley. Sproat (1868:268) was unable to gather any specific information on these images from Tseshaht and Hupacasath informants, who could tell him only that "Quawteaht [Kwatyat] made them." Similarly, Boas, in an early article in a German journal, noted that the rock bluff into which the images were carved was said by his informants to be "the house of Quotiath [Kwatyat]" (Lundy 1974:312).

Although none of the rock art sites have been dated, they do not give an impression of great age. Few of the petroglyphs show signs of extensive erosion. Some of the pictographs are faded and indistinct, but others are still clear. Most images are assumed to date to the late precontact period. Ellison (1977), in an analysis of the petroglyphs near Ozette, links the style and motifs of the rock art to the late precontact artworks excavated in the

46   Sailing ship and vulvic image carved on beach boulder, Wedding Rocks site (45CA31). *Photo by author*

buried house deposits. Some images, however, clearly postdate contact with Europeans. Several glyphs, at Clo-oose Hill and Ozette, appear to have been cut with metal blades (Lundy 1974:330; Ellison 1977:52), while others display items introduced by Europeans. Depictions of men on horseback occur in a pictograph at the end of Muchalat Inlet (Marshall 1992a:79; 1993:60) and in a petroglyph near Clo-oose (Hill and Hill 1974:76). An image at Wedding Rocks appears to be a man using a firearm (Hill and Hill 1974:66; Ellison 1977:43). Four detailed depictions of sailing ships occur on a rock ledge near Clo-oose (Hill and Hill 1974:72-73), while another is carved on a boulder at Wedding Rocks (Figure 46). The Clo-oose Blowhole site also contains the detailed image of a steamship, almost certainly the *Beaver*, a Hudson's Bay Company ship that first appeared along the west coast in 1836 (Hill and Hill 1974:77; Lundy 1974:326). The arrival of this first steamer, belching black smoke as it traversed the coast, must have seemed an event worth commemorating.

Once again, the Sproat Lake petroglyphs may be an exception. Carlson (1993) has attempted to establish a chronology for rock art styles based on comparison with art from dated archaeological contexts. The bold curvilinear style of carving that characterizes the Sproat Lake and Nanaimo images is linked to art recovered from Marpole period sites in the Strait of Georgia. Through this analysis, Carlson (1993:8) places the Sproat Lake petroglyphs in the period between 2500 BP and 1000 BP.

Questions of the function and meaning of rock art defy complete resolution, and certainly no one explanation encompasses all known rock art sites. Shamanism undoubtedly provides the underlying motivation behind the creation of many rock art images (Carlson 1993; Hill and Hill 1974). Shamanic rituals, however, involved secret knowledge, and many of the rock art sites are in such prominent and public locations that other explanations must be sought. A similar motivation involves ritual attempts to gain supernatural control over the creatures and wealth of the sea (Hill and Hill 1974:283; Ellison 1977:172). This fits well with the Ditidaht and Makah petroglyphs, with their open-ocean locations and frequent depictions of whales and fish, but cannot explain all images at these sites. One of the Nootka Sound pictographs (DjSo 1) is on a prominent rock face overlooking a rockshelter burial site and may have served as a grave marker or memorial (McMillan 1969:45-46, 50, 53; Marshall 1993:60). The large prominent petroglyph sites near the villages of Clo-oose and Ozette could possibly have functioned as boundary markers. Whatever the immediate motivation, the rock art sites symbolized the fundamental values of Nuu-chah-nulth, Ditidaht, and Makah society, including the vital role of whaling, sexuality, and the myths of founding ancestors.

Regional and Temporal Variation
The West Coast culture type, as defined by Mitchell (1990), was based almost entirely on artifacts from Yuquot and Hesquiat. As additional knowledge is gained from archaeological research on the west coast of Vancouver Island, variation in the culture type is becoming evident. Excavated data from Makah territory on the Olympic Peninsula, not considered in Mitchell's original formulation, can now also be encompassed within the culture type, although there are clearly differences as well. Regional variation, while evident, does not obscure the basic similarities in West Coast artifact assemblages, which are heavily dominated by small bone points, bone bipoints, bone splinter awls, the valves and points of composite toggling harpoon heads, and abrasive stones. Typical artifacts of the late West Coast culture type are shown in Figure 47.

The Shoemaker Bay site remains outside the culture type for its entire period of occupation. The most recent component, Shoemaker Bay II, begins about 1500 BP (McMillan and St. Claire 1982). Abrasive stones are by far the most common artifacts, comprising 27.6 percent of the total. Chipped stone points, ground stone points, and ground stone knives suggest close ties to sites of equivalent age in the Strait of Georgia. In fact, Shoemaker Bay II is best considered a component of the Strait of Georgia culture type. There are a few traits, however, such as the presence of bone fishhook shanks, that give this assemblage a distinct West Coast flavour.

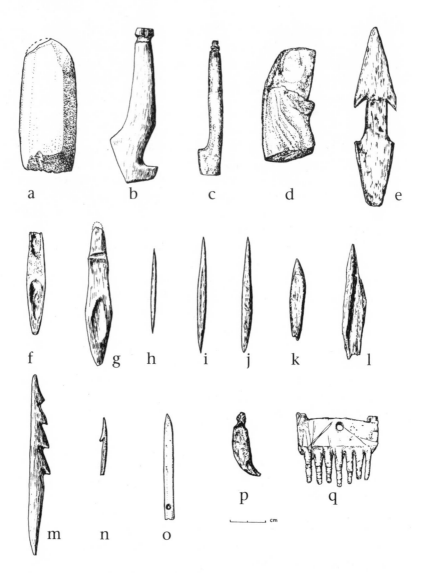

47   Artifacts of the late West Coast culture type: *a*, stone celt (Yuquot); *b*, stone fishhook shank (Yuquot); *c*, bone fishhook shank (Ch'uumat'a); *d*, mussel shell celt (T'ukw'aa); *e*, bilaterally barbed harpoon head (Ch'uumat'a); *f*, channelled valve for composite harpoon head (T'ukw'aa); *g*, slotted valve for composite harpoon head (Yuquot); *h* and *i*, bone bipoints (T'ukw'aa); *j*, bone point, probably a fishhook barb (T'ukw'aa); *k*, bone point, probably for arming a composite toggling harpoon head (T'ukw'aa); *l*, bone splinter awl (T'ukw'aa); *m*, barbed bone point, possibly an arrow point (Yuquot); *n*, single barb point, probably a fishhook barb (T'ukw'aa); *o*, bone needle (Ch'uumat'a); *p*, canine tooth pendant (T'ukw'aa); *q*, bone comb (T'ukw'aa). Length of *a* is 7.1 cm; rest are drawn to same scale. Yuquot artifacts are redrawn from Dewhirst 1980; all others are drawn from originals.

Table 12 summarizes the artifact assemblages from five major, largely contemporaneous, excavated West Coast sites. T'ukw'aa and Hesquiat Village were both occupied from about 1,200 years ago into the early Historic Period. Zone III at Yuquot, dating from about 1200 BP to the beginning of European contact, is also considered here. At Ch'uumat'a, only the later levels, from about 2000 BP to European contact, are included. The Ozette midden trench, although poorly dated, spans roughly the same period, although its initial date may be somewhat less.

For the purposes of comparison, some changes had to be made to the original investigators' artifact typologies. Reclassification has resulted in a certain amount of "lumping," which has reduced the total number of artifact categories. Differences in analytical procedures have also inhibited comparisons. At Yuquot and Ozette, for example, where artifacts were categorized according to presumed function, fragments that could not be assigned categories were eliminated from the analysis. As most of these fragments would have been bone, this reduces the total percentage of bone in relation to other raw material categories as compared to the other three sites.   One of the distinguishing features of the West Coast culture type as originally defined is the near absence of any flaked stone artifacts or flaking detritus. No such materials came from Zone III at Yuquot, and they are rare at T'ukw'aa and the later period at Ch'uumat'a. Although still only a small portion of the total, chipped stone was more abundant at Hesquiat Village. This site also had a wider range of items and materials, including a chipped jasper projectile point fragment, quartz crystal core fragments and possible microblade, and a cobble tool. Of the five sites, the Ozette midden trench had the largest numbers of chipped stone objects, consisting primarily of scrapers and other tools based on cortex flakes. Cores, scrapers, cobble tools, and other chipped stone implements were also relatively common at the Late Period Hoko River Rockshelter (D. Croes, pers. comm. 1995).

Ground stone tools, with the exception of numerous abrasive stones, are considered "comparatively infrequent" in West Coast culture type assemblages (Mitchell 1990:356). Stone celts and fishhook shanks occur in most West Coast sites. Ground stone points are restricted to the Toquaht sites, where they are found in small numbers. Ground slate knives, found at Ozette, are considered to be characteristic of late precontact shell middens on the Olympic Peninsula (Wessen 1990:414). Pecked and ground stone artifacts include grooved sinkers, found only at Ozette in this sample, and hand mauls, found only at Hesquiat Village despite their inclusion in Mitchell's (1990:356) list of characteristic West Coast culture type artifacts. One unique stone object is a small, beautifully carved image of a whale, only 4.2 cm in length, found at T'ukw'aa (McMillan and St. Claire 1992).

Major differences are evident in the relative importance of stone in the artifact assemblages of the five sites. At Yuquot and Hesquiat Village

Table 12

Comparison of artifacts from five excavated sites

	Yuquot Zone III		Hesquiat Village		T'ukw'aa		Ch'uumat'a (post-2000 BP)		Ozette trench	
	No.	%	No.	%	No.	%	No.	%	No.	%
Chipped stone										
chipped projectile point			1	0.1						
pebble/cobble tools			1	0.1					8	1.4
cores			12	1.3						
flakes/flake tools			2	0.2	3	0.2	2	0.5	28	4.9
pièces esquillées									8	1.4
Subtotal	*0*	*0*	*16*	*1.7*	*3*	*0.2*	*2*	*0.5*	*44*	*7.7*
Ground stone										
ground slate points					2	0.1	1	0.3		
ground stone knives	1	0.1							2	0.4
celts	3	0.4	3	0.3	1	0.1	2	0.5		
fishhook shanks	7	0.8	27	3.0	2	0.1	6	1.5	4	0.7
pendant/bead	1	0.1	1	0.1						
small stone sculpture					1	0.1				
misc. ground stone			4	0.4	1	0.1	3	0.8	4	0.7
edge-ground cobble					1	0.1				
saws	10	1.2	4	0.4			2	0.5		
abrasive stones	471	54.7	433	47.9	61	4.3	23	5.8	21	3.7
Subtotal	*493*	*57.3*	*472*	*52.2*	*69*	*4.9*	*37*	*9.3*	*31*	*5.4*
Pecked/misc. stone										
hammerstones					11	0.8	1	0.3	3	0.5
hand mauls			2	0.2						
grooved sinkers									10	1.7
perforated stones	10	1.2	1	0.1	1	0.1				
mica					1	0.1				
Subtotal	*10*	*1.2*	*3*	*0.3*	*13*	*0.9*	*1*	*0.3*	*13*	*2.3*
Bone and antler										
harpoon valves	48	5.6	22	2.4	53	3.8	22	5.5	43	7.5
harpoon arming points	44	5.1	16	1.8	66	4.7	15	3.8	39	6.8
other unipoints	84	9.8	18	2.0	171	12.2	48	2.0	42	7.3
bipoints	32	3.7	66	7.3	345	24.5	56	14.0	194	33.7
awls	38	4.4	10	1.1	42	3.0	22	5.5	31	5.4
needles	9	1.0					8	2.0	2	0.4
pointed bone frags			93	10.3	407	28.9	85	21.3		
single barb points	20	2.3			4	0.3	8	2.0	1	0.2
barbed fixed points	13	1.5	6	0.7	11	0.8	3	0.8	13	2.3

▶

◄ *Table 12*

	Yuquot Zone III		Hesquiat Village		T'ukw'aa		Ch'uumat'a (post-2000 BP)		Ozette trench	
	No.	%	No.	%	No.	%	No.	%	No.	%
barbed harpoons	4	0.5					4	1.0		
harpoon foreshafts	5	0.6								
wedges or chisels	4	0.5	4	0.4	12	0.9	3	0.8	33	5.7
knives/ scrapers									21	3.7
picks									8	1.4
fishhook shanks	17	2.0			2	0.2	9	2.3		
bird bone beads					3	0.2				
bird bone tubes	4	0.5			3	0.2	2	0.5	2	0.4
decorated combs					2	0.2	1	0.3	3	0.5
pendants	1	0.1			8	0.6	1	0.3	1	0.2
misc. decorated bone					12	0.9				
hafts							1	0.3	12	2.1
whorls									4	0.7
whalebone bark beater	1	0.1			1	0.1				
whalebone bark shredder							1	0.3	12	2.1
whalebone clubs	1	0.1			3	0.2			5	0.9
misc. bone and antler	11	1.3	175	19.4	157	11.2	66	16.5	4	0.7
Subtotal	*336*	*39.0*	*410*	*45.4*	*1302*	*92.5*	*355*	*89.0*	*470*	*81.7*
Tooth										
beaver incisor tools	2	0.2	1	0.1	2	0.2				
decorated beaver teeth									3	0.5
canine tooth pendants	11	1.3			5	0.4	2	0.5		
harpoon valve					1	0.1				
misc. worked teeth	7	0.8			4	0.3	1	0.3	11	1.9
Subtotal	*20*	*2.3*	*1*	*0.1*	*12*	*0.9*	*3*	*0.8*	*14*	*2.4*
Shell										
mussel shell celts	1	0.1			2	0.2				
mussel shell knives	1	0.1			1	0.1				
mussel shell point			1	0.1						
misc. mussel shell			1	0.1	2	0.2			1	0.2
dentalium shell beads					1	0.1	1	0.3		
Olivella shell beads					2	0.2				
other shell artifacts									2	0.4
Subtotal	*2*	*0.2*	*2*	*0.2*	*8*	*0.6*	*1*	*0.3*	*3*	*0.5*
Site totals	**861**		**904**		**1407**		**399**		**575**	

Sources: Dewhirst 1980; Haggarty 1982; McMillan and St. Claire 1996; McKenzie 1974

implements of stone make up over 50 percent of the artifact totals, while stone objects comprise only 6 percent to 15 percent of the total at the other three sites. The elimination of unclassifiable worked bone fragments from the artifact totals at Yuquot would have raised the relative importance of stone somewhat, but this was not the case at Hesquiat. The high values for stone in these two sites is almost entirely attributable to the great quantities of abrasive stones that were excavated. Abrasive stones alone make up almost 55 percent of the artifact total at Yuquot and 48 percent at Hesquiat. By comparison, abrasive stones at the other three sites range from 3.7 percent to 5.8 percent of the totals. If abrasive stones were removed, then stone artifacts would drop to very modest levels at all five sites. The abundance of abrasive stones, of varying sizes, coarseness, and degree of finish, indicates their vital role in the manufacture of most other objects found at these sites (as well as those of wood, which have not been preserved).

The great importance in the technology of bone and antler, particularly the former, is clearest at T'ukw'aa, where 92.5 percent of all excavated artifacts were of these materials. Particularly abundant are bone points of several styles and presumed functions, bipoints, bone splinter awls, and pointed bone fragments from such implements. At T'ukw'aa these together comprise over 70 percent of the artifact total. Bone bipoints, most presumably used as gorges for fishing, although some may have served as barbs on composite fishing hooks or teeth on herring rakes, were particularly abundant at T'ukw'aa and Ozette, comprising 24.5 percent and 33.7 percent of the artifact totals, respectively. Valves for composite harpoon heads, of varying sizes and styles, were also common artifacts at all five sites. Other bone

48   Grooved bark beater of whalebone, found in late precontact deposits at T'ukw'aa. *Photo by author*

artifacts characteristic of this period, although occurring in smaller numbers, include fixed barbed points, chisels or wedges, fishhook shanks, and bird bone tubes. The technology for producing clothing and basketry of woven cedar bark is indicated by a small number of distinctive tools, such as whalebone bark beaters (Figure 48), found at Yuquot and T'ukw'aa, and bark shredders, from Ch'uumat'a and Ozette. Sections of whalebone also served as simple undecorated clubs at T'ukw'aa, Yuquot, and Ozette. Pendants and other decorative items of bone or antler were found at all sites except Hesquiat, while small decorative combs came from the two Toquaht sites and Ozette.

Artifacts of tooth are relatively rare, although they occur at all five sites. Canine tooth pendants, perforated or grooved at the root end for suspension, are the most common type. Beaver incisors, modified as small cutting tools, were found at three of the five sites, while decorated examples from Ozette have been identified as gaming pieces (McKenzie 1974:74). One unique artifact from T'ukw'aa is a harpoon valve blank, 7.9 cm in length, made from an unidentified tooth of considerable size.

Shell artifacts, most commonly of mussel shell, occurred at all five sites, although in small numbers. At the Hoko River rockshelter, however, mussel shell knives were one of the most common artifact types. Ethnographically, mussel shell was an important raw material for knives and harpoon cutting blades. The comparative rarity of mussel shell tools at most excavated sites almost certainly stems from problems of recognition and recovery in middens consisting largely of mussel shell, often in a very poor state of preservation. Dentalium shells, presumably used as ornaments, were rare in these sites, as was discussed earlier in this chapter, although they were more frequently encountered in the late precontact house deposits at Ozette. Olivella shells, with one end ground off to allow stringing as beads, came only from T'ukw'aa in this sample. They were found in some quantity in the Ozette house deposits (Wessen 1994b:352) and the Hoko River rockshelter (D. Croes, pers. comm. 1995), however, and in historic times, due to their ornamental value, they were widely used by the Makah. Red ochre stains on a large clam shell from the Ozette midden show the use of such objects as containers, but this can rarely be detected archaeologically.

Artifacts from the five sites listed in Table 12, plus the contemporaneous assemblage from Shoemaker Bay II (see McMillan and St. Claire 1982: Table 29), were further compared through multi-dimensional scaling, which produced the plot shown in Figure 49. The degree of similarity between the assemblages is indicated by their spatial relationships in this diagram. As expected, the two Toquaht sites of T'ukw'aa and Ch'uumat'a, plus Hesquiat Village and Yuquot (Zone III), cluster quite closely. Yuquot's slight separation from the other three sites may be largely a result of the different classification used. While categories such as "pointed bone fragments" and

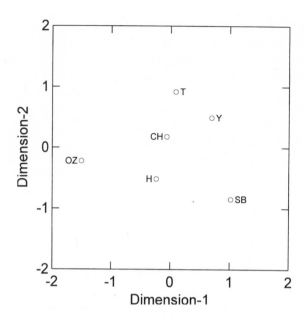

49   Plot showing relative similarity of six site assemblages by multidimensional scaling, based on relative frequency (percent) of 65 artifact classes. *T* = T'ukw'aa; *Y* = Yuquot (Zone III); *CH* = Ch'uumat'a (last 2,000 years); *H* = Hesquiat Village; *OZ* = Ozette trench; *SB* = Shoemaker Bay II. (No data standardization. Spearman rank order correlation used to measure inter-assemblage similarity. Analysis accomplished using SYSTAT for Windows [Wilkinson et al. 1996]). *Prepared by Jack Nance, Simon Fraser University*

"miscellaneous bone and antler" comprise a large part of the artifact total for T'ukw'aa, Ch'uumat'a, and Hesquiat, they were simply removed from the analysis at Yuquot. Shoemaker Bay II is further removed, differing primarily in the presence of several distinctive stone tool types. The artifact assemblage from the Ozette trench excavation is not closely linked to any of the Vancouver Island sites, although again the different classification system used may exaggerate its distinctiveness. Ozette appears particularly dissimilar to Shoemaker Bay II.

Unfortunately, faunal analysis is incomplete for most sites, frustrating attempts at broader comparisons than those allowed simply by artifact types. Differing levels of intensity of maritime adaptation were noted earlier in this chapter. At Yuquot, the most abundant mammalian remains were from coast deer (Dewhirst 1979), while whale and fur seal dominate the mammalian fauna from Hesquiat Village (Calvert 1980) and Ozette (Huelsbeck 1988, 1994a, 1994b). Resources from the land, such as deer and elk, played only a very minor role in the economy at Ozette. The outer coast Toquaht sites also clearly had a highly maritime economy, although no data yet exist for the full range of species exploited.

Some change over time is also evident, although most tools that characterized this area at contact were present at the beginning of the period considered here (about 2000 BP). Chipped stone implements disappear from the Ch'uumat'a assemblage around this time. On the Olympic Peninsula, however, chipped stone tools declined in importance over the two millennia of midden accumulation at Ozette but continued in small quantities into recent levels and were common at the Late Period Hoko River rockshelter. Stone fishhook shanks appear relatively late in Zone III at Yuquot, substantially later than do shanks of bone. At Ch'uumat'a, however, stone fishhook shanks occur somewhat earlier than at Yuquot and are about the same age as bone examples, while all fishhook shanks at Hesquiat Village and the Ozette midden trench are of stone. Stone celts greatly decline in number over time at the Toquaht sites. The large excavated sample from T'ukw'aa, all postdating 1200 BP, contains a single stone celt, a reworked greenstone example that differs considerably from all other stone celts found. Stone celts were much more abundant in the smaller artifact sample from Ch'uumat'a, with all but one found in levels that predate the earliest deposits at T'ukw'aa. It is possible that stone celts were largely replaced in Barkley Sound during the Late Period by celts of mussel shell, although only a few such implements were recovered, while at Yuquot stone celts continued into the Historic Period. Similarly, bone needles in Barkley Sound came only from Ch'uumat'a and only from deposits that predate the other excavated Toquaht sites, while they are found into historic levels at Yuquot.

The minor nature of temporal changes within the last two millennia can be seen at one of the Hesquiat sites, DiSo 9, a habitation cave in the upper harbour (Map 5). Two precontact components have been identified within the midden deposits underlying historic surface burial materials (Calvert 1980; Haggarty 1982). The earliest has four radiocarbon dates clustering around 1800 BP, while the later has three clustering around 1200 BP. Faunal analysis shows few differences between the two. In each case, fish elements dominate the faunal remains by bone count, with herring comprising just over half the total. Salmon elements increase slightly at the expense of midshipman from the earliest component to the later. Among the birds, ducks similarly increase at the expense of loons. Sea mammals are marginally more important in the earlier component. Artifact assemblages from the two components also differ only slightly.

Excavated materials from West Coast sites of this age reflect Nuu-chah-nulth culture prior to the disruptions of the early contact period. The temporal changes that can be shown to occur in this late period are, in general, few and gradual. After contact with Europeans late in the eighteenth century, cultural change became abrupt, pronounced, and, for some groups, catastrophic. The nature of these changes is discussed in the next chapter.

6
The Transition to Recorded History

The late eighteenth-century arrival of European ships off the west coast of Vancouver Island brought profound changes to the Aboriginal inhabitants. It also brought a new concept of history – something based on written documents. Aboriginal concepts of history, maintained through oral narratives, received little attention. History became the study of European achievements, as recorded in written documents, while indigenous populations around the globe became "people without history" (Wolf 1982), relegated to the subject matter of anthropology and perceived as essentially unchanging. Trigger (1980, 1984, 1989a), among others, has rejected this dichotomy between history and anthropology, instead advocating a holistic approach to Native history that incorporates all available knowledge.

This chapter examines the impact of the early contact period on the Nuu-chah-nulth people and the nature of the cultural adaptations that they pursued in these changing circumstances. It integrates data from historic records, indigenous oral histories, and archaeological research, putting them into a historical anthropological perspective in an attempt to understand the events and cultural adjustments following contact. In assessing the magnitude of change over the past two centuries, this chapter evaluates the extent to which ethnographic information collected in the early twentieth century can be used as analogy for the reconstruction of late precontact and early contact period lifeways.

The Meeting of Two Cultures

Brief History
The first recorded encounter between the Nuu-chah-nulth and Europeans occurred on 8 August 1774, as the Spanish ship *Santiago*, under the command of Juan Pérez, anchored somewhere near Estevan Point at the entrance to Nootka Sound (Howay 1941:59; Gunther 1972:11; Cook 1973:63; Pethick 1976:42-43; Beals 1989:144-149). This early meeting was incorporated into Native oral histories, which were recounted to subsequent European arrivals (Haswell in Howay 1941:59; Ingraham in Beals 1989:216;

Moziño 1970:65-66). Although initially fearful, some Nuu-chah-nulth soon paddled their canoes out to examine what they perceived to be a huge floating house with people walking on top (Moser 1926:164; Efrat and Langlois 1978a:59-60).[1] The Spanish conducted a brisk trade with these Natives, exchanging iron knives and abalone shells from California for sea otter skins and Native garments, including the distinctive Nuu-chah-nulth woven hats (Gunther 1972:12; Pethick 1976:43; Beals 1989:89; Moser 1926:162). This was a brief encounter, after which the Spanish departed without entering the sound or observing a Native village. A second Spanish voyage in 1775 passed the west coast of Vancouver Island well out to sea and in poor weather, without coming into contact with Native people.

It was the arrival of Captain James Cook on 29 March 1778 that ushered in the period of intensive contact between the Nuu-chah-nulth and outsiders. The famed British mariner, on his third voyage of discovery, spent nearly a month in Nootka Sound. He and his officers became the first Europeans to enter and describe a Native village on the Northwest Coast, and the journals from this expedition provide invaluable observations on Nuu-chah-nulth life at this early period of contact. The Nootka Sound Natives showed not "the least mark of fear or distrust" (Cook in Beaglehole 1967:295), eagerly going out in their canoes to guide Cook's ships into the harbour (Figure 50). Trade was the basis for much of the subsequent interaction between the two races. In exchange for metal objects so desired by the Native people, the British obtained furs, artworks, and items of food. The extent of the Native concept of ownership soon became clear to the British, as payment was demanded for wood, water, and any other use of the land, and John Webber, the expedition artist, had to surrender the brass buttons from his jacket before he was allowed to sketch the carved figures inside a house. Cook's initial impression that a profitable fur trade could be established was confirmed when the ships reached China and it was discovered that the thick, soft pelts of the sea otter obtained from the Nuu-chah-nulth could be sold at high prices. This was a discovery of momentous consequence for Northwest Coast peoples, turning Nootka Sound into a scene of international commerce in only a few years.

By the mid-1780s the rush for fur trade wealth had begun. The first of the commercial traders to arrive was Captain James Hanna in 1785, in a ship fittingly renamed the *Sea Otter*. Anchoring in Nootka Sound, he soon procured a "valuable cargo of Furs" (Gibson 1992:23), stimulating further commerce. British, French, Spanish, and American vessels soon were vying for pelts along the coast, but the trade was dominated by the British (called "King George Men" by the coastal peoples) and the Americans (known as

---

1 In the Nuu-chah-nulth language the word *mamalhni*, meaning "living on the water," is still the term applied to any person of European descent.

50 In this 1778 drawing by Cook expedition artist John Webber, Nuu-chah-nulth canoes encircle Cook's ship, the *Resolution*, at anchor in Nootka Sound. Chiefs stand in their canoes, singing and making speeches in ceremonial welcome prior to initiating trade. *By permission of the British Library, Add. 15514 folio 10*

"Boston Men" for their home port). Nootka Sound remained the major trade centre, although the American captains favoured Clayoquot Sound. In the twenty-year period between 1785 and 1805, nearly fifty trading expeditions arrived at Nootka Sound (Inglis and Haggarty 1987).

Hunting for sea otters was an ancient practice for the Nuu-chah-nulth, who highly valued the soft fur for their own robes or cloaks. These garments are described in several early historic accounts, which note that they were held in high esteem and were generally the mark of the noble class (Meares 1790:251; Moziño 1970:14; Jewitt 1967:38). Ethnographic accounts also associate such clothing with high-status or wealthy individuals (Koppert 1930:51; Drucker 1951:103). These items virtually disappeared along the coast, however, as the fur trade made them too valuable to wear. Hunting techniques also changed, as single hunters with harpoons or bows and arrows were replaced by communal hunts under the direction of the chiefs, using lines of canoes to sweep across a broad area and to surround the animals (Drucker 1951:46-48; Mills 1955:38; Moon 1978:71; Arima 1983:47; Brabant 1977:94; Gibson 1992:8). As the Nuu-chah-nulth were already traders and sea otter hunters at contact, they required only the intensification of long-established skills to take advantage of the European desire for furs.

As early as Cook's arrival in Nootka Sound it was clear that Nuu-chah-nulth chiefs regarded the newcomers as an owned economic resource, in the same way that they would claim drift rights over anything that floated into their territory. Cook was well aware that the presence of his ships was causing some dispute between the people at Yuquot and their neighbours and that the former were monopolizing the trade, requiring others to go through them to obtain items of European manufacture. It also became evident that the people of Yuquot were immediately exchanging the items they received from the British for additional trade commodities. As Cook (1784:278) noted: "Many of the principal natives, who lived near us, carried on a trade with more distant tribes, in the articles that they procured from us. For we observed, that they would frequently disappear for four or five days at a time, and then return with fresh cargoes of skins and curiosities." Walker (1982:110), at Nootka Sound in 1786, noted the same control of the trade as Cook had earlier: "These Savages wished to secure all the advantages of our Commerce to themselves. They claimed the exclusive priviledge of buying or selling any thing. They carefully watched and excluded Strangers from any intercourse with us. At last indeed after they had sold all their own commodities, and exhausted the resources of the Sound, they admitted the other Neighbouring tribes to a Share in the Trade. But even this was done under restrictions. They constituted themselves the Agents or Brokers, and assumed the prerogative of introducing the new Comers to us." Walker (1982:110) also reports the harsh measures taken by the residents of Yuquot when other Natives attempted to violate this trade monopoly. Similarly, Meares (1790:142) describes the violent retribution exacted by Wickaninish at Clayoquot Sound when a stranger attempted to trade directly with the ship.

Three powerful Native leaders, each controlling a large trade block, emerged early in the maritime fur trade period. Maquinna (Figure 51) consolidated his political and economic power through his trade monopoly in Nootka Sound. He also dominated the trade of the more northerly Nuu-chah-nulth. In Clayoquot Sound, Wickaninish had expanded his power and territory through a series of aggressive wars. Even the important Chief Hanna of Ahousaht had to surrender his furs to Wickaninish before they could be sold (Meares 1790:146). Wickaninish controlled the trade at least as far south as Barkley Sound. As a result, this area was never able to emerge as a trading centre like Nootka or Clayoquot Sounds, as few furs were available, most being gathered by Wickaninish for his own trading purposes (Howay 1941:79; Magee 1794; Bishop 1967:106; Gibson 1992:115). According to Meares (1790:230), Wickaninish's domain extended as far south as "Nitta-natt."[2]

---

2 This would be the Nuu-chah-nulth pronunciation of "Ditidaht," referring to the large open-ocean villages of Whyac and Clo-oose.

51   Chief Maquinna of Nootka Sound, from a
sketch by Spanish artist Tomás de Suria in 1791.
Maquinna is wearing a woven hat decorated with
whaling scenes and a cedar bark cape edged with
fur. Only individuals of chiefly status wore the
knob-topped whaler's hat. *Canadian Museum of
Civilization 99730*

The third major economic force was Tatoosh, the powerful leader of the
Cape Flattery villages (Figure 52). These three prominent chiefs maintained
close social ties; their frequent visits to each other's villages are remarked
upon in the eighteenth-century accounts. Furthermore, they were all linked
by ties of marriage (Marshall 1993:213), which served to consolidate alliances. Maquinna had acquired nine wives by 1803, each symbolizing the
formation of an alliance with another group (Wike 1951:99).

Ritual elements featured prominently in the Nuu-chah-nulth view of the
fur trade, at least at its inception. Canoeloads of people met Cook's ships,
giving them a ceremonial welcome to Nootka Sound through speeches,

52 Chief Tatoosh of the Cape Flattery area, as drawn
by the Spanish artist José Cardero in 1791. Tatoosh
wears a fur robe and the knob-topped whaler's hat.
Royal BC Museum PN4805

songs, and dances. Cook (1784:266) noted a large decorated canoe carrying
a prominent individual who appeared to be a chief and who shook a rattle
carved in the form of a bird. This individual is described by one of Cook's
officers (King in Beaglehole 1967:1394): "He stood upright in the middle of
the boat, & upon a plank laid across to be more conspicuous; the naked
parts of his body & arms were painted with a red, & his face with a whitish
paint, his head was wildly Ornamented with large feathers, which were
tyed to a stiff string or sinew & fastened to the hair, so that they hung in
different directions projecting from the head." Another individual danced
in his canoe, using two masks and wearing a wolf skin, while others sang,
shook rattles, and threw feathers and red ochre on the water (Cook 1784:266;
King in Beaglehole 1967:1394; Samwell in Beaglehole 1967:1089-90;
Gunther 1972:19-20). Such actions must have seemed incomprehensible to

the British, who had no knowledge of Native rituals for welcoming guests. As new groups arrived, each initiated trade with a ceremonial greeting.

> On their first coming, they generally went through a singular mode of introducing themselves. They would paddle, with all their strength, quite round both ships, a Chief, or other principal person in the canoe, standing up with a spear, or some other weapon, in his hand, and speaking, or rather hollowing, all the time. Sometimes the orator of the canoe would have his face covered with a mask, representing either a human visage, or that of some animal; and, instead of a weapon, would hold a rattle in his hand ... After making this curcuit round the ships, they would come along-side, and begin to trade without further ceremony. Very often, indeed, they would first give us a song, in which all the canoe joined, with a very pleasing harmony. (Cook 1784:273-274)

A formal protocol, involving ceremonial greetings, gift exchange, and negotiations over price, characterized the actual trading. In 1788, Wickaninish honoured Meares with a feast and presented him with prime sea otter skins (Meares 1790:139-142). Such generosity required reciprocal gift-giving. The Europeans began attempting to evade such gifts, as they cost more than did those received in trade (Howay 1941:265). Formalities might also involve the exchange of names; an Ahousaht chief took the name Hanna after such an exchange with the first of the European traders to appear. The new arrivals often resented such formalities, considering them to be time-consuming and unproductive. For the Nuu-chah-nulth, however, trade had important political and social elements, rather than consisting merely of commercial transactions.

As European goods became commonplace, Native demands shifted. Cook (1784:267) remarked that the Natives of Nootka Sound "were more desirous of iron, than of any other of our articles of commerce." The market quickly became glutted, and by 1787 sheet copper was about the only article in steady demand at Nootka Sound (Wike 1951:39). In 1791 an American trader on the *Columbia* ruefully stated that "iron they would scarcely take as a gift" (Howay 1941:187). Colnett (1940:202) in 1790 was trading sheets of copper, blankets, and "ear shells" (almost certainly abalone from California), along with muskets. Boit, on the *Columbia* in 1791, noted that they "got many Sea Otter and Land furs" from the Chicklisaht "for Copper, Iron and Cloth" and that they also bartered with beads and fishhooks for food supplies (Howay 1941:371). At Tatoosh Island the Natives demanded copper for their furs and exchanged halibut and salmon for nails and beads (Howay 1941:371-372).

Glimpses into these early trade practices are also evident in the archaeological record. In the Toquaht sites, for example, ornaments rolled from thin sheet copper precede all other European objects. A finely made rolled copper tinkler, the only object of European materials, was found at DfSj 30 on the George Fraser Islands, along with two small shell pendants that are almost certainly of imported California abalone. This confirms Colnett's account of trade in sheet copper and "ear shells" along the coast. The two main village sites of T'ukw'aa and Ch'uumat'a yielded rolled copper objects at earlier levels than they did other introduced materials. A small rectangle of ferrous metal also dates to the very early trade period at T'ukw'aa. Unfortunately, the abundant historic artifacts from Hesquiat Village and Ozette have not been analyzed, and reports are available for only a few categories of those from Yuquot. A small number of the glass and ceramic fragments from Yuquot have been dated to the late eighteenth century (Jones 1981; Lueger 1981), although these may relate to the Spanish settlement at that site rather than reflect Nuu-chah-nulth trade preferences.

Firearms also became major items of trade that were supplied primarily by the American traders. The demand for muskets and gunpowder was such that Colnett (1940:202), at Clayoquot Sound in 1790, noted that "few Bargains can be made without it." By 1791 Wickaninish had acquired over 200 firearms and a large quantity of ammunition (Howay 1941:312). Maquinna had sufficient muskets to trade them, along with other European goods, across Vancouver Island by the overland trail from Tahsis, receiving additional furs in return. Menzies, with Vancouver in Queen Charlotte Strait in 1792, observed that the Kwakwaka'wakw were well supplied with muskets, which he determined had been obtained through trade with Maquinna, the "grand agent" of commerce (Newcombe 1923:80). Moziño (1970:48), at Nootka Sound in 1792, noted that firearms had replaced the bow and arrow for hunting land animals and shore birds. The new weapons also made inter-tribal warfare more deadly and posed a threat to the European traders.

Relations between the Nuu-chah-nulth and outsiders worsened considerably in the decades following Cook. This was to a large degree a result of the high-handed and violent tactics employed by some of the traders. Driven by the desire to make a large profit in a short period of time, some unscrupulous traders stooped to plundering Native villages for their furs (Ingraham 1971:225; Kendrick 1991:87; Jane 1930:22; Jewitt 1967:92) or for supplies (Howay 1941:53), leaving the next arrivals to face the hostility of the victimized Natives. The Spanish in Nootka Sound stole house planks from Native villages to use in their own buildings (Moziño 1970:79; Cook 1973:285), while Native thefts from European ships led to violent retribution. After the Native theft of a chisel, for example, Captain Hanna fired on Native canoes in Nootka Sound, reportedly killing upwards of twenty people and forcing Maquinna to leap overboard and swim for his life (Jewitt 1967:92). In Barkley Sound, thefts from the *Jefferson* led its crew members to attack the Native village of Seshart, where they killed several people, ransacked the houses, and took several of the best canoes (Magee 1794). On several occasions chiefs were forcefully held as hostages aboard the ships (Magee 1794; Colnett 1940:191; Howay 1941:186, 188). Many "unprovoked attacks" reported by European traders stemmed from such behaviour by their predecessors. Jewitt, held as a captive in Nootka Sound after such an attack, was well aware that his misfortune was largely a result of such Native grievances: "I have no doubt that many of the melancholy disasters have principally arisen from the imprudent conduct of some of the captains and crews of the ships employed in this trade, in exasperating them by insulting, plundering, and even killing them on slight grounds" (Jewitt 1967:93).

Even more disastrous for the Nuu-chah-nulth was the traders' violent reaction to perceived threats to their ships. In 1790, when Colnett (1940:201) feared that canoeloads of Natives in Clayoquot Sound planned to attack his vessel, he drove them off with a volley of musket shot, then fired his cannon into the major village of Opitsat. Much greater destruction came at the hands of an American trader, Captain Gray of the *Columbia*, in 1792. In response to a failed plot against his ship, Gray ordered the complete destruction of Opitsat by cannon fire (Howay 1941:390-391). Later, he used his cannon against "a large Canoe with at least 20 Men in her" and "no doubt kill'd every soul in her" (Howay 1941:395). He also attacked a village in Esperanza Inlet, killing several Natives and taking their sea otter skins after a dispute over trading rates (Gibson 1992:163; Cook 1973:343; Jane 1930:22).

The destruction of Opitsat deserves special comment. Meares (1790:203) visited this village in 1788 and described it as "very large and populous," with houses "commodiously constructed, possessing a greater share of their rude magnificence than any which we had yet seen." The latter refers to his earlier observation of another of Wickaninish's villages, where he had been astonished at the vast size of the chief's house, and commented on the "gigantic images, carved out of huge blocks of timber" that supported the "rudely carved and painted" rafters (1790:138). The American traders stated that the Clayoquot villages were "larger and more numerously inhabited" than those at Nootka Sound (Howay 1941:69), with about 200 houses at Opitsat in 1792 (Howay 1941:391). The house occupied by Wickaninish was so large that Hoskins (in Howay 1941:263) estimated that 600 persons attended a ceremony there, with nearly twice as many observing from outside. Boit, who was charged by Gray with carrying out the destruction, expressed his regret:

> I ... am greived to think Capt. Gray shou'd let his passions go so far. This Village was about half a mile in Diameter, and Contained upwards off 200 Houses, generally well built for Indians ev'ry door that you enter'd was in resemblance to an human and Beasts head, the passage being through the

mouth, besides which there was much more rude carved work about the dwellings some of which was by no means innelegant. This fine Village, the Work of Ages, was in a short time totally destroy'd. (Howay 1941:390-391)

In addition to such attacks, in some cases land was usurped by the European arrivals. An area at one end of the village of Yuquot was appropriated in 1788, when Meares set up an onshore facility for building a boat. In the following year the Spanish, under Martinez, established a garrison at Yuquot in an attempt to enforce their claims to sovereignty over the coast (Figure 53). The seizure of British ships in Nootka Sound at that time precipitated an international incident. When Maquinna and his people moved to another village on the outer coast, the Spanish took over the village site, taking some building materials from the abandoned Native houses. Martinez's autocratic manner alienated the Native occupants of the sound, and his murder of Callicum, the second-ranked chief, led to the complete abandonment of the site by Maquinna, who went to Wickaninish for protection (Moziño 1970:75-76; Colnett 1940:62; Wagner 1930:162). Not until the Spanish finally departed in 1795 did Maquinna and his people reclaim the site and rebuild their village. A second Spanish fort, constructed at Neah Bay in 1792, also led to hostilities with the local people. In retaliation for the death of a Spanish pilot, the commander fired on two canoes, killing most of the occupants (Wagner 1933:64; Howay 1941:409; Cook 1973:351). The Neah Bay fort was also short-lived, being abandoned after only a few months.

53 The Spanish settlement at Yuquot in 1791. Note the fortification on the rocks at the entrance to the cove (upper left). Engraving from a drawing by José Cardero. *Royal BC Museum PN7230*

Such incidents fostered Native desires for vengeance, leading to two well known incidents of fur trade violence. In 1803, Maquinna reacted to being insulted by Captain Salter of the *Boston* by seizing the ship and killing all on board, with the exception of John Jewitt, the ship's armourer, and one other crewman (Jewitt 1967, 1988; Brathwaite and Folan 1972). Maquinna's reduced economic situation following his prolonged expulsion from Yuquot may have stimulated this attack as much as did Salter's insult. The capture of this ship with its full trading cargo provided Maquinna with new wealth for trading and potlatching, restoring his diminished status. Jewitt (1967:38-40) describes the arrival of other Nuu-chah-nulth groups and the distribution of goods from the *Boston*:

> When the ceremony was concluded, Maquina invited the strangers to a feast at his house, consisting of whale blubber, smoked herring spawn, and dried fish and train oil, of which they eat most plentifully ... On this occasion Maquina gave away no less than one hundred muskets, the same number of looking glasses, four hundred yards of cloth, and twenty casks of powder, besides other things ... In this manner tribes of savages from various parts of the coast, continued coming for several days, bringing with them, blubber, oil, herring spawn, dried fish and clams, for which they received in return, presents of cloth, &c.

In 1811 the American ship *Tonquin* was attacked in Clayoquot Sound, where it exploded and sank, leaving no survivors.

By this time the fur trade had long been in decline. Fewer skins and higher prices resulted in the trade gradually shifting northward. As early as 1793 Moziño (1970:91) noted that the Natives of Nootka Sound had killed so many sea otters that they had destroyed the basis of the trade. Yuquot had become primarily a safe port to take on water and supplies. The massacre of the crew of the *Boston* may have temporarily enhanced Maquinna's economic position, but it put an end to Nootka Sound's reputation as a safe haven. Few ships passed this way in the ensuing several decades and the Nuu-chah-nulth lived in near-isolation until the mid-nineteenth century, when a demand for dogfish oil to service the growing logging industry brought about a resumption of trade.

The Toquaht Case

It was the maritime sea otter trade that first brought the Nuu-chah-nulth of Barkley Sound into contact with Europeans. The first to arrive was Captain Charles William Barkley in the British trading vessel *Imperial Eagle*, who sailed into the sound in 1787. He named the sound after himself, and a number of prominent landmarks, such as Cape Beale, after members of his ship's company. Both Barkley and Captain John Meares, who arrived the

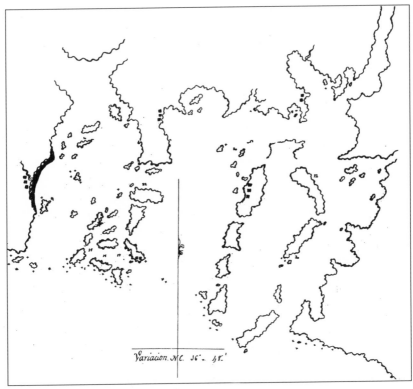

Map 11 Spanish map of Barkley Sound in 1791, showing five settlements, including one in Toquaht territory. *BC Archives, Maps Collection CM/ A1415*

following year aboard the *Felice Adventurer*, anchored among the Broken Group Islands in the central sound, near the large Native village of *Huumuuwa*, where they traded for furs.

The earliest information that pertains directly to Toquaht traditional territory comes from the Spanish explorations under the command of Don Francisco Eliza in 1791. In May of that year the vessel *Santa Saturnina*, commanded by José Maria Narvaez, entered Barkley Sound, which they termed the "Boca de Carrasco" (Wagner 1933:146). The map of the sound produced by this expedition is reasonably accurate, showing such features of Toquaht territory as the Stopper Islands, the George Fraser Islands, and the lower portions of Toquart Bay and Pipestem Inlet (Map 11). Five Native villages are shown in the sound, one of which is in Toquaht territory. It is placed about halfway along the western shore of the sound, immediately south of a major river. It seems likely that this would be Macoah, the major ethnographic Toquaht village. However, as Macoah is not situated on a river, this may have been the ethnographic fishing camp (*Ch'itkis*; DfSi 66) near the mouth of the Maggie River.

In 1793 Captain Josiah Roberts arrived in the *Jefferson* and wintered over near the head of Toquart Bay. An unpublished journal kept by his first officer, Bernard Magee, describes a village on the west side of the sound that was "still larger than any we had before visited" (Magee 1794). Magee described visits to the ship by "Hiuquis the Cheeff of Tooquot."[3] He noted that furs were difficult to obtain, as trade throughout the area was controlled by Wickaninish, the powerful chief of Clayoquot Sound to the north. Wickaninish himself, along with several of his brothers, appears among Magee's list of important chiefs who arrived in Toquaht territory to trade with the ship, as does Hanna, chief of the Ahousaht. He also reports the visit of "a Canoe from Clahaset," showing that the Makah were travelling this far to trade. Relations between the European traders and the Nuu-chah-nulth were occasionally uneasy, and at one point the chiefs "Hiuquis" and "He:che:nook" were seized and held until restitution was made for various items stolen from the ship.

The next ship to enter the sound – the *Ruby* under Captain Charles Bishop – arrived in 1795. Sailing into the western edge of the sound, it was met by Chief "Hyhocus," who came out to the ship "in a Large cannoe attended by many Smaller ones." Hyhocus acknowledged that he was subject to "Wiccannanish at Cloaqoit," who arrived within a few days to take part in the trade (Bishop 1967:106).

Several decades elapsed before another trading vessel is known to have entered western Barkley Sound. Pressures of the fur trade drove the sea otter to near extinction on this part of the coast, forcing the trade to move north. Even within Nuu-chah-nulth territory, Barkley Sound saw few trading vessels compared to the major fur trade centres of Nootka and Clayoquot Sounds. Ethnohistoric documents for the Toquaht area are lacking until resumption of contact in the second half of the nineteenth century. By this time the fur trade was long over, and contact centred on European settlement, commercial exploitation of the land, and restriction of Native people to small reserves within their traditional territories.

A brief resumption of trade by the 1850s was brought about by the demand for dogfish oil, which was required for lubrication by the developing lumber mills in the Fraser Valley and Puget Sound. A number of trading schooners, primarily American, visited Barkley Sound, and the various Nuu-chah-nulth groups there industriously caught and processed large quantities of dogfish for this trade. William Eddy Banfield, a British trader and later a colonial government agent, wrote a series of letters and articles describing the country and people of Barkley Sound. These provide comments and population estimates for all Native groups in the sound. He refers specifically to "a small tribe of Indians ... called Taquats," noting with approval

---

3 Elsewhere in the journal "Hiuquis" is written as "Hyuquis."

the natural abundance of their territory (Banfield 1858). By 1860 the first trading store in Barkley Sound was established in Ucluelet. The same year saw logging operations begin for the first export sawmill in British Columbia, which was established at the head of Alberni Inlet.

After British Columbia entered Confederation, attention turned to the Aboriginal land issue. In 1874 George Blenkinsop was sent to Barkley Sound by the federal Indian commissioner to gather information on Native needs and desires with regard to land. A map of tribal territories that he prepared shows the boundaries of Toquaht territory as confirmed by modern informants. "Hi.yoo.meek" is listed as chief of the Toquaht. Blenkinsop (1874:34) commented favourably on the resources in Toquaht territory, stating, "Fish and game are abundant: their country is without exception beyond anything in this respect I have yet seen."

Peter O'Reilly, the Indian reserve commissioner, visited the various Barkley Sound groups to allocate reserves in 1882. He described the Toquaht as "solely fishermen, gaining their living by sealing and selling fish oil; in addition to which they subsist largely on salmon, halibut and herring, which are found here in profusion" (O'Reilly 1883:100). Five reserves were laid out for the Toquaht, who at this point numbered only twenty-five individuals led by a chief named "New-cha-na." These reserves included their main villages of Macoah and T'ukw'aa, plus their major salmon fishery on the lower Toquart River, and two other fishing stations but not the large village site of Ch'uumat'a, which had lapsed into disuse by this time. O'Reilly considered it unnecessary to allocate any further lands, as the people looked to the sea for their existence.

The Twin Spectres: Disease and Warfare

Encounters with the new arrivals during this early period of trade were to have unforeseen and catastrophic effects on the Nuu-chah-nulth. Intensification of indigenous patterns of warfare, plus a number of disastrous encounters with European cannons and muskets, claimed many Native lives. Even more deadly was exposure to a variety of introduced diseases, which exacted a great toll from earliest contact. The resulting depopulation forced major changes in fundamental aspects of Nuu-chah-nulth culture.

Various afflictions brought by early European explorers and traders plagued Aboriginal communities. The most deadly, however, was smallpox, which had a catastrophic effect on Native populations throughout the Americas. On the Northwest Coast this lethal disease began its destruction of Native life shortly after initial contact with Europeans (Boyd 1990, 1994; Harris 1994). It was present among the Ditidaht prior to 1791, when Hoskins (in Howay 1941:196) noted smallpox scars on Cassacan, the chief of "Nittenat" (the Ditidaht village of Whyac). Boit (in Howay 1941:371), on the same vessel, noted that "these Natives had been visited by that scourge of mankind the

Smallpox," indicating that the evidence was fairly widespread. The first documented epidemic, which Boyd (1990, 1994) dates to the late 1770s and Harris (1994) to 1782, affected the Ditidaht and their Halkomelem- and Straits-speaking Salish neighbours on Vancouver Island. There is no evidence that the Nuu-chah-nulth and Makah were affected this early, but they were not to be so fortunate when subsequent epidemics swept the coast. Makah oral traditions describe the bodies of smallpox victims covering the beach at Neah Bay, while the survivors fled to their relatives on Vancouver Island or to the remote beaches of the Olympic Peninsula (Colson 1953:48). An epidemic in 1852-53 reduced an already depleted population (Drucker 1951:12; Boyd 1990:141). As late as 1875 Brabant (1977:38-41) described an outbreak of smallpox among the Mowachaht and Hesquiaht, which presumably affected other Nuu-chah-nulth groups as well.

Other infectious diseases, such as measles and influenza, spread rapidly among all coastal groups. Measles played a major role in reducing the Makah population throughout the 1840s, and an 1848 outbreak also affected the northern Nuu-chah-nulth (Boyd 1990:145). Tuberculosis also made an early historic appearance among the Nuu-chah-nulth (Schulting and McMillan 1995). Although this disease is known to predate European arrival in the Americas, there is no convincing evidence from the Northwest Coast prior to the early historic period (Boyd 1990:137; Cybulski 1990:57; 1994:83). Tuberculosis was present among Captain Cook's crew at Nootka Sound in 1778, and a Nuu-chah-nulth individual with this ailment was observed at this same location by Menzies in 1793 (Boyd 1990:137). As late as 1887 Brabant (1977:104-105) was lamenting the loss of many Hesquiaht and Mowachaht children to measles, noting that many of the survivors then succumbed to "consumption" (tuberculosis). Makah children also suffered from the combined effect of these two diseases, according to the Indian agent at Neah Bay in 1888 (Gillis 1974:106). ·

Venereal diseases, transmitted by European seamen, were also rampant in this early period. Hoskins (in Howay 1941:196) noted in 1791 that Chief Cassacan of "Nittenat" was "troubled with the venereal." In the following year the Spanish at Nootka Sound observed that the Nuu-chah-nulth there were "beginning to experience the terrible ravages of syphilis" (Jane 1930:115). Venereal diseases not only killed many, but they also rendered large numbers of others infertile (Duff 1964:43; Moziño 1970:43), further contributing to a declining population.

Intensification of warfare in the early Historic Period, stimulated by the introduction of firearms and new trade rivalries as well as by a destabilized economy (as many groups concentrated on hunting sea otters and trading furs), also resulted in widespread and catastrophic loss of life. Groups such as the Tla-o-qui-aht were able to expand militarily at the expense of their neighbours due to their early superiority in firearms. In a war tradition dating to the late eighteenth century, at a time when the Barkley Sound groups did not yet have muskets, the Ucluelet used their alliance with the Tla-o-qui-aht to seize Effingham Inlet and eliminate the former occupants (Swadesh 1948:79; Sapir and Swadesh 1955:373-377). In a well known war of expansion, the Ahousaht nearly exterminated the Otsosaht and absorbed their territory early in the nineteenth century (Drucker 1951:344-345; Arima 1983:107-117; Webster 1983:59-64; Bouchard and Kennedy 1990:224-241). Several decades later, around the 1840s, the Barkley Sound groups became embroiled in a deadly series of hostilities known as the Long War (discussed below). Intergroup warfare resulted in the extinction of some groups and forced the amalgamation of others, greatly reducing the number of independent political units among the Nuu-chah-nulth.

Population levels at European contact are unknown. Recent intensive archaeological surveys on western Vancouver Island (e.g., Inglis and Haggarty 1986; Marshall 1992a) give the impression of a "filled landscape" prior to contact, with populations greatly exceeding those of the ethnographic period, although the problem of demonstrating site contemporaneity is a difficult one. An important early historic population estimate comes from Meares (1790:229-231), who in 1788 calculated the number of people under the authority of each of the major chiefs. Maquinna, in his estimation, had about 10,000 subjects, while Wickaninish had 13,000; Hanna and Detootche, two Ahousaht chiefs, were considered independent and credited with 1,500 subjects each; Tatoosh, at Cape Flattery, had another 5,000. This makes a total of about 31,000 people for the three "Nootkan" divisions. Arima et al. (1991:1-2) accept Meares's estimates as reasonably accurate, concluding that the early contact population was approximately 30,000. Boyd (1991) takes a more conservative approach, estimating that at contact the Nuu-chah-nulth population was at least 6,000, while the Ditidaht and Makah together had another 4,320 people. Epidemic diseases and intensified warfare rapidly resulted in great population losses. By 1885, when the first accurate census data became available for the Canadian groups, the combined Nuu-chah-nulth and Ditidaht population was about 3,500 (Duff 1964:39). The population continued to decline until 1939, at which time the Nuu-chah-nulth and Ditidaht were reduced to a total of only 1,605 people.

Turning to Barkley Sound, and more specifically to the Toquaht, we get a glimpse of the magnitude of destruction wrought by warfare and disease. The Toquaht loss of life is detailed in several of the war texts recorded by Edward Sapir during his linguistic and ethnographic research among the Barkley Sound groups. His primary Ucluelet informant, Kwishanishim, was the son of a Ucluelet war chief and a Toquaht mother. Kwishanishim noted that the Toquaht had "become few" as a result of the hostilities he described.

Kwishanishim's story "Ucluelets seize Effingham Inlet" (Swadesh 1948; Sapir and Swadesh 1955) took place sometime before the end of the eighteenth century, shortly after the Tla-o-qui-aht had obtained firearms but before these were available to the Barkley Sound groups. The war started over a territorial dispute between the Toquaht and the people of Effingham Inlet, the "A'uts" (*A7uts'ath*) and "Hachaa" (*Hach'aa7ath*). To determine the boundary between them a contest was held that involved men from both sides attempting to jump the furthest across the rocks of the disputed area. After the Toquaht claimed victory, the Effingham people attacked them to take their land. Toquaht losses were considerable, reducing them to only a small group. These raids brought the Ucluelet and their powerful Tla-o-qui-aht allies into the war, resulting in the destruction of the Effingham Inlet groups and the seizure of their land by the Ucluelet.

The most lengthy and important of Kwishanishim's war texts is "The Long War in Barkley Sound." Kwishanishim's father, Angryface, played a role in this conflict, which took place around the 1840s. This lengthy war began at the Toquaht village of Macoah, where a Ucluelet chief demanded compensation for a runaway slave. When this was refused, the Ucluelets decided to punish the Toquaht, roughing up some of the men and damaging houses and canoes but not killing anyone. The Toquaht forged an alliance with the Tseshaht, Huu-ay-aht, and other Barkley Sound groups through presents of women. Many of the Ucluelet were killed in the ensuing attack by the combined forces, and the survivors retreated to a strongly fortified location. After a number of raids, they dispersed, some to live with their Tla-o-qui-aht relatives, others to join the neighboring Toquaht (despite the recent hostilities). Hearing of a plot by the Toquaht to help the Huu-ay-aht in the war, the Ucluelet turned on their hosts. The Tla-o-qui-aht aided the Ucluelet by hiding in the woods and killing the Toquaht as they fled. Kwishanishim estimated that sixty men were killed and beheaded and that many women and children were taken as slaves. The surviving Toquaht scattered to their relatives among the other Barkley Sound groups. Mistreatment at their hands, however, led the Toquaht to return to Macoah and eventually to rejoin the Ucluelet. Their combined village was attacked by the other groups, particularly the Huu-ay-aht, and a lengthy period of reciprocal raiding followed. The Ucluelet then moved into Toquaht territory, settling with the remaining Toquaht at a village on the Toquart River. Kwishanishim noted that the Toquaht and Ucluelet "had now become one tribe. They no longer had separate villages" (Sapir and Swadesh 1955:427). Finally, after the Ucluelet gave gifts of women, the wars were stopped.

The narrative, however, continues past the end of the Long War. Desiring to own the rights to the Toquart River, a Ucluelet man decided to kill the Toquaht chief, despite being married to his sister. The other Ucluelet were opposed but reluctantly agreed to his plan. The plot failed but several Toquaht were killed and the two tribes moved apart. According to Kwishanishim: "There were only a few Tukwaa [Toquaht] people now." Seeking revenge, the Toquaht survivors invited the Ucluelet to join them. The initiator of the plot returned to his wife's village and was killed, and another Ucluelet group was ambushed. The Toquaht then moved to their fishing village at the falls on the Toquart River. They were followed by the Ucluelet, who wanted to exterminate them, "leaving none of them alive, because they were now few" (Sapir and Swadesh 1955:433). After the Ucluelet killed one of the Toquaht chiefs, the two groups finally ceased hostilities and "war was no longer in season."

Euro-Canadian observers in the late nineteenth century noted the diminished state of the Toquaht and their neighbours and were well aware of the forces that caused their reduced numbers. Banfield (1858) stated that the Toquaht were "once a much larger tribe, but some ten years since they were engaged in an intertribal war with the Nitnats [Ditidaht], and in consequence were reduced to their present small number." Blenkinsop (1874:10) commented on the "numerous old village sites," which he felt proved "incontestably that the population of Barclay [sic] Sound must have been at no very remote period ten times its present number." He attributed this great population loss to "war in former years, and disease ... in latter years." Turning specifically to the Toquaht, Blenkinsop (1874:32-33) commented that they were "dwindling away from a once powerful tribe to scarcely a tenth of what they were fifty years since." He further stated: "Continual wars with their more powerful neighbours and disease have reduced them to their present weak state. On one occasion Dysentery swept off more than half the tribe, and smallpox and measles decimated them frequently. They are now the smallest tribe on the Sound." Sproat (1868:104-105) refers to the Toquaht as "the remnant of a large tribe ... now reduced by war to a comparatively small number." By the time the reserve commissioner enumerated the Toquaht in 1882, their population had declined to a mere twenty-five people (O'Reilly 1883).

Political and Settlement Pattern Changes

Depopulation forced major cultural adjustments, particularly in the political and economic realms. One of the most evident effects was the disappearance of many independent political groups. Some were forcefully incorporated into other polities by warfare, while others sought voluntary alliance with related groups when their populations sank to levels that could not be sustained. In the latter case they often retained their name and a sense of separate identity, becoming a ranked component group of a larger political unit. The number of independent political groups among the Nuu-chah-nulth and Ditidaht continued to drop throughout the Historic Period, in a process extending well into the twentieth century.

The amalgamation of small local groups into larger "tribal" units brought about shifts in resource use and settlement pattern. Independent local groups, the basic Nuu-chah-nulth political form, tended to exploit a relatively small, culturally constrained territory from a year-round base. Amalgamation of several local groups produced a larger consolidated territory that could not be managed effectively from a single location. The development of the ethnographic seasonal round, with a fixed pattern of movement to specific locations to exploit seasonal resources, was an outcome of such amalgamations. This seasonal round became particularly pronounced when outside groups obtained rights to salmon rivers on the inside, establishing late summer and fall camps at such locations. This stimulated further warfare, as groups lacking productive salmon streams attempted to acquire them by force. A Nuu-chah-nulth ideal became the control of a variety of resource areas, including both inside and outside locations. Expansion of group territories by the forceful seizure of such resource areas is a dominant theme in Nuu-chah-nulth oral traditions spanning the late eighteenth and first half of the nineteenth centuries (Swadesh 1948; Sapir and Swadesh 1955; Drucker 1951:37; Inglis and Haggarty 1986:321; St. Claire 1991:81-84).

While the above was a common pattern throughout the Nuu-chah-nulth area, considerable variation existed. The people of Hesquiat Harbour and Muchalat Inlet remained at the local group level of political organization until late in the nineteenth century, while those from Kyuquot Sound to Nootka Sound formed confederacies. In Barkley Sound a series of bitter wars and conquests shaped the nature of the five existing tribal groups and their ethnographic territories, while the amalgamation that led to the formation of the modern Ditidaht appears to have proceeded primarily through peaceful means. Two specific areas, Nootka Sound and Barkley Sound, with differing patterns of postcontact political adaptations, are examined here.

Nootka Sound

The four northern Nuu-chah-nulth political units – the Mowachaht, Ehattesaht, Nuchatlaht, and Kyuquot – all formed confederacies early in the Historic Period. Such federated polities characteristically emerged after a period of warfare, when peace was established and rights to residential and resource locations were exchanged. Joint residence at a confederacy village during the summer months enhanced group solidarity, as did an integrated ranking of the chiefs, but individual political units within the confederacy maintained considerable autonomy and held their own village locations, to which they retired during much of the year.

Warfare continued to play a role in confederacy formation, as once such groups emerged their neighbours were either forced to form similar political units or were absorbed. The Nuchatlaht confederacy, for example, appears to have been created from the groups that remained after the Ehattesaht and Mowachaht confederacies emerged (Drucker 1951:228). Surrounded by these two newly formed and powerful confederacies, the groups that comprise the historic Nuchahtlaht would have had little choice but to amalgamate for common defence. The Chicklisaht in the north and the Muchalaht in Nootka Sound survived as independent groups into the late nineteenth century but ultimately joined the Kyuquot and Mowachaht, respectively.

The history of the Mowachaht confederacy is complex and occurred in a number of stages. Its formation, however, is better documented than is that of any other Nuu-chah-nulth confederacy (Drucker 1951; Folan 1972; Dewhirst 1990; Marshall 1993). It provides a good example of the role of both warfare and alliances in creating more complex polities. It also illustrates the state of flux in political organization and territorial holdings experienced by Nuu-chah-nulth groups in the first century of contact.

Legendary history gives a dominant role to groups on the outside of Nootka Island. These were the people who invented whaling techniques and who received from the Wolves the major Nuu-chah-nulth ceremony (Drucker 1951:228). These were also the people who took the first steps in confederacy formation. Through alliances with independent local groups on Tahsis Inlet, each living year-round at a village on a salmon river, they gained their first holdings on the inside of the sound. Control of the upper portion of Tahsis Inlet, with its major salmon rivers and the entrance to the overland trail across Vancouver Island, was bequeathed to a chief of the outer coast people when the former occupants moved into Esperanza Inlet to join the Nuchatlaht confederacy (Drucker 1951:228; Dewhirst 1990:39; Marshall 1993:198). Warfare also played a role, as the outer coast people forcefully seized Yuquot (Folan 1972:43; Dewhirst 1990:38; Marshall 1993:197), driving out a group that formerly had been "the sole owners of Yuquot, and the largest tribe on the sound" (Curtis 1916:184). The resulting consolidated territory stretched from upper Tahsis Inlet to Yuquot and the open-ocean sites of Nootka Island. Chiefs exchanged rights to build houses at the major villages of Yuquot, Kupti, and Tahsis, and an economic round of seasonal movement between them developed. Folan (1972) and Dewhirst (1990) refer to this consolidated group as the "Yuquotaht," while Marshall (1993) terms this "the Yuquot-Tahsis confederacy."

This confederacy, along with a seasonal pattern of movement throughout the consolidated territory, was established before the arrival of Europeans in Nootka Sound (Curtis 1916:185; Folan 1972:42). In fact, Marshall (1993:156-160, 198) argues that it emerged as early as 300 to 400 years ago. She notes archaeological evidence for the expansion of Kupti and possibly Yuquot in the late precontact period, attributing this to seasonal occupation by a larger confederated population. At the same time, E'as, one of the original outside villages, appears to have declined in importance as the economic focus of the confederacy shifted to resources of the sound and inlet.

Certainly the early historic descriptions make clear that the people of Yuquot in the late eighteenth century were engaged in a seasonal round of movement that took them from the outer coast beaches to upper Tahsis Inlet. In 1778 Cook speculated that the houses he observed at Yuquot were only seasonally occupied, stating that "one cannot look upon their houses to be any thing more than temporary habitations for the summer season when the fishery calls them down to the Sea coast. And it is very probable ... that they have others farther inland which they retire to in the winter" (Cook in Beaglehole 1967:318). This speculation was confirmed by such subsequent visitors to Nootka Sound as the American traders on the *Columbia*, who visited Tahsis in 1789 and described it as "the winter village of the Uquat [Yuquot] Inhabitants" (Haswell in Howay 1941:83).

The relative rank of the chiefs of the confederated groups, publicly expressed through the order of seating in potlatches, became fixed. The highest ranked position belonged to the head of a lineage from E'as, one of the outside villages (Drucker 1951:230). Throughout the early historic period the chief who held this position took the hereditary name of Maquinna. The second ranked position belonged to Callicum, who traced his origin to Tahsis, an inside location (Dewhirst 1990:43). Visitors to Yuquot in the 1780s noted the chiefly authority of both men but recognized that Maquinna held the superior position (Walker 1982:67-68; Meares 1790:108) (Figure 54). The other component groups also held ranked positions within the confederacy, retaining their individual identities and some measure of influence within the larger polity.

At the time of the early European observations at Yuquot, the villages in the eastern part of the sound were politically separate from the Yuquot-Tahsis confederacy. In fact, a state of warfare existed for at least part of this period, as Haswell (in Howay 1941:55) commented in 1788 that the inhabitants of Yuquot were at war with "the people of the opposite side of the sound." The villages in Tlupana Inlet had also politically amalgamated, bringing together a number of formerly independent local groups, each associated with a village at the mouth of a salmon stream. This tribal organization emerged as one group became dominant and offered its neighbours residential rights at the village of O'wis in the upper sound (Drucker 1951:230). An integrated system of ranking for its chiefs and joint occupation of O'wis during the winter months consolidated this tribal grouping. Its chief, the head of the dominant local group, was Tlupananutl, who is frequently mentioned in the early historic documents for Nookta Sound. Tlupananutl's village is shown at the head of Tlupana Arm in a Spanish map of 1791 (in Moziño 1970: plate 4). Menzies, at Yuquot with Vancouver in 1792, refers to an "aged Chief named *Floopannanoo* [Tlupananutl], whose Tribe occupied one of the North west branches of the Sound" (Newcombe 1923:115). Vancouver's account of his 1794 visit to Tlupananutl's village of "Mooetchee"

54 Maquinna and Callicum, chiefs at Nootka Sound. Maquinna derived his hereditary position from an outer coast village, while Callicum was chief of Tahsis, at the end of an inlet in the upper sound. Both men wear sea otter robes, and Maquinna wears a woven whaler's hat. The European convention of the handshake shown in this picture is surely a fanciful addition by the artist. This engraving appeared in the journal of John Meares's voyages, published in 1790. *Royal BC Museum PN4720*

(*Muwach'a*) clearly recognizes the people of Tlupana Inlet as distinct from those at Yuquot, noting "the superiority of *Maquinna's* authority, when compared with that of the neighbouring chiefs; amongst whom *Clewpaneloo* [Tlupananutl] was reputed to be one of the first in wealth and power" (1984:1,406).

The Mowachaht confederacy emerged through political amalgamation of the Tlupana Inlet people with the Yuquot-Tahsis confederacy. Tlupananutl was linked by marriage to Maquinna, and it was through transfer of marriage rights at a potlatch that the Tlupana Inlet people acquired house sites and potlatch seats at Yuquot (Drucker 1951:230-231; Folan 1972:45; Marshall 1993:257). They continued, however, to winter separately at O'wis and to retire seasonally to their fishing stations in Tlupana Inlet. This union appears to have taken place early in the nineteenth century, as Jewitt's descriptions of visitors to Yuquot from Tlupana Inlet indicate that these were still separate polities as late as 1804 (Dewhirst 1990:41); yet the Tlupana people are said to have moved to Yuquot during the time of Tlupananutl (Curtis 1916:183), an aged chief when described by Vancouver and the Spanish in the 1790s. It took a considerable period of time to work out an integrated series of ranking for their chiefs. In fact, Drucker (1951:230-231) states that it was not until the middle of the nineteenth century, when people began to live at Yuquot for much of the year and the occupants were invited as a single group to potlatches held by other Nuu-chah-nulth, that this was finally achieved. At this point the Mowachaht confederacy, as known through ethnographic descriptions, was established. Why the confederacy derived its name from Tlupananutl's village of *Muwach'a* is unknown (Drucker 1951:231; Folan 1972:37; Dewhirst 1990:40; Marshall 1993:257), but it reflects the shift in emphasis from outside resources to those of the inner sound and inlets.

A late stage in political union involved the Muchalaht, whose villages were along Muchalat Inlet at the eastern side of the sound and along the major rivers near its head. These villages existed as independent local groups, occasionally warring among themselves, until forced by outside aggression to consolidate (Drucker 1951:232). Around the mid-nineteenth century the Mowachaht initiated a lengthy war of attrition, with the rich salmon fisheries of the Gold and Burman Rivers on Muchalat Inlet providing the incentive for attempted conquest. A leading figure in these hostilities was Shewish, the Mowachaht war chief who had taken political leadership when his elder brother, who held the title Maquinna, had died. The beleaguered Muchalaht faced additional threats, as the Hupacasath crossed overland to attack villages on Gold River, as did the Namgis Kwakwaka'wakw from across the island, while the Ahousaht were raiding villages along Muchalat Inlet (Drucker 1951:234, 354, 356, 359). The death of Shewish at the hands of a Muchalaht war chief removed one of the chief instigators of the war and possibly saved the Muchalaht from annihilation. By the time the hostilities came to an end around the early 1870s, the Muchalaht survivors had consolidated at the village of Ahaminaquus (*Aa7aminkis*; DkSm 4), at the mouth of Gold River, where they had built a palisaded fort of cedar timbers (Drucker 1951:234, 363). The two small defensive sites (DkSm 2 and 3) recorded by Marshall (1992a:17-18; 1993:51-52) on either side of Gold River may also relate to these hostilities, particularly since at the time Shewish was killed the Muchalaht were living "at an old site just across the river [from Ahaminaquus] which they considered more defensible" (Drucker 1951:361). After building a large house at Ahaminaquus, the Muchalaht chief invited the Mowachaht and Ahousaht to a potlatch, at which he sprinkled eagle down on his guests and formally established peace (Drucker 1951:353-365).

In the final decades of the nineteenth century the Muchalaht who had survived the war consolidated into a single group, although without an integrated ranking of potlatch seats (Drucker 1951:235). The marriage of a Muchalaht chief's daughter to the second-ranking Mowachaht chief led many of her relatives to follow her to Yuquot (Drucker 1951:231). When the primary Mowachaht chief died early in the twentieth century, the position, including the name of Maquinna, passed to a Muchalaht man and most of the remaining Muchalaht joined the Mowachaht at Yuquot (Drucker 1951:231; Marshall 1993:263). The Muchalaht were never formally integrated into the Mowachaht confederacy, however, instead establishing and maintaining their own ranked series of potlatch seats. As joint residence encouraged continued intermarriage, individuals came to acquire potlatch seats and other privileges from both groups. Finally, in 1951 the Muchalaht formally joined the Mowachaht as a single band under the Canadian administrative system. Later, the federal government encouraged the entire band to move to the former Muchalaht site of Ahaminaquus at Gold River. Even today, however, traditions of separate histories are strong, and in 1994 the band was formally renamed the Mowachaht/Muchalaht.[4]

Marshall (1993:166, 265) maintains that historic settlement patterns in Nootka Sound remained relatively stable compared to Nuu-chah-nulth areas to the south. Archaeological surveys of Nootka Sound revealed that most large shell midden sites continued to be occupied into the Historic Period, often into the twentieth century. Furthermore, most ethnographic village locations had archaeological evidence of earlier use, indicating that few new sites had been established in this late period. People continued to return to previously established village locations, although the intensity and duration of occupation would have changed over time, as would have the political composition of the site residents. The lack of evidence for widespread abandonment of older sites and the rarity of ethnographic sites with no archaeological presence suggests a different pattern of events than that seen from surveys in Hesquiat Harbour and Barkley Sound. It seems likely that the more complex political organization achieved by the northern Nuu-chah-nulth allowed them to make a more orderly transition to the contractions and amalgamations caused by historic depopulation than could be realized by the southern Nuu-chah-nulth, whose postcontact history was marked by many violent and disruptive events.

4 A similar situation exists among the northernmost Nuu-chah-nulth. The Chicklisaht formally merged with the Kyuquot band under the Canadian legal system but continued to maintain their own chiefs and identity. Today both groups are members of the Kyuquot band, but they have begun to refer to themselves as the Kyuquot/Chicklisaht (often written as K̲a:yu:'k't'h'/Che:k̲'tles7et'h̲') First Nation.

A prominent theme running throughout these early historic changes is the shift in emphasis from outer ocean resources to those of the protected inner sound and inlets. Outer coast sites such as E'as, dominant in legendary history and the home of the highest ranked division of the Mowachaht, declined in use throughout the historic period. Archaeological evidence comes from Yuquot, where excavation in the historic levels shows that less emphasis was placed on the procurement of open-ocean fauna. Albatross, the dominant avian fauna throughout earlier levels, is reduced in importance, while Canada goose remains become much more common; in addition, mussel shells, which form much of the midden matrix from precontact levels, are largely replaced by clams of several species (Dewhirst 1979; McAllister 1980; Clarke and Clarke 1980). Large quantities of land mammal bones also show the historic importance placed on hunting deer (Dewhirst 1980:347). The name of the nineteenth-century confederacy, taken from the Tlupana Inlet village of *Muwach'a*, indicates the increasing importance of the upper sound and inlet locations. The Mowachaht, literally "the People of the Deer," were by this time focused on deer and salmon, while the whales that had preoccupied their ancestors played a role only in the oral traditions of a glorious past.

Barkley Sound

The first century of contact was a tumultuous period for the Barkley Sound Nuu-chah-nulth, who were devastated by warfare and disease. Most of the independent political units occupying the sound at contact were eliminated by these catastrophic forces. The few surviving political units are primarily nineteenth-century amalgamations of formerly autonomous groups. Such amalgamations resulted in the abandonment of many large, formerly year-round village sites, while the larger territorial holdings of each amalgamated group stimulated an economic round of seasonal movement.

Unlike Nootka Sound, no single polity assumed control over all of Barkley Sound. In the late eighteenth century, however, Wickaninish exerted a trade hegemony over the sound. Captains Barkley (in 1787) and Meares (in 1788) were able to trade successfully for furs in the sound (Meares 1790:180; Hill 1978:37), but after that time Wickaninish forced local chiefs to trade their furs through him. Many of the early European visitors noted this control of trade exerted by the powerful Tla-o-qui-aht chief (Magee 1794; Bishop 1967:106; Haswell in Howay 1941:79). Wickaninish enforced his control through military power, telling the crew of the *Jefferson* at Barkley Sound that he had been forced to kill forty local people to keep them in line (Magee 1794). The list of tributary groups given by Wickaninish to Meares (1790:230) in 1788 includes the Ucluelet and Uchucklesaht, with "Qu-quaet" probably referring to the Toquaht. Wickaninish's overlordship may not have extended to the eastern shores of the sound, however, as Bishop (1967:108) observed in 1795: "We where [sic] visited by two Chiefs from the East shore, their Names where [sic] Yapasuet & Annathat. They made some trade with us, and Promised to return ... I believe these People are independant of Wiccannanish, but speak the same language and are of the Same Manners." This trade hegemony seems to have collapsed when the maritime fur trade came to an end. Wickaninish is not mentioned in the written accounts of the next period of contact in Barkley Sound, which began around the mid-nineteenth century, nor is his influence recognized in the ethnographic traditions.

Evidence for extensive disruption and displacement shortly after contact is evident in the archaeological landscape of Barkley Sound. The areas that have been intensively surveyed provide evidence for a shift in settlement pattern in the recent period. In Toquaht territory, a number of ethnographically important village locations, occupied seasonally for salmon fishing, have no archaeological deposits (McMillan and St. Claire 1991:69-70), suggesting a late development of the ethnographic pattern of seasonal movement. The same may be true for Alberni Inlet (McMillan and St. Claire 1982:32). In the Broken Group Islands of the central sound, a number of large shell midden sites lack any ethnographic information (Inglis and Haggarty 1986:265, 279), suggesting early historic abandonment. Other large village sites, remembered by informants as origin places of various Tseshaht subgroups, were reduced to occasional seasonal use when the surviving occupants left to join other groups. During the process of amalgamation, sites that offered superior defensive capabilities or the best access to valued economic resources continued to be occupied, while those less favoured fell into disuse. By the time the reserve commissioner examined Native land-use patterns late in the nineteenth century, many large village sites in the Broken Group and elsewhere in Barkley Sound were no longer being used.

The Tseshaht (*Ts'ishaa7ath*) offer the best documented example of the process of amalgamation in Barkley Sound. At least six formerly independent political groups coalesced in the century following European contact to form the modern Tseshaht (Map 12). Inglis and Haggarty (1986:279) suggest that there may once have been as many as fifteen separate local groups in the Broken Group Islands, based on the presence of that number of large village sites, indicating that the ethnographic data may refer only to the later stages of a lengthy process of amalgamation. From a small area in the outer islands of the Broken Group occupied by the original Tseshaht local group, the amalgamated Tseshaht grew to become one of the dominant political units in the sound, occupying all of the Broken Group, the western portion of the Deer Group Islands, most of the northern shore of Barkley Sound, and much of the Alberni Inlet and the lower Somass River in the Alberni Valley. Sapir (1922:307) describes the Tseshaht as:

a cluster of various smaller tribal units, of which the Ts'isha'ath, that gave their name to the whole, were the leading group. The other subdivisions were originally independent tribes that had lost their isolated distinctness through conquest, weakening in numbers, or friendly removal and union. Each of the tribal subdivisions or "septs" had its own stock of legends, its distinctive privileges, its own houses in the village, its old village sites and distinctive fishing and hunting waters that were still remembered in detail by its members. While the septs now lived together as a single tribe, the basis of the sept division was really a traditional local one.

The process of amalgamation that brought the component groups known ethnographically into the larger Tseshaht polity began shortly after European contact. The *Maḵtli7ii7ath̲*, neighbouring the original Tseshaht in the

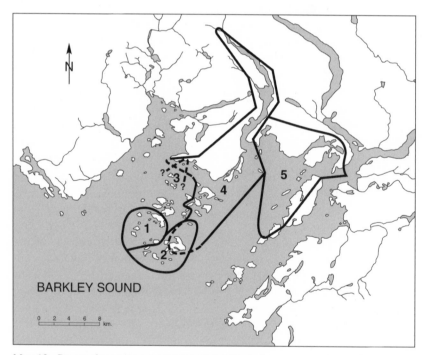

Map 12   Pre-amalgamation territories of the Tseshaht component groups (after St. Claire 1991):

1   original Tseshaht (*Ts'ishaa7ath̲*) territory

2   *Maḵtli7ii7ath̲*

3   *Nash7as7ath̲* (winter village at east end of *Hiikwis*; rest of territory unknown)

4   *Hach'aa7ath* (after conquest of Effingham Inlet from *A7uts'ath̲* and Effingham [Village] Island from *Maḵtli7ii7ath̲*)

5   Ekoolthaht (*Hikwuulh7ath̲*)

outer islands of the Broken Group, were among the first to be absorbed, probably in the late eighteenth century (St. Claire 1991:26). Wars with the *Hach'aa7ath* had so reduced their numbers that they could no longer sustain an independent existence. The *Hach'aa7ath* wars also nearly destroyed the *Waanin7ath*, originally an offshoot of the *Maktli7ii7ath* (Golla 1987:83, 88; St. Claire 1991:40), who were forced to rejoin their parent group and then move with them to merge with the Tseshaht. Somewhat later, wars with the *Hach'aa7ath* and possibly the Tseshaht brought the *Nash7as7ath* of the upper sound into the Tseshaht polity (St. Claire 1991:41-44). All these groups lost their autonomy, becoming subordinate to the Tseshaht, and their former territories were incorporated into the holdings of the larger political unit.

At the beginning of the historic period the *Hach'aa7ath* were a large and successful group, waging wars of expansion against most of their neighbours in Barkley Sound and raiding as far away as the Ahousaht and Ditidaht (St. Claire 1991:28). Their territory included some of the eastern Broken Group Islands and the Vancouver Island shore along Sechart Channel, including the important site of *Hiikwis*. A war of subjugation against the *A7uts'ath* reduced the latter to a subordinate group and added Effingham Inlet to *Hach'aa7ath* territory. Along with the neighbouring Ekoolthaht (*Hikwuulh7ath*), the *Hach'aa7ath* expanded up Alberni Inlet, seizing by conquest the rich salmon fishery of the lower Somass River (McMillan and St. Claire 1982:14; Inglis and Haggarty 1986:130-131; St. Claire 1991:30). After some conflict between the two groups, the *Hach'aa7ath* occupied the eastern bank of the Somass River, while the Ekoolthaht took the western bank. Before the end of the eighteenth century, however, *Hach'aa7ath* fortunes dramatically turned. In a war with the Toquaht over the location of their boundary, the *Hach'aa7ath* inadvertently killed a Ucluelet man. This brought the Ucluelet, along with their powerful Tla-o-qui-aht allies, into the war (Sapir and Swadesh 1955:373-377). Using trade muskets recently acquired by the Tla-o-qui-aht, the allies struck a devastating blow against the *Hach'aa7ath*. The few survivors eventually joined the Tseshaht, leaving the *Hach'aa7ath* to exist only as a component group of the larger polity.

The final group to join the amalgamated Tseshaht was the Ekoolthaht (*Hikwuulh7ath*). This once powerful group held territory in the upper sound (Figure 55) and later seized land along the lower Somass River. The Ekoolthaht had become greatly weakened by warfare, losing many in the Qualicum Salish raids against the Hupacasath and other residents along the Somass River (St. Claire 1991:37). Blenkinsop (1874:41) referred to them in 1874 as "once a large tribe now numbering only forty eight men, women and children." As their population dropped they became increasingly associated with the Tseshaht, but they were still considered to be a separate and independent group when observed by Blenkinsop in 1874 and Brabant (1977:52-

55   This carved house post and beam are part of
house remains standing in upper Barkley Sound at
Ekool (*Hikwuulh*), the main village of the Ekoolthaht
(*Hikwuulh7at̲h̲*), in this 1912 photograph by C.F.
Newcombe. *Royal BC Museum PN1255*

53) in 1876. Blenkinsop (1874:41) described their situation: "About sixty
years since being hard pressed by the other Indians, and having through
sickness and war become unable to cope with their enemies, they of their
own accord joined the Se.shah.ahts [Tseshaht], as they say for protection
only and did not at the time surrender the right to control their own lands.
The latter however seem to look on them as a conquered race." The
Ekoolthaht complained to Blenkinsop that the Tseshaht had sold the
Ekoolthaht land near the mouth of the Somass River to the new mill company without their consent, leaving them "living a wandering life and having no village they can call their own either for summer or winter."
Blenkinsop recommended that they be assigned a separate reserve adjacent
to that of the Tseshaht on the lower Somass River. Despite this recommenda-
tion, when Reserve Commissioner O'Reilly (1883) laid out the reserves in

1882 he failed to provide separate land for the Ekoolthaht, forcing their final amalgamation with the Tseshaht.

Although these formerly independent local groups were absorbed into the Tseshaht, they did not disappear. They retained their names and separate traditions, with their chiefs holding ranked potlatch seats within the larger grouping. Their primary role among the amalgamated Tseshaht, however, was that of being ceremonial units. Sayaach'apis, Sapir's main Tseshaht informant, described the ceremonies taking place at Hiikwis:

> When living there, when all had come together, someone gave a potlatch. They went to dance with the other divisions possessing names in the village. When a Nashas [Nash7as7ath] person gave a potlatch, the whole Tsishaa [Tseshaht] Band danced into the house ... Then the Wanin [Waanin7ath] Band danced in ... Then the large Maktlii [Maktli7ii7ath] Band would all dance in. And they gave gifts to the Nashas. The Nachimwas [Nach'imuuwas7ath] Band also danced in. The Hikuuthl [Hikwuulh7ath] people also danced in. The Hachaa [Hach'aa7ath] people also danced in. That was the complete number of bands in the village of Hiikwis. (Sapir and Swadesh 1955:43-44)

Even after the Tseshaht became an amalgamated group, considerable changes took place in their territories. During the Long War around the 1840s, when the Tseshaht were greatly suffering from losses at the hands of the Ucluelet, they largely abandoned the Broken Group Islands, instead wintering at a village on Sarita River in modern Huu-ay-aht territory (Inglis and Haggarty 1986:133, 137). The site of Hiikwis at this time was held by the Ucluelet, as Sayaach'apis indicated that "the Ucluelet houses filled the space from end to end at Hiikwis" (Sapir and Swadesh 1955:412). By the end of the war the Tseshaht had regained Hiikwis and made it their main winter village site. From Hiikwis people moved to *Huumuuwa*, a former *Maktli7ii7ath* site in the outer Broken Group that became the major summer village of the amalgamated Tseshaht. Sayaach'apis described how the people stayed together because of fear of the Ucluelets: "We always moved away [from Hiikwis] when the herring finished spawning. We would go to Huumuuwa (Village Island), the whole Tsishaa Tribe staying together because the war had ended only recently. We did not want to get separated" (Sapir and Swadesh 1955:39).

As tensions eased in the following years the individual component groups began to revisit their origin places in the Broken Group Islands, using them as seasonal resource camps, while Hiikwis and Huumuuwa continued as the amalgamation sites (Sapir and Swadesh 1955:44-45; Inglis and Haggarty 1986:137). As the Tseshaht acquired rights to the Somass River through amalgamation with the Ekoolthaht and *Hach'aa7ath* they began to winter along the Somass, reducing Hiikwis to a seasonal camp used in the spring (St. Claire 1991:135). By the end of the nineteenth century the amalgamated Tseshaht were spending the winter on the Somass River at the Tsahaheh reserve, near the growing Euro-Canadian community of Port Alberni, and travelling to various seasonal resource locations along Alberni Inlet and the Broken Group Islands from spring to fall. This set of activities was the seasonal pattern of movement that has been documented ethnographically (Sapir and Swadesh 1955:27-46; McMillan and St. Claire 1982:17-23). It reflects, however, only a late stage in a changing pattern of political organization and resource use in central Barkley Sound.

The modern Ucluelet (*Yuulhuu7ilh7ath*) are also the result of historic amalgamations, incorporating at least six formerly independent local groups (Inglis and Haggarty 1986:142; St. Claire 1991:56). Three of these groups once occupied the open-ocean shores of the Ucluth Peninsula and extended as far north as Green Point on Long Beach, where they bordered on the Tla-o-qui-aht. The remaining three had villages along the sheltered water of Ucluelet Inlet. That these were year-round villages is made clear by Kwishanishim, who told Sapir: "They were called the Ucluelet Arm Tribe because they lived there all the time. They only occasionally moved outside of that place" (Sapir and Swadesh 1955:362). Once again it was an outside local group that gave its name to the amalgamated polity, yet residence shifted to an inside location, in the territory of the *Hitats'u7ath* local group.

Early in the Historic Period, the Ucluelet embarked on several aggressive wars of expansion. Allied with the Tla-o-qui-aht, the Ucluelet destroyed the Effingham Inlet people and seized their territory (Sapir and Swadesh 1955:373-377). Their search for a productive salmon river also led the Ucluelet to wipe out the *Namint7ath*, an independent local group at the mouth of the Nahmint River on Alberni Inlet, in a series of raids (Sapir and Swadesh 1955:362-367). That this was carried out primarily by the *Hitats'u7ath*, prior to full amalgamation of the Ucluelet, is clear in Kwishanishim's comment that "only the Ucluelet Arm people without the other Ucluelets went on the war party" (Sapir and Swadesh 1955:363). The long journey to fish at Nahmint River hastened the process of amalgamation, as it made the *Hitats'u7ath* vulnerable to attacks from the Huu-ay-aht. The *Hitats'u7ath* offered the outer coast groups fishing rights at Nahmint and house sites at their village of *Hitats'u* in exchange for assistance against the Huu-ay-aht (St. Claire 1991:60; Inglis and Haggarty 1986:157). The amalgamated Ucluelet then developed a seasonal pattern of movement throughout their consolidated territory, from the outer coast beaches to Alberni Inlet. During the Long War of the mid-nineteenth century, the Ucluelet seized portions of Tseshaht territory and began to winter at the village of *Hiikwis*. These lands were lost by the end of the war and the Ucluelet, considerably reduced in numbers, consolidated at Hitats'u. By the late nineteenth century this was their principal community, although the outer coast villages were still seasonally occupied for halibut fishing, and the Nahmint River remained their primary salmon fishery. Today the entire band resides on Ucluelet Inlet at the Ittatsoo (*Hitats'u*) reserve.

The modern Huu-ay-aht (*Huu <u>Z</u>ii7at<u>h</u>*), whose territory covered all of eastern Barkley Sound, were also formed through the amalgamation of independent local groups. According to Sapir's informants, this process had begun prior to European arrival (St. Claire 1991:68-69; Inglis and Haggarty 1986:179). A war text collected by Sapir, "Uchucklesits Exterminate Kiihin" (Swadesh 1948; Sapir and Swadesh 1955), describes a war of expansion by the Uchucklesaht (*<u>H</u>uuchu<u>k</u>wtlis7at<u>h</u>*) against the *Kiix7in7at<u>h</u>*, who occupied the coastline from Banfield Inlet nearly to Cape Beale. In fact, the war affected all the groups of eastern Barkley Sound, who were defeated and made into subject peoples, while the Uchucklesaht seized the entire eastern coastline of the sound to Cape Beale and along the outer coast as far as Tsusiat River, well within modern Ditidaht territory (Inglis and Haggarty 1986:186, 189; St. Claire 1991:75; Clamhouse et al. 1991:231). Several of the outer coast local groups disappeared as independent polities at that time, either due to losses in warfare or as a result of a natural catastrophe – an earthquake and tsunami that destroyed a village in Pachena Bay (Clamhouse et al. 1991:230-231). By the time the Uchucklesaht were driven out, only two separate polities remained, the *Kiix7in7at<u>h</u>* along the coastline and the Huu-ay-aht in the Deer Group Islands and along the Sarita River. Later, a bitter war with the Clallum further reduced their numbers and forced the survivors to retreat to the Sarita River (Inglis and Haggarty 1986:190; Clamhouse et al. 1991:209). The Long War in Barkley Sound brought further losses, primarily at the hands of the Ucluelet. By this time the Huu-ay-aht were a single amalgamated polity. When Blenkinsop described them in 1874 they were wintering at "Noo.muk.em.e.is" (*Numa<u>k</u>amiis*), at the mouth of the Sarita River, and spending the summers at "Keh.ahk.in" (*Kiix7in*), the former village of the *Kiix7inat<u>h</u>* near Banfield Inlet (Figure 56). Shortly after, *Kiix7in* was abandoned as the Huu-ay-aht moved around the trading post at Dodger Cove in the Deer Group Islands. In recent times the largest Huu-ay-aht community has been on the Anacla reserve at Pachena Bay.

Like the Uchucklesaht, the Toquaht saw their former dominance greatly diminished in the early Historic Period. Formerly the most powerful group in the western sound, their fortunes declined as their population dwindled through disease and warfare and as they became eclipsed by the rising power of the Ucluelet. Modern Toquaht informants maintain, as mentioned in Chapter 1, that the Toquaht once protected the inhabitants of Ucluelet Inlet. Certainly their large fortified village of T'ukw'aa, controlling the entrance to Ucluelet Inlet, put them in a position of dominance. However, this likely refers to a period prior to the amalgamation of the Ucluelet Inlet

56   A house frame and two large carved figures still stand at the Huu-ay-aht village of *Kiix7in* in this photograph, taken circa 1900. *Royal BC Museum PN495*

groups with the outer coast people. After amalgamation sometime early in the Historic Period, the Ucluelet presented a much more formidable political and military force. It was likely at that time that the Toquaht shifted their main village from T'ukw'aa, which was reduced to use as a seasonal resource camp, to Macoah, which is further up the sound and more distant from the Ucluelet. This move also would have allowed the Toquaht to protect their major salmon fishery on the Toquart River. Despite moving further away from the Ucluelet, however, continued close relations with that group and declining Toquaht numbers nearly led to the disappearance of the Toquaht as a separate polity. During the Long War the Ucluelet had settled with the remaining Toquaht at a village on the Toquart River. Kwishanishim, Sapir's Ucluelet-Toquaht informant, noted that the two groups "had now become one tribe" (Sapir and Swadesh 1955:427). Had the Ucluelet not initiated further fighting in an attempt to take ownership of the Toquart River, the Toquaht may have been absorbed peacefully by their larger neighbour.

The Toquaht may have been at a competitive disadvantage as other groups in Barkley Sound amalgamated. It is not clear whether Toquaht history involved amalgamation of independent local groups. Certainly their ethnographic territory is as large as are several of the known amalgamations. Sayaach'apis, Sapir's main Tseshaht informant, maintained that the people of Macoah, the *Ma7akwuu7ath*, were once a distinct group that amalgamated and became subordinate to the Toquaht (Sapir 1910-1914; St. Claire 1991:54). Arima (1983:5) also claims that the *Ma7akwuu7ath* were a separate group, joining the Toquaht only in the nineteenth century. Another of Sapir's Tseshaht informants, William, credited the *Ch'uumat'a7ath*, at the large village of Ch'uumat'a, with once being a separate tribe. Unlike the other Barkley Sound groups, however, no oral traditions of amalgamation remain among the Toquaht, nor are there separate ranked chiefly positions or potlatch seats. The relative lack of large abandoned shell midden sites, particularly when compared to the Broken Group Islands, also suggests that amalgamation, if it occurred at all, involved only a few component groups. Opportunities for further peaceful amalgamation and consolidation of territory dwindled when the people of Ucluelet Inlet joined with those of the outer coast of the Ucluth Peninsula. The Toquaht were then caught between two powerful and expansionist amalgamations, the Ucluelet and the Tseshaht, and this contributed to their early historic decline in population and influence.

In summary, the postcontact period in Barkley Sound, as at Nootka Sound, was marked by a shift from outer coast locations and resources to those of the upper sound and inlets. The original Tseshaht were a small local group occupying several outer coast islands. Eventually they became part of a much larger amalgamated polity with a greatly increased territory, shifting their winter residence first to the upper sound and then to the end of Alberni Inlet, along the Somass River. The limited nature and extent of archaeological deposits along Alberni Inlet suggest that this pattern of seasonal movement developed only recently. The Ucluelet, who also take their name from an outer coast local group, consolidated on Ucluelet Inlet while maintaining their important salmon fishery on Alberni Inlet. The Toquaht moved from the large outer coast village and fortress from which they derive their name to their nineteenth-century principal residence on the upper sound. These shifts of residence entailed changed patterns of resource use, and this required the development of a seasonal round of movement.

Barkley Sound and Nootka Sound were examined here as specific examples of a more widespread pattern. Similar changes, involving a reduction in the number of independent local groups and a shift from outer coast to inside locations, were taking place throughout the territories of the Nuu-chah-nulth and their relatives. The Ditidaht remained a cluster of independent polities, many residing in outer coast villages, until quite recent times, but they eventually consolidated at their modern village on Nitinat Lake. Even the Makah, whose territory lacks inside sounds or inlets, eventually abandoned the outer coast villages such as Ozette and Tsoo-yess for the comparatively sheltered location on Neah Bay, where their modern community is situated. Although such factors as better access to schools, roads, and jobs played a role in these more recent movements, the effect was to continue what had become a well established pattern.

Culture Change and the Ethnographic Present

Pioneering anthropologists among the Nuu-chah-nulth, as among other Native peoples, assumed the presence of an earlier traditional culture that could be recovered and recorded through gaining access to the knowledge held by elderly informants. Working early in the twentieth century, anthropologists such as Sapir, Drucker, Curtis, and Koppert believed that they were in a race with "progress" and that their task was to record the traditional knowledge of Native communities before it was irretrievably lost. The memories of their oldest informants, however, could extend back only to the mid- or late nineteenth century. This period of time then became the "ethnographic present," characterized by an essentially unchanging "traditional culture," minimizing changes that had occurred earlier in the Historic Period. In fact, as the ethnographic present floated in a timeless state, indigenous cultures were rarely viewed in a historical perspective. Little recognition was accorded to cultural changes that occurred before the late advent of extensive acculturation to Euro-Canadian society.

Yet, as outlined in this chapter, aspects of Native cultures were subject to constant restructuring throughout the period following European contact. Disease and warfare were driving factors, as declining populations destabilized economies and forced new political accommodations. Small local groups living year-round in one place were transformed into amalgamated units with larger territories, requiring a seasonal round of activities in order to manage resources effectively. In the "traditional culture," as it became ethnographically known, the seasonal round was a universal Nuu-chah-nulth pattern. Even the political units of ethnographic study, such as the Mowachaht and the Tseshaht, were nineteenth-century amalgamations that do not represent the nature of the societies encountered in the same areas during the first decades of recorded contact.

Similar patterns of change were occurring among other coastal groups during the early contact period. Galois (1994) has documented extensive early historic shifts in settlement pattern among the neighbouring Kwakwaka'wakw. Recent archaeological research among the Haida of the southern Queen Charlotte Islands also shows a shift from numerous small year-round settlements in the period prior to European contact to the large seasonally occupied villages that were recorded ethnographically (Acheson 1995).

The ethnographic documentation of a fixed pattern of seasonal movement is suspect even for quite late periods. Among the Makah, for example, Swan (1870) lists five winter villages, yet, through analysis of faunal remains recovered archaeologically, Huelsbeck and Wessen (1995) argue that at least some people were living at these sites throughout the year. Even place name research with modern Nuu-chah-nulth informants suggests that the pattern was more flexible than is indicated by the ethnographies. For example, a Toquaht informant maintained that some people lived at Macoah year-round, as "a sort of headquarters for all the creeks around" (St. Claire 1991:71). Although populations certainly would have fluctuated with the availability of seasonal food resources in other locations, it is likely that many of the major Nuu-chah-nulth villages had a permanent core of residents.

Recognition of extensive cultural change in the early contact period debunks the myth of an unchanging traditional culture stuck in the ethnographic present. Although few would argue that Native life had been static, the ahistorical nature of these concepts discouraged consideration of the nature and extent of culture change. Ethnohistoric and ethnographic observations spanning a considerable period of time have frequently been conflated into a single description of "traditional" Native lifeways. Such anthropological perceptions implicitly served to perpetuate the colonialist myth of the "unchanging Native," so effectively attacked by Trigger (1980, 1981, 1985).

Evidence of early historic cultural change poses problems for the use of ethnographic data in interpreting the archaeological past. As argued in this chapter, the cultures observed by Cook and Vancouver differed markedly from those carried in the memories of Nuu-chah-nulth individuals interviewed by Curtis and Drucker. Imposition of ethnographic data on the archaeological past precludes the recognition of differing earlier patterns, a problem that Wobst (1979) refers to as "the tyranny of the ethnographic record in archaeology." Similarly, Marshall (1990:124) maintains that such an exercise serves only "to colonize the past from the present." Trigger (1981:13; 1985:28) argues that any ethnographic present, if it is meant to describe cultures prior to European-induced changes, will have to be defined archaeologically.

Clearly the lack of historical perspective inherent in the concept of the ethnographic present must be countered, and caution must be exercised in how ethnographic data are used in archaeology. Despite these concerns, however, there are many aspects of Nuu-chah-nulth culture that appear to have a lengthy continuity. Many archaeological discoveries at Yuquot, for example, have direct counterparts among the historic Nuu-chah-nulth of Nootka Sound. While the Nuu-chah-nulth pattern of resource use across the landscape appears to have changed considerably during the historic period, the technology of resource procurement remained relatively constant until very recent times. Belief systems, ceremonial practices, rules for tracing descent, and other basic aspects of Nuu-chah-nulth life seem to have survived the tumultuous years of rapid change relatively intact. Even political groups that had lost their independence survived as ceremonial units within the larger polities. Oral traditions collected by the ethnographers also hold great value, providing insights into history from a Native perspective. Although ethnographic information cannot be extended uncritically into the past, such data provide a rich body of knowledge that may be compared with that generated archaeologically. The integration of these distinct sets of data, along with contributions from fields such as historical linguistics, provides the basis for a holistic archaeology.

7
Recent History and the Modern Communities

The resilience shown by the Nuu-chah-nulth and their relatives in meeting the challenges of changing conditions, as discussed for the early contact period in the last chapter, carries on into the modern world. They continue to adapt to new conditions in their lives, while asserting control after the demoralizing effects of colonization and taking steps to ensure the maintenance of their cultures. A holistic approach to their study requires a long-term view, continuing past the devastating effects of population loss and the suppression of culture following contact to show their survival and vitality as living cultures. Otherwise, we run the risk of stereotyping Native peoples as occupants of a timeless past, thus neglecting their living presence and Aboriginal rights in the modern world.

Much of Nuu-chah-nulth culture came under intensified assault in the late nineteenth century. This was the period of reserve allocations, imposition of federal government authority, continued outbreaks of disease, and conversion to Christianity. The first sustained missionary effort among the Nuu-chah-nulth was that of Reverend A.J. Brabant, who established a mission among the Hesquiaht in 1875 (Brabant 1977; Moser 1926). Brabant encountered considerable resistance to his missionizing efforts but eventually succeeded in converting most of the Hesquiaht to Roman Catholicism. During this time, Roman Catholic missions were established in other Nuu-chah-nulth communities, particularly among the northern groups. Several Protestant denominations were also active, establishing mission schools among the Ahousaht, Ditidaht, and Alberni groups before the end of the century. The missionaries attacked traditional Native beliefs and embarked on zealous programs of enforced cultural change. They encouraged the Nuu-chah-nulth to abandon the large plank-clad houses that traditionally sheltered extended families and to reside in small, single-family, European-style houses. Brabant confronted the chiefs and shamans, using the concept of Christian equality to erode their former power and appointing converts as police to enforce the new order (Moser 1926). Missionaries were instrumental in lobbying the federal government to legislate prohibitions on traditional customs such as the potlatch. They also used their positions in charge of the newly established schools to suppress Nuu-chah-nulth language and culture among the children. Such acculturative forces were at work even earlier among the Makah, with the establishment of a school and an Indian agency in Neah Bay by the 1860s (Colson 1953; Gillis 1974; Renker and Gunther 1990).

In the early decades of the twentieth century, the Nuu-chah-nulth, Ditidaht, and Makah continued to seek new economic opportunities, which often involved using traditional skills in commercial enterprises. Many men signed on aboard sealing schooners as fur seal hunters, providing their own canoes and hunting equipment on voyages that took them as far afield as the Bering Sea and Japan. A few of the Native sealers acquired and operated their own schooners. This industry collapsed in 1911, when an international treaty halted commercial sealing, although Native sealers were allowed to continue for some time (Kirk 1986; Arima and Dewhirst 1990). Many individuals were employed in the commercial fishery, while others left to find work in the hop fields and lumber camps that sprang up around the new centres, particularly in the Fraser Valley and Puget Sound. Fish canneries provided employment for large numbers of Nuu-chah-nulth men and women, often entailing the seasonal movement of families. The closure of canneries all along the coast by the mid-twentieth century meant the loss of a major source of income for many Nuu-chah-nulth. The production of traditional crafts, in demand by non-Native collectors, was another source of revenue for many; Nuu-chah-nulth and Makah women produced large numbers of small baskets for sale, while some men carved model canoes and other wooden artworks.

The Vancouver Island groups, as a result of Canadian Indian policy, are divided into a number of separate political-administrative units known as bands. Amalgamations, continuing into the mid-twentieth century, have reduced the number of such units, but today there are thirteen Nuu-chah-nulth bands, plus the Ditidaht and the Pacheedaht, on Vancouver Island. Each band holds a considerable number of small, scattered reserves, corresponding to the location of villages, fishing stations, and other traditional land uses at the time of the reserve commissioner's visit in the late nineteenth century. In all, the Nuu-chah-nulth hold over 160 widely dispersed reserves, many of which can be reached only by boat or float plane. The total area encompassed in all these reserves is only slightly over 12,000 acres (Arima and Dewhirst 1990:409), about half the size of the single large reservation held by the Makah. Such a scattered pattern of small land holdings inhibits any effective economic development.

On the American side of the border, the five autonomous village communities that comprised the Makah were incorporated as a single political unit.

They were assigned one main reservation, covering much of the Cape Flattery area and encompassing four of the original villages. Ozette, however, lay well to the south of its borders. Although a small reservation was created in 1882 for those who remained at Ozette (Colson 1953:78), it was sold when the last inhabitants moved to Neah Bay early in the twentieth century, not to be officially returned to the Makah until 1970 (Renker and Gunther 1990:429). The large block of land on the main reservation provides the Makah better economic opportunities than exist among their Nuu-chah-nulth counterparts. Logging of forests within the reservation, for example, generates considerable revenue, which can be used to support tribal programs.

The Makah also differ from their Canadian relatives today in that they have a historic treaty with the federal government. In the 1855 treaty signed in Neah Bay, the Makah ceded much of their traditional lands in exchange for their reservation and educational and health benefits (Renker and Gunther 1990:427). The treaty also guaranteed the protection of Makah fishing rights. Recent court decisions have upheld the treaty rights of the Makah and other western Washington groups that signed such agreements, allocating them half the total amount of fish harvested in their territorial waters.

To provide a stronger, more unified, voice for political action, the Nuu-chah-nulth bands formed an alliance in 1958. After several name changes, in 1978 this organization became the Nuu-chah-nulth Tribal Council. The Ditidaht, along with all thirteen Nuu-chah-nulth bands, are members of the tribal council, although the Pacheedaht are not politically affiliated. There are three regional branches, with the main council offices centrally located on the Tseshaht reserve in Port Alberni. In addition to its political and economic functions, the tribal council provides community health, child welfare, and counselling services. It also publishes a newspaper, *Ha-Shilth-Sa*, which provides a common voice for the separate Nuu-chah-nulth and Ditidaht communities.

The plummeting populations that characterized much of the contact period were arrested and began to rebound by the end of the 1930s (Duff 1964:39). Population levels for all groups have increased markedly in recent years. In Canada, changes in the federal Indian Act are responsible for some of this increase, as many additional people have become eligible for membership. Like other small bands, the Toquaht have been able to use the changed rules to enrol more members, almost doubling their population. Total populations remain small, however, as six of the fifteen bands have fewer than 250 members, and the Toquaht remain the smallest of the Nuu-chah-nulth groups.

In total, there are approximately 6,400 Nuu-chah-nulth (in thirteen bands) and 750 Ditidaht (in two bands) in Canada today (Canada, Indian and Northern Affairs 1998), along with 2,200 Makah in the United States (Makah Cultural and Research Center; G. Wessen, pers. comm. 1997). These are the legally enrolled populations, however, and not all reside in their home communities. The isolated nature of many western Vancouver Island reserves, with their limited economic opportunities, has encouraged off-reserve movement to such urban centres as Campbell River, Port Alberni, Victoria, and Vancouver. In fact, only a minority (37.7 percent) of Nuu-chah-nulth and Ditidaht are reserve residents (Canada, Indian and Northern Affairs 1998). The on-reservation rate appears to be much higher for the Makah.

Until recently, government policy in both Canada and the United States promoted the assimilation of indigenous peoples into the general society. Control of education was used as a primary instrument in achieving this goal. Residential schools were established among the Nuu-chah-nulth at Alberni, Ahousaht, and near Tofino. Such schools enforced the norms of the dominant society, punishing children for speaking their own languages or practising Native customs. Generations of Native people were removed from their families and alienated from their cultures. Although these schools were clearly educational failures as well as repressive institutions, they were maintained until several decades ago. Charges of physical, emotional, and sexual abuse have recently emerged, with highly publicized trials of former staff members at the Alberni residential school bringing this disgrace to public attention. A major demand of the Nuu-chah-nulth Tribal Council in its modern negotiations with the Canadian government involves the recognition of residential school abuses and an apology for this misguided program.

Native ceremonial life was also suppressed through the administration of government policy on reserves. Masked dances, public gift-giving, and other elements of the potlatch became offences under the Indian Act in Canada, remaining illegal from 1884 until 1951. Such practices were also actively discouraged by government agents among the Makah (Colson 1953:14). Despite such prohibitions, the Nuu-chah-nulth, Ditidaht, and Makah carried on with their traditions, particularly in the more isolated communities. Hupacasath elder Winifred David recalled what it was like for the Alberni groups at that time.

> I was in the boarding school when the potlatch was forbidden ... But I know we used to go out during the holidays ... There's an island way out in the Pacific, right at the mouth of Barkley Sound, and we would go out there, it's called Village Island. The whole of the two reserves in Port Alberni went down there for the summer. The men would go out fishing and the women would dry fish. No white man ever came there, so they did have their potlatches and feasts ... Nobody could stop them because there was no

policeman around or anything. But when they got back they couldn't do them because there was a policeman around. (Efrat and Langlois 1978b:34)

As the assimilationist policies of the national governments fell from favour and power began to shift to the band or tribal governments, a resurgence of ceremonial life took place. Potlatches and dancing are again prominent features of Nuu-chah-nulth and Ditidaht life, while Makah Days brings together a number of Canadian and American Native groups for an annual festival celebrating Makah culture in Neah Bay (Figures 57 to 60). Traditional dances and ceremonies frequently follow such church events as weddings, and memorial potlatches are still held to honour the memories of deceased relatives. These are the occasions for speeches, the performance of inherited dances, and the transference of hereditary names to children and grandchildren. Guests at these events must be fed, with the menu often featuring traditional seafood delicacies as well as more ordinary fare. Hosts present gifts to their high-status guests, while everyone present shares in a general distribution of goods, typically consisting of such domestic items as dishes and towels.

In the absence of historic treaties, one of the most pressing modern concerns of the Nuu-chah-nulth and the Ditidaht is to reach a negotiated settlement with the governments of Canada and British Columbia. In common with many other First Nations in British Columbia, negotiations are proceeding through the British Columbia Treaty Commission. Two agreements are being sought, as the Ditidaht and Pacheedaht bands have joined forces to

57 Makah children dancing at Makah Days celebrations, 1997. *Photo by author*

58 (above) Makah Days celebrations, 1977, showing women wearing modern replicas of hats excavated from the waterlogged house deposits at Ozette. *Photo by author*

59 (left) Makah woman wearing large headdress in Makah Days parade, 1982. *Photo by author*

negotiate separately from the Nuu-chah-nulth Tribal Council. Ongoing discussions involve such vital issues as title to lands and resources, compensation for past loss of resources, and the powers of Aboriginal governments. Other concerns involve protection of traditional heritage sites and the repatriation of heritage objects from distant museums to Nuu-chah-nulth and Ditidaht communities. As treaty negotiations are complex and multifaceted, considerable time will be required before final agreements can be reached.

60 Nuu-chah-nulth men play lahal, the "bones game," on the beach at Neah Bay during Makah Days, 1975. The late Ahousaht chief Peter Webster holds the bones, while Aylmer Thompson (Ditidaht) drums. Chief Edward Shewish of the Tseshaht is at the right. *Photo by author*

The unresolved nature of Aboriginal title in Nuu-chah-nulth territory has led to numerous land-use disputes. The establishment of Pacific Rim National Park, as well as numerous small parks in Nuu-chah-nulth traditional territory, has been contentious in treaty negotiations, complicating discussions of available land for eventual settlements. Aquaculture has also been a concern for many Nuu-chah-nulth, who believe that commercial fish farms pollute the water and threaten the wild salmon stocks. The most acrimonious debates, however, have involved logging, particularly the large clearcut operations that have denuded the mountainsides surrounding the Nuu-chah-nulth communities. Plans to log Meares Island in Clayoquot Sound in 1984 led to protests by Nuu-chah-nulth and non-Native environmentalists, and to the Tla-o-qui-aht and Ahousaht declaring the island a "tribal park." The Nuu-chah-nulth Tribal Council launched court action, obtaining a 1985 injunction that stops the logging until the Nuu-chah-nulth claim is settled. Continued logging elsewhere in Clayoquot Sound, however, led to further non-Native protests and blockades of logging roads, resulting in a large number of arrests in the summer of 1993. The Nuu-chah-nulth did not support these actions, as they were not totally opposed to logging in the area; instead, they sought more sustainable logging practices, a greater share in management, and a share in the economic benefits of logging. At the end of 1993 an agreement was signed between the government of British Columbia and the six central Nuu-chah-nulth nations, from the Hesquiaht to the Toquaht, that met these concerns and effectively brought a halt to the protests. This agreement was seen as an interim step towards the final resolution of Nuu-chah-nulth claims in this area.

Native groups are also taking control of their cultural heritage, including archaeological sites and resources. Several Nuu-chah-nulth nations have sponsored archaeological research in their traditional territories, establishing protocols for cooperative research. In several cases, the research was specifically directed to gather data on Aboriginal land use for treaty negotiations. With the opening of the Makah Cultural and Research Center in Neah Bay in 1979, the Makah have assumed control of the management and public interpretation of their heritage. This institution, which houses the extensive archaeological collections from the Ozette and Hoko River sites, exhibits the history and complexity of Makah culture as revealed by

61   A Nuu-chah-nulth whaling canoe (*Rainbow off the Beach*), carved by Hesquiaht artist Tim Paul (at rear of canoe) in 1997, is taken for a test run on Sproat Lake, near Port Alberni. *Photo by Bob Soderlund*

archaeological excavation and as corroborated by Makah oral history. It also acts as a cultural centre, developing community programs in Makah language and culture (Renker and Arnold 1988).

As part of reasserting control over their cultural heritage, the Makah have recently announced that they intend to resume the whale hunt that was so important in their ancestors' lives. Grey whale populations have rebounded after a successful conservation period, leading the Makah to maintain that a limited harvest would pose no threat to the species' survival. Accordingly, they began pressing for permission to resume hunting whales for food and ceremonial use. Although considerable opposition still exists, the International Whaling Commission recently ruled that the Makah could take up to five whales a year. The Nuu-chah-nulth are following such developments closely, making their own plans to resume whaling on a limited basis.

The skills to create large, graceful dugout canoes, essential to such traditional pursuits as whaling, have not been lost. A number of such sea-going craft, elegantly carved and beautifully painted, have appeared in Nuu-chah-nulth communities in recent years (Figure 61). Such canoes have become a vital part of a modern assertion of cultural identity for indigenous groups along the coasts of British Columbia and Washington. In coordinated events, young people from many coastal First Nations, including the Nuu-chah-nulth and the Makah, have paddled their large canoes to a common destination, being welcomed and feasted in Native communities along the way. The next planned "Canoe Quest" will feature the Nuu-chah-nulth as hosts, as canoeloads of participants paddle along the west coast to the Ahousaht village.

Revitalization of indigenous languages, which were severely affected by the years of official suppression, is a major concern for all groups along the west coast. A Canadian government study in the early 1980s categorized the Nuu-chah-nulth language as "moderately endangered," with 1,000 to 2,000 speakers, while Ditidaht was considered "extremely endangered," with perhaps only sixty speakers (Foster 1982). In the Aboriginal Peoples Survey that followed the 1991 federal census, approximately 1,000 people indicated that they could speak the "Nootka" (presumably including Ditidaht) language. This should be considered a minimum number of Native-language speakers among the Nuu-chah-nulth and Ditidaht today. The Makah language has also been reduced to only a few fluent speakers.

In an ironic reversal of the role the school system played in suppressing Native languages only a few decades ago, Native-run school programs are now helping to maintain and revitalize the languages. A number of Nuu-chah-nulth schools have integrated such language instruction as an important component of children's education. In Neah Bay, an ambitious educational effort is the Makah Language Program, operated by the Makah Cultural and Research Center, which conducts language training for on-reservation school children plus night classes for adults (Renker and Arnold 1988). Using a team-teaching approach involving an elder and a trained Makah teacher, this program has successfully increased the level of Makah language proficiency among the Makah.

Fishing and logging continue to be economic mainstays of many reserve communities, but increasingly tourism is taking a dominant role. The Nuu-chah-nulth Economic Development Corporation provides assistance to Aboriginal entrepreneurs, many of whom are developing tourist-related enterprises. The Tla-o-qui-aht operate a modern hotel near Tofino, while the Mowachaht/Muchalaht have constructed cabins and campgrounds for visitors to Yuquot. Backpackers are encouraged to hike the wilderness trail recently opened by the Ahousaht near their community. Heritage and eco-tourism are particularly attractive options, allowing the Nuu-chah-nulth to share their culture and environment with interested visitors. Nuu-chah-nulth individuals operate water taxis, whale watching expeditions, and fishing charters, to name just a few such enterprises. Tourists and sport fishers also swell the population of Neah Bay each summer.

Nuu-chah-nulth art also plays a significant economic, as well as cultural, role. A major gallery of Nuu-chah-nulth art in the tourist centre of Tofino is owned and operated by members of the Tla-o-qui-aht band, and many other galleries, some Native-run, prominently feature such work. Many individual artists have achieved recognition and some measure of financial reward for their works. Artists such as Joe David (Tla-o-qui-aht), Art Thompson (Ditidaht), Ron Hamilton (Hupacasath), Tim Paul (Hesquiaht), and Pat Amos (Mowachaht) have made the Aboriginal art from this region a widely recognized and acclaimed variant of Northwest Coast Native art. All have been innovators in their artistic production, experimenting with new media and taking the art in new directions, while maintaining a recognizable West Coast style. These artists are also very much involved in the culture of their people, creating masks and other artworks for ceremonial and social use in their villages as well as for sale to outsiders.

Despite the assimilationist policies of governments in both countries and the devastating impact of such institutions as the residential schools, the Nuu-chah-nulth, Ditidaht, and Makah have survived as distinct cultures. Essential elements of their traditional past are today being maintained or revived. Elders safeguard their ancient heritage, transmitting this knowledge to new generations. The Nuu-chah-nulth Tribal Council and the Makah Tribal Council provide the political strength to ensure control of their heritage, including the right to teach their languages and traditions to their children. Their history, as revealed by archaeological research, is lengthy, spanning at least the last four millennia. In their oral traditions, this history ties them to the ancestral lands they have occupied since transformers such as Kwatyat shaped their world.

References

Abbott, Donald N.
   1972   The Utility of the Concept of Phase in the Archaeology of the Southern Northwest Coast. *Syesis* 5:267-278.
Acheson, Steven R.
   1995   In the Wake of the Iron People: A Case for Changing Settlement Strategies Among the Kunghit Haida. *Journal of the Royal Anthropological Institute* 1(2):273-299.
Ackerman, Robert E.
   1992 Earliest Stone Industries on the North Pacific Coast of North America. *Arctic Anthropology* 29(2):18-27.
Ames, Kenneth M.
   1981   The Evolution of Social Ranking on the Northwest Coast of North America. *American Antiquity* 46(4):789-805.
   1994   The Northwest Coast: Complex Hunter-Gatherers, Ecology, and Social Evolution. *Annual Review of Anthropology* 23:209-229.
Andrews, Rebecca W.
   1989 Hiaqua: Use of Dentalium Shells by the Native Peoples of the Pacific Northwest. Unpublished MA thesis, Department of Anthropology, University of Washington, Seattle.
Apland, Brian
   1982 Chipped Stone Assemblages from the Beach Sites of the Central Coast. In *Papers on Central Coast Archaeology*, edited by Philip M. Hobler, pp. 13-63. Publication No. 10, Department of Archaeology, Simon Fraser University, Burnaby.
Arcas Associates
   1984 Meares Island Aboriginal Tree Utilization Study. Report on file, Archaeology Branch, Victoria.
   1986 Native Tree Use on Meares Island, BC. Unpublished report in four volumes prepared for the Ahousaht and Clayoquot Indian Bands, Ahousat and Tofino (on file, Archaeology Branch, Victoria).
   1988 Native Settlements on Meares Island, B.C. Report on file, Archaeology Branch, Victoria.
Arcas Consulting Archeologists Ltd.
   1991 Archaeological Investigations at Little Beach Site, Ucluelet, B.C. Report on file, Archaeology Branch, Victoria.
   1993 Archaeological Impact Assessment of Proposed Cheesish Campground: Hanna Channel, Nootka Sound, Vancouver Island, BC. Unpublished report prepared for British Columbia Ministry of Forests, Campbell River, and Mowachaht Indian Band, Gold River. Copy on file, Archaeology Branch, Victoria.
   1994 Archaeological Impact Assessment, Block H-1000, Allman Lagoon, Nootka Sound, Vancouver Island, BC. Unpublished report prepared for International Forest Products Limited, Tofino. Copy on file, Archaeology Branch, Victoria.

1998　Archaeological Investigations in Ucluelet Traditional Territory, 1994-1997: Final Report. Report prepared for the Ucluelet Band, Ucluelet, B.C. (copy filed with the Archaeology Branch, Victoria).

Arcas Consulting Archaeologists Ltd. and Archeotech Associates

1994 Cultural Heritage Resource Overview, Clayoquot Sound Land Use Decision Area. Report prepared for Archaeology Branch and Heritage Conservation Branch, Victoria.

Arima, Eugene Y.

1983 *The West Coast (Nootka) People*. BC Provincial Museum, Victoria.

1988　Notes on Nootkan Sea Mammal Hunting. *Arctic Anthropology* 25(1):16-27.

Arima, Eugene, and John Dewhirst

1990 Nootkans of Vancouver Island. In *Handbook of North American Indians*. Vol. 7, *Northwest Coast*, edited by Wayne Suttles, pp. 391-411. Smithsonian Institution, Washington, DC.

Arima, E.Y., D. St. Claire, L. Clamhouse, J. Edgar, C. Jones, and J. Thomas

1991 *Between Ports Alberni and Renfrew: Notes on West Coast Peoples*. Canadian Ethnology Service, Mercury Series Paper 121, Canadian Museum of Civilization, Ottawa.

Ayers, Jennifer

1980　Computer Summary of the Hoko River Artifacts. In *Hoko River: A 2500 Year Old Fishing Camp on the Northwest Coast of North America*, edited by Dale R. Croes and Eric Blinman, pp. 125-151. Reports of Investigations No. 58, Laboratory of Anthropology, Washington State University, Pullman.

Banfield, A.W.F.

1974 *The Mammals of Canada*. University of Toronto Press, Toronto.

Banfield, William E.

1858　Vancouver Island: Its Topography, Characteristics, etc. *Victoria Gazette*, Aug.-Sept. 1858. Victoria.

Barton, Andrew John

1994 Fishing for Ivory Worms: A Review of Ethnographic and Historically Recorded *Dentalium* Source Locations. Unpublished MA thesis, Department of Archaeology, Simon Fraser University, Burnaby.

Bates, Ann M.

1987 Affiliation and Differentiation: Intertribal Interactions Among the Makah and Ditidaht Indians. Unpublished PhD dissertation, Department of Anthropology, Indiana University.

Beaglehole, J.C. (editor)

1967 *The Journals of Captain James Cook on His Voyages of Discovery* (4 vols.). Cambridge University Press, Cambridge.

Beals, Herbert K. (translator and editor)

1989 *Juan Pérez on the Northwest Coast: Six Documents of His Expedition in 1774*. Oregon Historical Society Press, Portland.

Bernick, Kathryn

1987 The Potential of Basketry for Reconstructing Cultural Diversity on the Northwest Coast. In *Ethnicity and Culture*, edited by R. Auger, M.F. Glass, S. MacEachern, and P.H. McCartney, pp. 251-257. Proceedings of the 18th Annual Chacmool Conference, Archaeological Association, University of Calgary.

Bishop, Charles

1967 *The Journal and Letters of Captain Charles Bishop on the North-West Coast of America, in the Pacific and in New South Wales, 1794-1799* (edited by Michael Roe). Hakluyt Society, Cambridge University Press.

Blenkinsop, George

1874 Report to J.W. Powell, Indian Commissioner. Manuscript, National Archives of Canada, RG10, v. 3614, f. 4105, Ottawa.

Blinman, Eric

1980 Stratigraphy and Depositional Environment. In *Hoko River: A 2500 Year Old Fishing Camp on the Northwest Coast of North America*, edited by Dale R. Croes and Eric Blinman, pp. 64-89. Reports of Investigations No. 58, Laboratory of Anthropology, Washington State University, Pullman.

Boas, Franz
1891 The Nootka. In Second General Report on the Indians of British Columbia. *Report of the Sixtieth Meeting of the British Association for the Advancement of Science, 1890*, pp. 582-715. London.
1905 The Jesup North Pacific Expedition. *Proceedings of the International Congress of Americanists*, 13th Session, pp. 91-100.
1907 Clubs Made of Bone of Whale. In *Archaeology of the Gulf of Georgia and Puget Sound*, by Harlan I. Smith, pp. 403-412. Jesup North Pacific Expedition, *Memoirs of the American Museum of Natural History* 4(6):301-441. New York.
1916 Myths of the Nootka. In *Tsimshian Mythology*, pp. 888-935. Thirty-first Annual Report of the U.S. Bureau of Ethnology, Smithsonian Institution, Washington. (Johnson Reprint, New York, 1970).
1927 *Primitive Art*. Harvard University Press, Cambridge. (Dover Publications Reprint, New York, 1955).
1930 A Nootka Ceremonial House. In *The Religion of the Kwakiutl Indians*, pp. 261-269. Contributions to Anthropology 10, Columbia University, New York (AMS Press reprint, New York, 1969).
1974 Legends of the Nutka [Nootka]. In Indian Legends of the North Pacific Coast of America, pp. 159-208. Unpublished manuscript, translated by Dietrich Bertz for the British Columbia Indian Language Project, Victoria. (Originally published as *Indianische Sagen von der Nord-Pacifischen Küste Amerikas*, Berlin, 1895.)

Bobrowsky, P.T., and J.J. Clague
1991 Neotectonic Investigations on Western Vancouver Island, British Columbia (92F/4). In *Geological Fieldwork 1990*, pp. 307-313. British Columbia Ministry of Energy, Mines and Petroleum Resources, Paper 1991-1, Victoria.
1992 Neotectonic Investigations on Vancouver Island (92B,F). In *Geological Fieldwork 1991*, pp. 325-329. British Columbia Ministry of Energy, Mines and Petroleum Resources, Paper 1992-1, Victoria.

Borden, Charles E.
1951 Facts and Problems of Northwest Coast Prehistory. *Anthropology in British Columbia* 2:35-52.
1975 *Origins and Development of Early Northwest Coast Culture to About 3000 BC*. Archaeological Survey of Canada Paper No. 45, National Museum of Man Mercury Series, National Museums of Canada, Ottawa.
1979 Peopling and Early Cultures of the Pacific Northwest. *Science* 203:963-971.

Bouchard, Randy
1971 A Proposed Practical Orthography for Nootka-Nitinat. Unpublished manuscript, British Columbia Indian Language Project, Victoria.

Bouchard, Randy, and Dorothy Kennedy
1990 Clayoquot Sound Indian Land Use. Report prepared for MacMillan Bloedel Limited, Fletcher Challenge Canada, and the British Columbia Ministry of Forests.
1991 Preliminary Notes on Ditidaht Land Use. Report prepared for Millennia Research, Ditidaht Indian Band, and British Columbia Heritage Trust. Copy on file, Archaeology Branch, Victoria.

Boyd, Robert T.
1990 Demographic History, 1774-1874. In *Handbook of North American Indians*. Vol. 7, *Northwest Coast*, edited by Wayne Suttles, pp. 135-148. Smithsonian Institution, Washington.
1994 Smallpox in the Pacific Northwest: The First Epidemics. *BC Studies* 101:5-40.

Brabant, Augustin Joseph
1977 *Mission to Nootka: 1874-1900*, edited by Charles Lillard. Gray's Publishing, Sidney, BC.

Brathwaite, Jean, and W.J. Folan
1972 The Taking of the Ship *Boston*: An Ethnohistoric Study of Nootkan-European Conflict. *Syesis* 5:259-266.

British Columbia
   1914   Royal Commission on Indian Affairs for the Province of BC, West Coast Agency –
      Evidence from Hearings. National Archives of Canada/British Columbia Archives and
      Records Service, RG 10, v. 11025, f. AH13.
   1916 *Report of the Royal Commission on Indian Affairs for the Province of British Columbia*.
      Acme Press, Victoria.
British Columbia Ministry of Crown Lands
   1894 Plan of the To-quart Indian Reserves, Clayoquot District, British Columbia. Manu-
      script, Maps and Plans Vault, Surveyor General Branch, BC Ministry of Crown Lands,
      Victoria.
Brolly, Richard P.
   1992 Little Beach Site, Ucluelet, BC: 1991 Archaeological Investigations. *The Midden*
      24(1):2-4.
Burley, David V.
   1980   *Marpole: Anthropological Reconstructions of a Prehistoric Northwest Coast Culture
      Type*. Publication No. 8, Department of Archaeology, Simon Fraser University,
      Burnaby.
   1981   Inter-Regional Exchange in the Gulf of Georgia During the Marpole Phase, 490 BC
      to AD 500. In *Networks of the Past: Regional Interaction in Archaeology*, edited by Peter D.
      Francis, F.J. Kense, and P.G. Duke, pp. 397-410. Proceedings of the 12th Annual
      Chacmool Conference, Archaeological Association, University of Calgary.
Burley, David V., and Owen B. Beattie
   1987 Coast Salish Origins: Ethnicity and Time Depth in Northwest Coast Prehistory. In
      Ethnicity and Culture, edited by R. Auger, M.F. Glass, S. MacEachern, and P.H. McCartney,
      pp. 199-207. Proceedings of the 18th Annual Chacmool Conference, Archaeological
      Association, University of Calgary.
Burley, David V., and Christopher Knusel
   1989 Burial Patterns and Archaeological Interpretations: Problems in the Recognition of
      Ranked Society in the Coast Salish Region. Paper presented at the Circum-Pacific Pre-
      history Conference, Seattle.
Buxton, Judith M.
   1969 Earthworks of Southwestern British Columbia. Unpublished MA thesis, Depart-
      ment of Archaeology, University of Calgary.
Calvert, Sheila Gay
   1980 A Cultural Analysis of Faunal Remains from Three Archaeological Sites in Hesquiat
      Harbour, BC. Unpublished PhD dissertation, Department of Anthropology and Soci-
      ology, University of British Columbia.
Calvert, Gay, and Susan Crockford
   1982 Analysis of Faunal Remains from the Shoemaker Bay Site (DhSe 2). Appendix IV in
      *Alberni Prehistory: Archaeological and Ethnographic Investigations on Western Vancouver
      Island*, edited by A.D. McMillan and D.E. St. Claire, pp. 174-219. Theytus Books,
      Penticton.
Canada, Atmospheric Environment Service
   1982 *Canadian Climate Normals, Temperature and Precipitation, 1951-1980*. Environment
      Canada, Ottawa.
Canada, Indian and Northern Affairs
   1998 *Indian Register Population by Sex and Residence 1997*. Department of Indian Affairs
      and Northern Development, Ottawa.
Cannon, Aubrey
   1991 *The Economic Prehistory of Namu*. Publication No. 19, Department of Archaeology,
      Simon Fraser University, Burnaby.
Carlson, Catherine
   1979 The Early Component at Bear Cove. *Canadian Journal of Archaeology* 3:177-194.
Carlson, Roy L.
   1979 The Early Period on the Central Coast of British Columbia. *Canadian Journal of
      Archaeology* 3:211-228.

1983a Prehistory of the Northwest Coast. In *Indian Art Traditions of the Northwest Coast*, edited by R.L. Carlson, pp. 13-32. Archaeology Press, Simon Fraser University, Burnaby, BC.

1983b The Far West. In *Early Man in the New World*, edited by Richard Shutler, Jr., pp. 73-96. Sage Publications, Beverly Hills.

1990 Cultural Antecedents. In *Handbook of North American Indians*. Vol. 7, *Northwest Coast*, edited by Wayne Suttles, pp. 60-69. Smithsonian Institution, Washington.

1991 The Northwest Coast Before AD 1600. In *Proceedings of the Great Ocean Conferences*, vol. 1, pp. 109-136. Oregon Historical Society Press, Portland.

1993 Content and Chronology of Northwest Coast (North America) Rock Art. In *Time and Space: Dating and Spatial Considerations in Rock Art Research*, edited by Jack Steinbring and Alan Watchman, pp. 7-12. Occasional AURA Paper No. 8, Australian Rock Art Research Association, Melbourne.

1994 Trade and Exchange in Prehistoric British Columbia. In *Prehistoric Exchange Systems in North America*, edited by Timothy G. Baugh and Jonathon E. Ericson, pp. 307-361. Plenum Press, New York.

1996a Prologue to British Columbia Prehistory. In *Early Human Occupation in British Columbia*, edited by Roy L. Carlson and Luke Della Bona, pp. 3-10. UBC Press, Vancouver.

1996b Early Namu. In *Early Human Occupation in British Columbia*, edited by Roy L. Carlson and Luke Della Bona, pp. 83-102. UBC Press, Vancouver.

Carlson, Roy L., and Philip M. Hobler

1976 Archaeological Survey of Seymour Inlet, Quatsino Sound, and Adjacent Localities. In *Current Research Reports*, edited by Roy L. Carlson, pp. 115-141. Publication No. 3, Department of Archaeology, Simon Fraser University, Burnaby.

1993 The Pender Canal Excavations and the Development of Coast Salish Culture. *BC Studies* (Special Issue, *Changing Times: British Columbia Archaeology in the 1980s*, edited by Knut Fladmark) 99:25-52.

Carmichael, Alfred

1922 *Indian Legends of Vancouver Island*. Musson, Toronto.

Carter, Lionel

1973 Surficial Sediments of Barkley Sound and the Adjacent Continental Shelf, West Coast Vancouver Island. *Canadian Journal of Earth Sciences* 10:441-459.

Cavanagh, Deborah May

1983 Northwest Coast Whaling: A New Perspective. Unpublished MA thesis, Department of Anthropology and Sociology, University of British Columbia.

Chapman, Margaret Winnifred

1982 Archaeological Investigations at the O'Connor Site, Port Hardy. In *Papers on Central Coast Archaeology*, edited by Philip M. Hobler, pp. 65-132. Publication No. 10, Department of Archaeology, Simon Fraser University, Burnaby

Chard, Chester S.

1960 Northwest Coast-Northeast Asiatic Similarities: A New Hypothesis. In *Men and Cultures: Selected Papers of the Fifth International Congress of Anthropological and Ethnological Sciences*, edited by Anthony F.C. Wallace, pp. 235-240. University of Philadelphia Press, Philadelphia.

Clague, J.J., J.E. Armstrong, and W.H. Mathews

1980 Advance of the Late Wisconsin Cordilleran Ice Sheet in Southern British Columbia Since 22,000 Yr B.P. *Quaternary Research* 13:322-326.

Clague, John J., and Peter T. Bobrowsky

1990 Holocene Sea Level Change and Crustal Deformation, Southwestern British Columbia. In Current Research, Part E, Geological Survey of Canada, Paper 90-1E, pp. 245-250.

1994a Tsunami Deposits Beneath Tidal Marshes on Vancouver Island, British Columbia. *Geological Society of America Bulletin* 106(10):1,293-1,303.

1994b Evidence for a Large Earthquake and Tsunami 100-400 Years Ago on Western Vancouver Island, British Columbia. *Quaternary Research* 41:176-184.

Clague, John J., Peter T. Bobrowsky, and T.S. Hamilton
  1994   A Sand Sheet Deposited by the 1964 Alaska Tsunami at Port Alberni, British Columbia. *Estuarine, Coastal and Shelf Science* 38:413-421.
Clague, John, John R. Harper, R.J. Hebda, and D.E. Howes
  1982 Late Quaternary Sea Levels and Crustal Movements, Coastal British Columbia. *Canadian Journal of Earth Sciences* 19:597-618.
Clamhouse, Louis, Joshua Edgar, Charles Jones, John Thomas, and E.Y. Arima
  1991 From Barkley Sound Southeast. In *Between Ports Alberni and Renfrew: Notes on West Coast Peoples*, pp. 203-315. Canadian Ethnology Service, Mercury Series Paper 121, Canadian Museum of Civilization, Ottawa.
Clarke, Louise R., and Arthur H. Clarke
  1975 Mollusk Utilization by Nootka Indians, 2300 BC to AD 1966. *Bulletin of the American Malacological Union* 1974:15-16.
  1980   Zooarchaeological Analysis of Mollusc Remains from Yuquot, British Columbia. In *The Yuquot Project*, vol. 2, edited by W.J. Folan and J. Dewhirst, pp. 37-57. History and Archaeology 43, Parks Canada, National Historic Parks and Sites Branch, Ottawa.
Clutesi, George
  1969   *Potlatch*. Gray's Publishing, Sidney, BC.
Coates, Clinton D., and Morley Eldridge
  1992 Bamfield Highways Aguilar Point Road Allowance Impact Assessment: 7O:ts'o:7a, Aguilar Inn Site, DfSg-2. Report on file, Archaeology Branch, Victoria.
Colnett, James
  1940 *The Journal of Captain James Colnett Aboard the Argonaut From April 26, 1789 to Nov. 3, 1791* (edited by F.W. Howay). The Champlain Society, Toronto.
Colson, Elizabeth
  1953   *The Makah Indians: A Study of an Indian Tribe in Modern American Society*. University of Minnesota Press, Minneapolis.
Cook, Captain James
  1784 *A Voyage to the Pacific Ocean: Undertaken by the Command of His Majesty, For Making Discoveries in the Northern Hemisphere; Performed Under the Direction of Captain Cook, Clerke, and Gore, in His Majesty's Ships the Resolution and Discovery, in the Years 1776, 1777, 1778 and 1780*. W. and A. Strahan, London.
Cook, Warren L.
  1973 *Flood Tide of Empire: Spain and the Pacific Northwest, 1543-1819*. Yale University Press, New Haven, CT.
Coupland, Gary
  1989 Warfare and Social Complexity on the Northwest Coast. In *Cultures in Conflict: Current Archaeological Perspectives*, edited by Diana Claire Tkaczuk and Brian C. Vivian, pp. 205-214. Proceedings of the 12th Annual Chacmool Conference, Archaeological Association, University of Calgary.
Cowan, Ian McTaggart, and Charles J. Guiguet
  1965 *The Mammals of British Columbia* (3rd edition). Handbook No. 11, British Columbia Provincial Museum, Victoria.
Crockford, Susan
  1994 New Archaeological and Ethnographic Evidence of an Extinct Fishery for Giant Bluefin Tuna (*Thunnus thynnus orientalis*) on the Pacific Northwest Coast of North America. In *Fish Exploitation in the Past: Proceedings of the 7th Meeting of the ICAZ Fish Remains Working Group*, edited by W. Van Neer, pp. 163-168. Annales du Musée Royal de l'Afrique Centrale, Sciences Zoologiques, Tervuren.
  1997 Archaeological Evidence of Large Northern Bluefin Tuna, *Thunnus thynnus*, in Coastal Waters of British Columbia and Northern Washington. *Fishery Bulletin* 95:11-24.
Croes, Dale R.
  1976 An Early "Wet" Site at the Mouth of the Hoko River, the Hoko River Site (45CA213). In *The Excavation of Water-Saturated Archaeological Sites (Wet Sites) on the Northwest Coast of North America*, edited by Dale R. Croes, pp. 201-232. National Museum of Man Mercury Series, Archaeological Survey of Canada Paper No. 50, Ottawa.

1977   Basketry from the Ozette Village Archaeological Site: A Technological, Functional, and Comparative Study. Unpublished PhD dissertation, Department of Anthropology, Washington State University, Pullman.

1980a *Cordage from the Ozette Village Archaeological Site: A Technological, Functional, and Comparative Study.* Project Reports No. 9, Laboratory of Archaeology and History, Washington State University, Pullman.

1980b Basketry Artifacts. In *Hoko River: A 2500 Year Old Fishing Camp on the Northwest Coast of North America*, edited by Dale R. Croes and Eric Blinman, pp. 188-222. Reports of Investigations No. 58, Laboratory of Anthropology, Washington State University, Pullman.

1980c Cordage. In *Hoko River: A 2500 Year Old Fishing Camp on the Northwest Coast of North America*, edited by Dale R. Croes and Eric Blinman, pp. 236-257. Reports of Investigations No. 58, Laboratory of Anthropology, Washington State University, Pullman.

1987 Locarno Beach at Hoko River, Olympic Peninsula, Washington: Wakashan, Salishan, Chimakuan or Who? In *Ethnicity and Culture*, edited by R. Auger, M.F. Glass, S. MacEachern, and P.H. McCartney, pp. 259-283. Proceedings of the 18th Annual Chacmool Conference, Archaeological Association, University of Calgary.

1988   The Significance of the 3000 BP Hoko River Waterlogged Fishing Camp in Our Overall Understanding of Southern Northwest Coast Cultural Evolution. In *Wet Site Archaeology*, edited by Barbara A. Purdy, pp. 131-152. Telford Press, Caldwell, NJ.

1989 Prehistoric Ethnicity on the Northwest Coast of North America: An Evaluation of Style in Basketry and Lithics. *Journal of Anthropological Archaeology* 8: 101-130.

1992a An Evolving Revolution in Wet Site Research on the Northwest Coast of North America. In *The Wetland Revolution in Prehistory*, edited by Bryony Coles, pp. 99-111. WARP (Wetland Archaeology Research Project) Occasional Paper 6, Department of History and Archaeology, University of Exeter, UK.

1992b Exploring Prehistoric Subsistence Change on the Northwest Coast. In *Long-Term Subsistence Change in Prehistoric North America*, edited by Dale R. Croes, Rebecca A. Hawkins, and Barry L. Isaac, pp. 337-366. *Research in Economic Anthropology*, Supplement 6. JAI Press, Greenwich, CT.

1993 Prehistoric Hoko River Cordage: A New Line on Northwest Coast Prehistory. In *A Spirit of Enquiry: Essays for Ted Wright*, edited by John Coles, Valerie Fenwick, and Gillian Hutchinson, pp. 32-38. Wetlands Archaeology Research Project (WARP) Occasional Paper No. 7, Department of History and Archaeology, University of Exeter, Exeter, England.

1995 *The Hoko River Archaeological Site Complex: The Wet/Dry Site (45CA213), 3000-1700 BP.* Washington State University Press, Pullman.

Croes, Dale R., and Eric Blinman (editors.)
1980 *Hoko River: A 2500 Year Old Fishing Camp on the Northwest Coast of North America.* Reports of Investigations No. 58, Laboratory of Anthropology, Washington State University, Pullman.

Croes, Dale R., and Jonathan O. Davis
1977 Computer Mapping of Idiosyncratic Basketry Manufacture Techniques in the Prehistoric Ozette House, Cape Alava, Washington. In *The Individual in Prehistory: Studies of Variability in Style in Prehistoric Technologies*, edited by James N. Hill and Joel Gunn, pp. 155-165. Academic Press, New York.

Croes, Dale R., and Steven Hackenberger
1988 Hoko River Archaeological Complex: Modeling Prehistoric Northwest Coast Economic Evolution. In *Prehistoric Economies of the Pacific Northwest Coast*, edited by Barry L. Isaac, pp. 19-85. *Research in Economic Anthropology*, Supplement 3. JAI Press, Greenwich, CT.

Curtis, Edward S.
1913 *The North American Indian.* Vol. 9, *Salishan Tribes of the Coast; The Chimakum and the Quilliute; The Willapa.* Johnson Reprint Corporation, New York (1970).

1916   *The North American Indian.* Vol. 11, *Nootka and Haida.* Johnson Reprint Corporation, New York (1970).

Cybulski, Jerome S.

1978   *An Earlier Population of Hesquiat Harbour, British Columbia.* Cultural Recovery Papers No. 1, British Columbia Provincial Museum, Victoria.

1980 Osteology of the Human Remains from Yuquot, British Columbia. In *The Yuquot Project,* vol. 2, edited by W.J. Folan and J. Dewhirst, pp. 175-192. History and Archaeology 43, Parks Canada, National Historic Parks and Sites Branch, Ottawa.

1990   Human Biology. In *Handbook of North American Indians.* Vol. 7, *Northwest Coast,* edited by Wayne Suttles, pp. 52-59. Smithsonian Institution, Washington.

1994 Culture Change, Demographic History, and Health and Disease on the Northwest Coast. In *In the Wake of Contact: Biological Responses to Conquest,* edited by G.R. Miller and C.S. Larsen, pp. 75-85. Wiley-Liss, New York.

Dahlstrom, Bruce

1997 Test Excavations at DdSc 12 on the Juan de Fuca Marine Trail. *The Midden* 29(2):4-6.

Dahlstrom, Bruce, and Ian R. Wilson

1996   Mitigative Archaeological Excavations: DdSc 12, Juan de Fuca Marine Trail, Port Renfrew, British Columbia. Report on file, Archaeology Branch, Victoria.

Dahm, Inge R.

1994 Cultural and Social Dimensions of the Prehistoric Gulf Islands Soapstone Industry. Unpublished MA thesis, Department of Archaeology, Simon Fraser University, Burnaby.

Daugherty, Richard D.

1988 Problems and Responsibilities in the Excavation of Wet Sites. In *Wet Site Archaeology,* edited by Barbara A. Purdy, pp. 15-29. Telford Press, Caldwell, NJ.

Daugherty, Richard, and Janet Friedman

1983   An Introduction to Ozette Art. In *Indian Art Traditions of the Northwest Coast,* edited by R.L. Carlson, pp. 183-195. Archaeology Press, Simon Fraser University, Burnaby, BC.

Daugherty, Richard D., and Roald Fryxell

n.d. Archaeological, Geochronological, and Ecological Investigations of the Ozette Village Site Complex on the Northwest Coast of Washington: II. Research proposal submitted to the National Science Foundation. Manuscript in possession of the author.

Davis, Stanley D.

1990 Prehistory of Southeastern Alaska. In *Handbook of North American Indians.* Vol. 7, *Northwest Coast,* edited by Wayne Suttles, pp. 197-202. Smithsonian Institution, Washington.

Densmore, Frances

1939 *Nootka and Quileute Music.* Bureau of American Ethnology Bulletin 124, Smithsonian Institution, Washington.

DePuydt, Raymond T.

1994 Cultural Implications of the Avifaunal Remains Recovered from the Ozette Site. In *Ozette Archaeological Project Research Reports.* Vol. 2, *Fauna,* edited by Stephan R. Samuels, pp. 197-263. Reports of Investigations 66. Department of Anthropology, Washington State University, Pullman, and National Park Service, Seattle.

Dewhirst, John

1969 Yuquot, British Columbia: the Prehistory and History of a Nootkan Village. Part 2, Prehistory. *Northwest Anthropological Research Notes* 3(2):232-239.

1977 The Origins of Nootkan Whaling: A Definition of Northern and Central Nootkan Ecological Orientation for the Past Four Millenia [sic]. Unpublished paper presented at the 10th Annual Meeting of the Canadian Archaeological Association, Ottawa.

1978 Nootka Sound: A 4,000 Year Perspective. In *Nu.tka.: The History and Survival of Nootkan Culture,* edited by Barbara S. Efrat and W.J. Langlois, pp. 1-29. *Sound Heritage,* vol. 7, no. 2. Provincial Archives of British Columbia, Victoria.

1979 An Archaeological Pattern of Faunal Resource Utilization at Yuquot, a Nootkan Outside Village: 1000 BC-AD 1966. Unpublished paper presented at the 44th Annual Meeting of the Society for American Archaeology, Vancouver.

1980 *The Indigenous Archaeology of Yuquot, a Nootkan Outside Village*. National Historic Parks and Sites Branch, Parks Canada, Ottawa.

1988 Yuquot Sequence. In *Historical Dictionary of North American Archaeology*, edited by Edward B. Jelks and Juliet C. Jelks, pp. 543-544. Greenwood Press, New York.

1990 Mowachaht Ownership and Use of Salmon Resources of the Leiner River and Upper Tahsis Inlet, Nootka Sound, BC. Unpublished report prepared by Archeotech Associates, Victoria (in possession of the author).

Donald, Leland
1983 Was Nuu-chah-nulth-aht (Nootka) Society Based on Slave Labor? In *The Development of Political Organization in Native North America*, edited by Elisabeth Tooker, pp. 108-119. American Ethnological Society, Washington, DC.

Donald, Leland, and Donald H. Mitchell
1975 Some Correlates of Local Group Rank Among the Southern Kwakiutl. *Ethnology* 14(4):325-346.

Drucker, Philip
1950 Culture Element Distributions: 26, Northwest Coast. *University of California Anthropological Records* 9:3.

1951 *The Northern and Central Nootkan Tribes*. Bureau of American Ethnology Bulletin 144, Smithsonian Institution, Washington.

1955a Sources of Northwest Coast Culture. In *New Interpretations of Aboriginal American Culture History*, pp. 59-81. Anthropological Society of Washington, Washington, DC.

1955b *Indians of the Northwest Coast*. Anthropological Handbook No. 10, American Museum of Natural History, NY. (Reprinted 1963 by Natural History Press, Garden City, NY.)

Duff, Wilson
1964 *The Indian History of British Columbia*. Vol. 1, *Impact of the White Man*. Anthropology in British Columbia Memoir No. 5, Provincial Museum of British Columbia, Victoria.

1965 Thoughts on the Nootka Canoe. In *Provincial Museum of Natural History and Anthropology: Report for the Year 1964*, pp. 24-31. Department of Recreation and Conservation, British Columbia, Victoria.

1975 *Images: Stone: BC*. Hancock House, Saanichton, BC.

Earle, Timothy K.
1994 Positioning Exchange in the Evolution of Human Society. In *Prehistoric Exchange Systems in North America*, edited by Timothy G. Baugh and Jonathon E. Ericson, pp. 419-437. Plenum Press, New York.

Efrat, Barbara S., and W.J. Langlois
1978a The Contact Period As Recorded by Indian Oral Tradition. In *Nu.tka.: Captain Cook and the Spanish Explorers on the Coast*, edited by Barbara S. Efrat and W.J. Langlois, pp. 54-61. *Sound Heritage*, vol. 7, no. 1. Provincial Archives of British Columbia, Victoria.

1978b Contemporary Accounts of Nootkan Culture. In *Nu.tka.: The History and Survival of Nootkan Culture*, edited by Barbara S. Efrat and W.J. Langlois, pp. 32-62. *Sound Heritage*, vol. 7, no. 2. Provincial Archives of British Columbia, Victoria.

Eldridge, Morley
1989 Bligh Island, Nootka Sound Forest Service Road Archaeological Impact Assessment. Unpublished report to the Ministry of Forests and Lands, Campbell River.

1992 Ditidaht Tribal Heritage Resources: An Inventory and Management Plan. Report prepared for the Ditidaht Band Council, Port Alberni, and the BC Heritage Trust, Victoria. Copy on file, Archaeology Branch, Victoria.

Eldridge, Morley, and Tal Fisher
1997 Archaeological Data Recovery from Wetsite Components at the Ditidaht Sites of *wikpalhuus* (295T, DeSf-9) and *hit'ilhta7sak* (296T), DeSf-10), Nitinat Lake, BC. Unpublished report to Archaeological Services, Parks Canada, Victoria.

Ellis, David W., and Luke Swan
1981 *Teachings of the Tides: Uses of Marine Invertebrates by the Manhousat People*. Theytus Books, Nanaimo.

Ellison, Jeffrey
   1977   The Ozette Petroglyphs. Unpublished MA thesis, Department of Anthropology, Washington State University, Pullman.
Elmendorf, William W.
   1990 Chemakum. In *Handbook of North American Indians*. Vol. 7, *Northwest Coast*, edited by Wayne Suttles, pp. 438-440. Smithsonian Institution, Washington.
Embleton, Sheila M.
   1985 Lexicostatistics Applied to the Germanic, Romance, and Wakashan Families. *Word* 36(1):37-60.
Ernst, Alice Henson
   1952 *The Wolf Ritual of the Northwest Coast*. University of Oregon Press, Eugene.
Fedje, D.W., A.P. Mackie, J.B. McSporran, and B. Wilson
   1996   Early Period Archaeology in Gwaii Haanas: Results of the 1993 Field Programme. In *Early Human Occupation in British Columbia*, edited by Roy L. Carlson and Luke Della Bona, pp. 133-150. UBC Press, Vancouver.
Ferguson, R. Brian
   1983   Warfare and Redistributive Exchange on the Northwest Coast. In *The Development of Political Organization in Native North America*, edited by Elisabeth Tooker, pp. 133-147. American Ethnological Society, Washington.
   1984   A Reexamination of the Causes of Northwest Coast Warfare. In *Warfare, Culture, and Environment*, edited by R.B. Ferguson, pp. 267-328. Academic Press, New York.
Fisken, Marian
   1994 Modifications of Whale Bones. Appendix D in *Ozette Archaeological Project Research Reports*. Vol. 2, *Fauna*, edited by Stephan R. Samuels, pp. 359-377. Reports of Investigations 66. Department of Anthropology, Washington State University, Pullman, and National Park Service, Seattle.
Fladmark, Knut R.
   1975 *A Paleoecological Model for Northwest Coast Prehistory*. Archaeological Survey of Canada Paper No. 43, National Museum of Man Mercury Series, National Museums of Canada, Ottawa.
   1979 Routes: Alternate Migration Corridors for Early Man in North America. *American Antiquity* 44(1):55-69.
   1982 An Introduction to the Prehistory of British Columbia. *Canadian Journal of Archaeology* 6:95-156.
   1986 *British Columbia Prehistory*. National Museum of Man, National Museums of Canada, Ottawa.
Fladmark, Knut R., Kenneth M. Ames, and Patricia D. Sutherland
   1990 Prehistory of the Northern Coast of British Columbia. In *Handbook of North American Indians*. Vol. 7, *Northwest Coast*, edited by Wayne Suttles, pp. 229-239. Smithsonian Institution, Washington.
Flenniken, J. Jeffrey
   1980 Systems Analysis of the Lithic Artifacts. In *Hoko River: A 2500 Year Old Fishing Camp on the Northwest Coast of North America*, edited by Dale R. Croes and Eric Blinman, pp. 290-307. Reports of Investigations No. 58, Laboratory of Anthropology, Washington State University, Pullman.
   1981 *Replicative Systems Analysis: A Model Applied to the Vein Quartz Artifacts from the Hoko River Site*. Reports of Investigations No. 59, Laboratory of Anthropology, Washington State University, Pullman.
Folan, William J.
   1969 Yuquot, British Columbia: The Prehistory and History of a Nootkan Village. Part 1, Introduction and Ethnohistory of the Village. *Northwest Anthropological Research Notes* 3(2):217-231.
   1972 The Community, Settlement and Subsistence Patterns of the Nootka Sound Area: A Diachronic Model. Unpublished PhD dissertation, Southern Illinois University, Carbondale.

Folan, William J., and John T. Dewhirst
   1970   Yuquot: Where the Wind Blows from all Directions. *Archaeology* 23(4):276-286.
Foster, Michael K.
   1982   Canada's First Languages. *Language and Society* 7:7-16.
   1996   Language and the Culture History of North America. In *Handbook of North American Indians*. Vol. 14, *Languages*, edited by Ives Goddard, pp. 64-110. Smithsonian Institution, Washington.
Fournier, Judith A., and John Dewhirst
   1980   Zooarchaeological Analysis of Barnacle Remains from Yuquot, British Columbia. In *The Yuquot Project*, vol. 2, edited by W.J. Folan and J. Dewhirst, pp. 59-102. History and Archaeology 43, Parks Canada, National Historic Parks and Sites Branch, Ottawa.
French, Diana E.
   1990   Archaeological Investigations at Chesterman Beach, Tofino, and Amphitrite Point, Ucluelet, Vancouver Island. Report on file, Archaeology Branch, Victoria.
Friedman, Edward
   1976 An Archaeological Survey of Makah Territory: A Study in Resource Utilization. Unpublished PhD dissertation, Department of Anthropology, Washington State University, Pullman.
   1980   Avian Faunal Remains from Archaeological Middens, Makah Territory, Washington. *Northwest Anthropological Research Notes* 14(1):91-106.
Friedman, Edward I., and Carl E. Gustafson
   1975 Distribution and Aboriginal Use of the Sub-Order Pinnipedia on the Northwest Coast As Seen from Makah Territory, Washington. Paper presented at the 28th Annual Northwest Anthropological Conference, Seattle.
Friedman, Janet L.
   1975   The Prehistoric Uses of Wood at the Ozette Archaeological Site. Unpublished PhD dissertation, Department of Anthropology, Washington State University, Pullman.
   1976   Archaeology and Wood Technology at the Ozette Archaeological Site. In *Primitive Art and Technology*, edited by J. S. Raymond, B. Loveseth, C. Arnold, and G. Reardon, pp. 109-120. Archaeological Association, University of Calgary.
Friele, Pierre A.
   1991 Holocene Relative Sea-Level Change: Vargas Island, British Columbia. Unpublished MSc thesis, Department of Geography, Simon Fraser University, Burnaby, BC.
Friele, Pierre A., and Ian Hutchinson
   1993 Holocene Sea-Level Change on the Central West Coast of Vancouver Island, British Columbia. *Canadian Journal of Earth Sciences* 30:832-840.
Fyles, J.G.
   1963 *Surficial Geology of Horne Lake and Parksville Map-Areas, Vancouver Island, British Columbia*. Geological Survey of Canada Memoir 318, Ottawa.
Galois, Robert
   1994 *Kwakwaka'wakw Settlements, 1775-1920*. UBC Press, Vancouver.
Gibson, James R.
   1992 *Otter Skins, Boston Ships, and China Goods: The Maritime Fur Trade of the Northwest Coast, 1785-1841*. McGill-Queen's University Press, Montreal and Kingston.
Gillis, Alix Jane
   1974 History of the Neah Bay Agency. In *Coast Salish and Western Washington Indians*, vol. 3, pp. 91-115. Garland Publishing, New York and London.
Gleeson, Paul F.
   1980 *Ozette Woodworking Technology*. Project Reports No. 3, Laboratory of Archaeology and History, Washington State University, Pullman.
Gleeson, Paul, and Gerald Grosso
   1976 Ozette Site. In *The Excavation of Water-Saturated Archaeological Sites (Wet Sites) on the Northwest Coast of North America*, edited by Dale R. Croes, pp. 13-44. National Museum of Man Mercury Series, Archaeological Survey of Canada Paper No. 50, Ottawa.

Golla, Susan
1987   He Has a Name: History and Social Structure Among the Indians of Western Vancouver Island. Unpublished PhD dissertation, Columbia University, New York.
1991 A Tale of Two Chiefs: Nootkan Narrative and the Ideology of Chiefship. *Société des Américanistes*, pp. 107-123.

Guinn, Stanley J.
1963 A Maritime Village on the Olympic Peninsula of Washington. Report of Investigations No. 22, Laboratory of Anthropology, Washington State University, Pullman.

Gunther, Erna
1942   Reminiscences of a Whaler's Wife. *Pacific Northwest Quarterly* 33:65-69.
1960   A Re-evaluation of the Cultural Position of the Nootka. In *Men and Cultures: Selected Papers of the Fifth International Congress of Anthropological and Ethnological Sciences*, edited by Anthony F.C. Wallace, pp. 270-276. University of Pennsylvania Press, Philadelphia.
1972 *Indian Life on the Northwest Coast of North America As Seen by the Early Explorers and Fur Traders during the Last Decades of the Eighteenth Century.* University of Chicago Press, Chicago and London.

Gustafson, Carl E.
1968   Prehistoric Use of Fur Seals: Evidence from the Olympic Coast of Washington. *Science* 161:49-51.

Gustafson, Carl E., Delbert Gilbow, and Richard D. Daugherty
1979 The Manis Mastodon Site: Early Man on the Olympic Peninsula. *Canadian Journal of Archaeology* 3:157-164.

Haggarty, James C.
1982 The Archaeology of Hesquiat Harbour: The Archaeological Utility of an Ethnographically Defined Social Unit. Unpublished PhD dissertation, Department of Anthropology, Washington State University.

Haggarty, James C., and Richard I. Inglis
1983a Westcoast Sites: An Archaeological and Macroenvironmental Synthesis. In *Prehistoric Places on the Southern Northwest Coast*, edited by Robert E. Greengo, pp. 11-33. Thomas Burke Memorial Washington State Museum, University of Washington, Seattle.
1983b Archaeological Survey of the Brooks Peninsula Yields Ten Sites. *The Midden* 15(2):1-6.
1984 Preliminary Results of the Archaeological Survey of Pacific Rim National Park, West Coast of Vancouver Island. *The Midden* 16(3):2-5.
1985 Historical Resources Site Survey and Assessment, Pacific Rim National Park. Unpublished report, Parks Canada, Calgary.
1997 Archaeology of Brooks Peninsula. In *Brooks Peninsula: An Ice Age Refugium on Vancouver Island*, edited by Richard J. Hebda and James C. Haggarty, pp. 14.1-14.27. Occasional Paper No. 5, Ministry of Environment, Lands and Parks, Victoria.

Haggarty, Jim, and Gay Boehm
1974 The Hesquiat Project. *The Midden* 6(3):2-12.

Harris, Cole
1994 Voices of Disaster: Smallpox around the Strait of Georgia in 1782. *Ethnohistory* 41(4):591-626.

Hebda, Richard J., and Glenn E. Rouse
1979 Palynology of Two Holocene Cores from the Hesquiat Peninsula, Vancouver Island. *Syesis* 12:121-130.

Hill, Beth
1978 *The Remarkable World of Frances Barkley: 1769-1845.* Gray's Publishing, Sidney, BC.

Hill, Beth, and Ray Hill
1974 *Indian Petroglyphs of the Pacific Northwest.* Hancock House Publishers, Saanichton, BC.

Hobler, Philip M.
1990 Prehistory of the Central Coast of British Columbia. In *Handbook of North American Indians*. Vol. 7, *Northwest Coast*, edited by Wayne Suttles, pp. 298-305. Smithsonian Institution, Washington.

Hoff, Ricky
   1980   Fishhooks. In *Hoko River: A 2500 Year Old Fishing Camp on the Northwest Coast of North America*, edited by Dale R. Croes and Eric Blinman, pp. 160-188. Reports of Investigations No. 58, Laboratory of Anthropology, Washington State University, Pullman.
Holland, Stuart S.
   1964 *Landforms of British Columbia: A Physiographic Outline*. British Columbia Department of Mines and Petroleum Resources Bulletin 48, Victoria.
Howay, Frederic W. (editor)
   1941   *Voyages of the "Columbia" to the Northwest Coast, 1787-1790 and 1790-1793*. The Massachusetts Historical Society, Boston.
Howes, Donald W.
   1982   Spatial Analysis at a Northwest Coast Fishing Camp: The Hoko River Site. Unpublished MA thesis, Department of Anthropology, Washington State University, Pullman.
Huelsbeck, David R.
   1980   Analysis of the Fish Remains. In *Hoko River: A 2500 Year Old Fishing Camp on the Northwest Coast of North America*, edited by Dale R. Croes and Eric Blinman, pp. 104-111. Reports of Investigations No. 58, Laboratory of Anthropology, Washington State University, Pullman.
   1981 *Utilization of Fish at the Ozette Site*. Project Reports No. 11, Laboratory of Archaeology and History, Washington State University, Pullman.
   1988a The Surplus Economy of the Central Northwest Coast. In *Prehistoric Economies of the Pacific Northwest Coast*, edited by Barry L. Isaac, pp. 149-177. *Research in Economic Anthropology*, Supplement 3. JAI Press, Greenwich, CT.
   1988b Whaling in the Precontact Economy of the Central Northwest Coast. *Arctic Anthropology* 25(1):1-15.
   1989 Food Consumption, Resource Exploitation and Relationships Within and Between Households at Ozette. In *Households and Communities*, edited by Scott MacEachern, David J.W. Archer, and Richard D. Garvin, pp. 157-167. Proceedings of the 21st Annual Chacmool Conference, Archaeological Association, University of Calgary.
   1994a Mammals and Fish in the Subsistence Economy of Ozette. In *Ozette Archaeological Project Research Reports*. Vol. 2, *Fauna*, edited by Stephan R. Samuels, pp. 17-91. Reports of Investigations 66. Department of Anthropology, Washington State University, Pullman, and National Park Service, Seattle.
   1994b The Utilization of Whales at Ozette. In *Ozette Archaeological Project Research Reports*. Vol. 2, *Fauna*, edited by Stephan R. Samuels, pp. 265-303. Reports of Investigations 66. Department of Anthropology, Washington State University, Pullman, and National Park Service, Seattle.
Huelsbeck, David R., and Gary C. Wessen
   1994 Twenty-Five Years of Faunal Analysis at Ozette. In *Ozette Archaeological Project Research Reports*. Vol. 2, *Fauna*, edited by Stephan R. Samuels, pp. 1-16. Reports of Investigations 66. Department of Anthropology, Washington State University, Pullman, and National Park Service, Seattle.
   1995 Late Prehistoric Settlement Seasonality in Makah Territory. *Archaeology in Washington*, in press.
Hupquatchew (Ron Hamilton)
   1981 Yahtshulthaht. In *The World Is As Sharp As a Knife: An Anthology in Honour of Wilson Duff*, edited by Donald N. Abbott, pp. 304-306. British Columbia Provincial Museum, Victoria.
Hutchinson, Ian, and Alan D. McMillan
   1997 Archaeological Evidence for Village Abandonment Associated with Late Holocene Earthquakes at the Northern Cascadia Subduction Zone. *Quaternary Research* 48: 79-87.
Inglis, Richard I., and James C. Haggarty
   1983   Provisions or Prestige: A Re-evaluation of the Economic Importance of Nootka

Whaling. Paper presented at the symposium on Megafauna of the Seas, 11th International Conference of Anthropological and Ethnological Sciences, Vancouver.

1984   The Yuquot Whalers Shrine: Rediscovery of Its Original Location. Paper presented at the 17th Annual Meeting of the Canadian Archaeological Association, Victoria.

1986   Pacific Rim National Park: Ethnographic History. Unpublished report, Parks Canada, Calgary.

1987 Cook to Jewitt: Three Decades of Change in Nootka Sound. In *Le Castor Fait Tout: Selected Papers of the Fifth North American Fur Trade Conference, 1985*, edited by Bruce G. Trigger, Toby Morantz, and Louise Dechene, pp. 193-222. Lake St. Louis Historical Society, Montreal.

Ingraham, Joseph

1971 *Voyage to the Northwest Coast of North America, 1790-92*, edited by Mark D. Kaplanoff. Imprint Society, Barre, MA.

Irvine, Albert

1921 *How the Makah Obtained Possession of Cape Flattery* (translated by Luke Markistun). Indian Notes and Monographs, Museum of the American Indian, Heye Foundation, New York.

Jacobsen, William H., Jr.

1979   Wakashan Comparative Studies. In *The Languages of Native America, Historical and Comparative Assessment*, edited by Lyle Campbell and Marianne Mithun, pp. 766-791. University of Texas Press, Austin.

Jane, Cecil

1930 *A Spanish Voyage to Vancouver and the North-West Coast of America Being the Narrative of the Voyage Made in the Year 1792 by the Schooners* Sutil *and* Mexicana *to Explore the Strait of Fuca*. Argonaut Press, London.

Jewitt, John R.

1967   *Narrative of the Adventures and Sufferings of John R. Jewitt, Only Survivor of the Crew of the Ship Boston, During a Captivity of Nearly Three Years Among the Savages of Nootka Sound*. Ye Galleon Press, Fairfield, Washington. (Reprint of the 1815 manuscript)

1988 *A Journal Kept at Nootka Sound*. Ye Galeon Press, Fairfield, Washington.

Jonaitis, Aldona

1988 *From the Land of the Totem Poles: The Northwest Coast Indian Art Collection at the American Museum of Natural History*. American Museum of Natural History, New York, and Douglas and McIntyre, Vancouver.

Jones, Chief Charles, with Stephen Bosustow

1981 *Queesto, Pacheenaht Chief by Birthright*. Theytus Books, Nanaimo.

Jones, Olive

1981 Glassware Excavated at Yuquot, British Columbia. In *The Yuquot Project*, vol. 3, edited by W.J. Folan and J. Dewhirst, pp. 3-77. History and Archaeology 44, Parks Canada, National Historic Parks and Sites Branch, Ottawa.

Jorgensen, Joseph G.

1969 *Salish Language and Culture: A Statistical Analysis of Internal Relationships, History, and Evolution*. Language Science Monographs, Indiana University Publications, Bloomington.

Kaeppler, Adrienne L.

1978 *"Artificial Curiosities": An Exposition of Native Manufactures Collected on the Three Pacific Voyages of Captain James Cook, RN*. Bishop Museum Press, Honolulu, HI.

Kane, Paul

1968 *Wanderings of an Artist Among the Indians of North America*. Hurtig Publishers, Edmonton.

Kendrick, John (translator and editor)

1991 *The Voyage of the Sutil and Mexicana 1792: The Last Spanish Exploration of the Northwest Coast of America*. The Arthur H. Clark Co., Spokane, WA.

Kenyon, Susan M.

1980   *The Kyuquot Way: A Study of a West Coast (Nootkan) Community*. Canadian Ethnology Service, Mercury Series Paper 61, National Museums of Canada, Ottawa.

King, J.C.H.
1981   *Artificial Curiosities from the Northwest Coast of America: Native American Artefacts in the British Museum Collected on the Third Voyage of Captain James Cook and Acquired Through Sir Joseph Banks.* British Museum Publications, London.

Kinkade, M. Dale
1990 History of Research in Linguistics. In *Handbook of North American Indians.* Vol. 7, *Northwest Coast,* edited by Wayne Suttles, pp. 98-106. Smithsonian Institution, Washington.
1991   Prehistory of the Native Languages of the Northwest Coast. In *Proceedings of the Great Ocean Conferences,* vol. 1, pp. 137-158. Oregon Historical Society Press, Portland.

Kinkade, M. Dale, and J.V. Powell
1976   Language and the Prehistory of North America. *World Archaeology* 8(1):83-100.

Kirk, Ruth
1986 *Wisdom of the Elders: Native Traditions on the Northwest Coast – The Nuu-chah-nulth, Southern Kwakiutl and Nuxalk.* Douglas and McIntyre, Vancouver.

Kirk, Ruth, with Richard D. Daugherty
1974   *Hunters of the Whale: An Adventure in Northwest Coast Archaeology.* William Morrow and Co., New York.

Kool, Richard
1982 Northwest Coast Indian Whaling: New Considerations. *Canadian Journal of Anthropology* 3(1):31-44.

Koppert, Vincent A.
1930 *Contributions to Clayoquot Ethnology.* Catholic University of America, Anthropological Series No. 1, Washington.

Kroeber, A.L.
1923   American Culture and the Northwest Coast. *American Anthropologist* 25(1):1-20.
1939   *Cultural and Natural Areas of Native North America.* University of California Press, Berkeley.

Langdon, Steve
1976 The Development of the Nootkan Cultural System. Paper presented at the Northwest Coast Studies Conference, Simon Fraser University, Burnaby.

Lantis, Margaret
1938 The Alaskan Whale Cult and Its Affinities. *American Anthropologist* 40:438-464.

Lueger, Richard
1981 Ceramics from Yuquot, British Columbia. In *The Yuquot Project,* vol. 3, edited by W.J. Folan and J. Dewhirst, pp. 103-170. History and Archaeology 44, Parks Canada, National Historic Parks and Sites Branch, Ottawa.

Lundy, Doris Marion
1974 The Rock Art of the Northwest Coast. Unpublished MA thesis, Department of Archaeology, Simon Fraser University, Burnaby.

Luternauer, J.L., John J. Clague, K.W. Conway, J.V. Barrie, B. Blaise, and R.W. Mathewes
1989 Late Pleistocene Terrestrial Deposits on the Continental Shelf of Western Canada: Evidence for Rapid Sea-Level Change at the End of the Last Glaciation. *Geology* 17:357-360.

Mackie, Alexander
1983 The 1982 Meares Island Archaeological Survey: An Inventory and Evaluation of Heritage Resources. Report on file, Archaeology Branch, Victoria (and Nuu-chah-nulth Tribal Council, Port Alberni).
1986 A Closer Look at Coastal Survey Results. *The Midden* 18(1):3-5.
1992 Nuu-chah-nulth Culture History: Is Something Missing? Paper presented at the 45th Annual Northwest Anthropology Conference, Simon Fraser University, Burnaby, BC.

Magee, Bernard
1794   Log of the *Jefferson.* Unpublished manuscript. Photocopy held in University of British Columbia Library, Vancouver.

Marshall, Yvonne

1989a The House in Northwest Coast, Nuu-chah-nulth, Society: the Material Structure of Political Action. In *Households and Communities*, edited by Scott MacEachern, David J.W. Archer, and Richard D. Garvin, pp. 15-21. Proceedings of the 21st Annual Chacmool Conference, Archaeological Association, University of Calgary.

1989b Whaling, Subsistence and Settlement Among the Westcoast People of Vancouver Island. In *Saying So Doesn't Make It So: Papers in Honour of B. Foss Leach*, edited by Douglas G. Sutton, pp. 258-276. New Zealand Archaeological Association Monograph 17, Aukland.

1990   The Mowachaht Archaeology Project, Phase 1, 1989. Unpublished report, British Columbia Heritage Trust and Archaeology Branch, Victoria.

1992a Mowachaht/Muchalat Archaeology Project: Final Report. Unpublished report, British Columbia Heritage Trust and Archaeology Branch, Victoria.

1992b Surveying in Nootka Sound: The Man in the Sun and Other Stories. *The Midden* 24(2):7-10.

1993 A Political History of the Nuu-chah-nulth People: A Case Study of the Mowachaht and Muchalaht Tribes. Unpublished PhD dissertation, Department of Archaeology, Simon Fraser University, Burnaby.

Marshall, Yvonne, and Heather Moon

1989 Fieldwork in Nootka Sound. *The Midden* 21(5):6-9.

Mathews, W.H., J.G. Fyles, and H.W. Nasmith

1970 Postglacial Crustal Movements in Southwestern British Columbia and Adjacent Washington State. *Canadian Journal of Earth Sciences* 7:690-702.

Matson, R.G.

1983   Intensification and the Development of Cultural Complexity: The Northwest Versus the Northeast Coast. In *The Evolution of Maritime Cultures on the Northeast and the Northwest Coasts of America*, edited by Ronald J. Nash, pp. 125-148. Publication No. 11, Department of Archaeology, Simon Fraser University, Burnaby.

1992 The Evolution of Northwest Coast Subsistence. In *Long-Term Subsistence Change in Prehistoric North America*, edited by Dale R. Croes, Rebecca A. Hawkins, and Barry L. Isaac, pp. 367-428. *Research in Economic Anthropology*, Supplement 6. JAI Press, Greenwich, CT.

1996 The Old Cordilleran Component at the Glenrose Cannery Site. In *Early Human Occupation in British Columbia*, edited by Roy L. Carlson and Luke Della Bona, pp. 111-122. UBC Press, Vancouver.

Matson, R.G. (editor)

1976 *The Glenrose Cannery Site*. Archaeological Survey of Canada Paper No. 52, National Museum of Man Mercury Series, National Museums of Canada, Ottawa.

Matson, R.G., and Gary Coupland

1995 *The Prehistory of the Northwest Coast*. Academic Press, San Diego.

Mauger, Jeffrey E.

1982 Ozette Kerf-Corner Boxes. *American Indian Art Magazine* 8(1):72-79.

1991 Shed-Roof Houses at Ozette and in a Regional Perspective. In *Ozette Archaeological Project Research Reports*. Vol. 1, *House Structure and Floor Midden*, edited by Stephan R. Samuels, pp. 29-173. Reports of Investigations 63. Department of Anthropology, Washington State University, Pullman, and National Park Service, Seattle.

Mayne, R.C.

1862 *Four Years in British Columbia and Vancouver Island*. John Murray, London.

McAllister, Nancy M.

1980 Avian Fauna from the Yuquot Excavation. In *The Yuquot Project*, vol. 2, edited by W.J. Folan and J. Dewhirst, pp. 103-174. History and Archaeology 43, Parks Canada, National Historic Parks and Sites Branch, Ottawa.

McKenzie, Kathleen H.

1974   Ozette Prehistory: Prelude. Unpublished MA thesis, Department of Archaeology, University of Calgary.

McLeod, Ann, and Mark Skinner
  1986   Analysis of Human Remains: Bamfield Teacherage Site Burial (DeSg 47). Report on file, Archaeology Branch, Victoria.
McMillan, Alan D.
  1969 Archaeological Investigations at Nootka Sound, Vancouver Island. Unpublished MA thesis, Department of Anthropology and Sociology, University of British Columbia.
  1975a Preliminary Report on Archaeological Survey in the Alberni Valley and Upper Alberni Inlet. Report on file, Archaeology Branch, Victoria.
  1975b Archaeological Survey in the Alberni Valley. *The Midden* 7(4):6-10.
  1979 Archaeological Evidence for Aboriginal Tuna Fishing on Western Vancouver Island. *Syesis* 12:117-119.
  1981   Archaeological Research in Nootka Territory: Barkley Sound to the Alberni Valley. *BC Studies* 48:86-102.
  1992 Recent Research in Barkley Sound: The Toquaht Archaeological Project. *The Midden* 24(2):3-5.
  1996a Since Kwatyat Lived on Earth: An Examination of Nuu-chah-nulth Culture History. Unpublished PhD dissertation, Department of Archaeology, Simon Fraser University, Burnaby, BC
  1996b Early Surface Collections from the Alberni Valley. In *Early Human Occupation in British Columbia*, edited by Roy L. Carlson and Luke Della Bona, pp. 211-214. UBC Press, Vancouver.
  1998 Changing Views of Nuu-chah-nulth Culture History: Evidence of Population Replacement in Barkley Sound. *Canadian Journal of Archaeology* 22(1): in press.
McMillan, Alan D., and Denis E. St. Claire
  1977   An Archaeological Resource Inventory in the Alberni-Barkley Sound Region of Vancouver Island. In *Annual Report for the Year 1975: Activities of the Archaeological Sites Advisory Board and Selected Research Reports*, edited by B.O. Simonsen, pp. 154-192. Government of British Columbia, Victoria.
  1982 *Alberni Prehistory: Archaeological and Ethnographic Investigations on Western Vancouver Island*. Theytus Books, Penticton, BC.
  1991 The Toquaht Archaeological Project: Report on the 1991 Field Season. Unpublished Report Submitted to the British Columbia Heritage Trust and Archaeology Branch, Victoria, and the Toquaht Band, Ucluelet.
  1992 The Toquaht Archaeological Project: Report on the 1992 Field Season. Unpublished Report Submitted to the British Columbia Heritage Trust and Archaeology Branch, Victoria, and the Toquaht Band, Ucluelet.
  1994 The Toquaht Archaeological Project: Report on the 1994 Field Season. Unpublished Report Submitted to the Toquaht Nation, Ucluelet, and the Archaeology Branch, Victoria.
  1996 The Toquaht Archaeological Project: Report on the 1996 Field Season. Unpublished Report Submitted to the Toquaht Nation, Ucluelet, and the BC Heritage Trust and Archaeology Branch, Victoria.
McPhatter, Blair
  1986 Analysis of Found Human Remains: Toquart Bay Historic Period Box Burial (DgSi 1). Report on file, Archaeology Branch, Victoria.
Meares, John
  1790 *Voyages Made in the Years 1788 and 1789, From China to the North West Coast of America*. J. Walter, London.
Miller, David Glen
  1984 The Hoko River Rockshelter: Intertidal Resources. Unpublished MA thesis, Department of Anthropology, Washington State University, Pullman.
Mills, John Edwin
  1955   The Ethnohistory of Nootka Sound, Vancouver Island. Unpublished PhD dissertation, University of Washington, Seattle.

Mitchell, Donald H.
1968   Excavations at Two Trench Embankments in the Gulf of Georgia Region. *Syesis* 1:29-46.
1971 Archaeology of the Gulf of Georgia Area, a Natural Region and Its Culture Types. *Syesis* vol. 4, supplement 1.
1981 Test Excavations at Randomly Selected Sites in Eastern Queen Charlotte Strait. *BC Studies* 48:103-123.
1983 Seasonal Settlements, Village Aggregations, and Political Autonomy on the Central Northwest Coast. In *The Development of Political Organization in Native North America*, edited by Elisabeth Tooker, pp. 97-107. American Ethnological Society, Washington, DC.
1984 Predatory Warfare, Social Status, and the North Pacific Slave Trade. *Ethnology* 23: 39-48.
1988   Changing Patterns of Resource Use in the Prehistory of Queen Charlotte Strait, British Columbia. In *Prehistoric Economies of the Pacific Northwest Coast*, edited by Barry L. Isaac, pp. 245-290. *Research in Economic Anthropology*, Supplement 3. JAI Press, Greenwich, CT.
1990   Prehistory of the Coasts of Southern British Columbia and Northern Washington. In *Handbook of North American Indians*. Vol. 7, *Northwest Coast*, edited by Wayne Suttles, pp. 340-358. Smithsonian Institution, Washington.
Monks, Gregory G.
1992 Preliminary Faunal Report. In The Toquaht Archaeological Project: Report on the 1992 Field Season, by Alan D. McMillan and Denis E. St. Claire, pp. 76-91. Unpublished report submitted to the BC Heritage Trust and Archaeology Branch, Victoria, and the Toquaht Band, Ucluelet.
Moogk, Susan Rosa Tovell
1980   The Wolf Masks of the Nootka Wolf Ritual: A Statement on Transformation. Unpublished MA thesis, Department of Anthropology and Sociology, University of British Columbia, Vancouver.
Moon, Barbara J.
1978 Vanished Companions: The Changing Relationship of the West Coast People to the Animal World. In *Nu.tka.: Captain Cook and the Spanish Explorers on the Coast*, edited by Barbara S. Efrat and W.J. Langlois, pp. 71-77. *Sound Heritage*, vol. 7, no. 1. Provincial Archives of British Columbia, Victoria.
Morgan, Robert Christopher
1980 The Economic Basis and Institutional Framework of Traditional Nootka Polities. Unpublished MA thesis, Department of Anthropology, University of Victoria.
Moser, Rev. Charles
1926 *Reminiscences of the West Coast of Vancouver Island*. Acme Press, Victoria.
Moss, Madonna L., and Jon M. Erlandson
1992 Forts, Refuge Rocks, and Defensive Sites: The Antiquity of Warfare Along the North Pacific Coast of North America. *Arctic Anthropology* 29:73-90.
Moziño, José Mariano
1970 *Noticias de Nutka: An Account of Nootka Sound in 1792* (translated and edited by Iris Higbie Wilson). McClelland and Stewart, Toronto.
Muller, J.E.
1980 Geological Outline of the Nootka Sound Region, with Notes on Stone Artifacts from Yuquot, British Columbia. In *The Yuquot Project*, vol. 2, edited by W.J. Folan and J. Dewhirst, pp. 3-14. History and Archaeology 43, Parks Canada, National Historic Parks and Sites Branch, Ottawa.
Nagorsen, David W., Grant Keddie, and Tanya Luszcz
1996 *Vancouver Island Marmot Bones from Subalpine Caves: Archaeological and Biological Significance*. Occasional Paper No. 4, Ministry of Environment, Lands and Parks, Victoria.
Nelson, D.E., J.M. D'Auria, and R.B. Bennett
1975   Characterization of Pacific Northwest Coast Obsidian by X-Ray Flourescence Analysis. *Archaeometry* 17(1):85-97.

Newcombe, C.F.
1907 Petroglyphs in British Columbia. *Victoria Daily Times*, Sept. 7.
Newcombe, C.F. (editor)
1923 *Menzies' Journal of Vancouver's Voyage, April to October, 1792*. Archives of British Columbia Memoir No. 5, Victoria.
Nuu-chah-nulth Tribal Council
1991 *Our World-Our Ways: T'aat'aaqsapa Cultural Dictionary* (compiled and edited by Jay Powell). Nuu-chah-nulth Tribal Council, Port Alberni.
Olson, Ronald L.
1927 Adze, Canoe, and House Types of the Northwest Coast. *University of Washington Publications in Anthropology* 2(1), Seattle.
O'Reilly, P.
1883 Letter to the Superintendent General of Indian Affairs. In *Annual Report of the Department of Indian Affairs 1882*, pp. 100-101. MacLean, Roger and Co., Ottawa.
Pethick, Derek
1976 *First Approaches to the Northwest Coast*. Douglas and McIntyre, Vancouver.
Powell, James V.
1990 Quileute. In *Handbook of North American Indians*. Vol. 7, *Northwest Coast*, edited by Wayne Suttles, pp. 431-437. Smithsonian Institution, Washington.
1993 Chimakuan and Wakashan: The Case for Remote Common Origin. In *American Indian Linguistics and Ethnography in Honor of Laurence C. Thompson*, edited by A. Mattina and T. Montler, pp. 451-470. University of Montana Occasional Papers in Linguistics No. 10, Missoula.
Renker, Ann M., and Greig W. Arnold
1988 Exploring the Role of Education in Cultural Resource Management: The Makah Cultural and Research Center Example. *Human Organization* 47(4):302-307.
Renker, Ann M., and Erna Gunther
1990 Makah. In *Handbook of North American Indians*. Vol. 7, *Northwest Coast*, edited by Wayne Suttles, pp. 422-430. Smithsonian Institution, Washington.
Riley, Carroll L.
1968 The Makah Indians: A Study of Political and Economic Organization. *Ethnohistory* 15:57-95.
St. Claire, Denis E.
1975 Report on the Archaeological Survey of the Barkley Sound area. Report on file, Archaeology Branch, Victoria.
1991 Barkley Sound Tribal Territories. In *Between Ports Alberni and Renfrew: Notes on Westcoast Peoples*, E.Y. Arima at al., pp. 13-202. Canadian Museum of Civilization, Mercury Series, Canadian Ethnology Service Paper 121, Ottawa.
Samuels, Stephan R.
1989 Spatial Patterns in Ozette Longhouse Floor Middens. In *Households and Communities*, edited by Scott MacEachern, David J.W. Archer, and Richard D. Garvin, pp. 143-156. Proceedings of the 21st Annual Chacmool Conference, Archaeological Association, University of Calgary.
Samuels, Stephan R. (editor)
1991 *Ozette Archaeological Project Research Reports*. Vol. 1, *House Structure and Floor Midden*. Reports of Investigations 63. Department of Anthropology, Washington State University, Pullman, and National Park Service, Seattle.
1994 *Ozette Archaeological Project Research Reports*. Vol. 2, *Fauna*. Reports of Investigations 66. Department of Anthropology, Washington State University, Pullman, and National Park Service, Seattle.
Samuels, Stephan R., and Richard D. Daugherty
1991 Introduction to the Ozette Archaeological Project. In *Ozette Archaeological Project Research Reports*. Vol. 1, *House Structure and Floor Midden*, edited by Stephan R. Samuels, pp. 1-27. Reports of Investigations 63. Department of Anthropology, Washington State University, Pullman, and National Park Service, Seattle.

Sapir, Edward

1910-14 Field Notes on Barkley Sound Native Groups. MS. on file, American Philosophical Society, Philadelphia. (Microfilm copy at Provincial Archives of British Columbia, Victoria.)

1911 Some Aspects of Nootka Language and Culture. *American Anthropologist* 13:15-28.

1912 Language and Environment. *American Anthropologist* 14:226-242.

1913 A Girl's Puberty Ceremony Among the Nootka Indians. *Royal Society of Canada, Proceedings and Transactions*, series 3, part 2:67-80.

1915   Abnormal Types of Speech in Nootka. *Geological Survey of Canada, Memoir* 62:1-21.

1916   Time Perspective in Aboriginal North American Culture: A Study in Method. *Geological Survey of Canada Memoir* 90. Ottawa. (Reprinted in *Selected Writings of Edward Sapir*, edited by David G. Mandelbaum, pp. 389-462. University of California Press, Berkeley and Los Angeles, 1949.)

1922   Sayach'apis, a Nootka Trader. In *American Indian Life*, edited by Elsie Clews Parsons, pp. 297-323. B.W. Huebsch, New York.

1924 The Rival Whalers: A Nitinat Story. *International Journal of American Linguistics* 3: 76-102.

1929   Central and North American Languages. *Encyclopedia Britannica* (14th ed.) 5:138-141. (Reprinted in *Selected Writings of Edward Sapir*, edited by David G. Mandelbaum, pp. 169-178. University of California Press, Berkeley and Los Angeles, 1949.)

1959 Indian Legends from Vancouver Island. *Journal of American Folklore* 72(284): 106-114.

Sapir, Edward, and Morris Swadesh

1939 *Nootka Texts*. Linguistic Society of America, University of Pennsylvania.

1955 *Native Accounts of Nootka Ethnography*. International Journal of American Linguistics, vol. 21, no. 4, pt. 2.

Savage, Howard

1973 Faunal Changes Through Time in British Columbia Coastal Sites and the Implications Thereof. Unpublished paper presented at the 6th Annual Meeting of the Canadian Archaeological Association, Burnaby, BC.

Schulting, Rick J., and Alan D. McMillan

1995 A Probable Case of Tuberculosis from a Burial Cave in Barkley Sound, Vancouver Island. *Canadian Journal of Archaeology* 19:149-153.

Scott, R. Bruce

1972 *Barkley Sound: A History of the Pacific Rim National Park Area*. Sono Nis Press, Victoria.

Singh, Ram Raj Prasad

1966 *Aboriginal Economic System of the Olympic Peninsula Indians, Western Washington*. Sacramento Anthropological Society Paper No. 4, Sacramento State College, Sacramento CA.

Sneed, Paul G.

1972 A Report of Archaeological Research Activity in Hesquiat Harbour, Vancouver Island, British Columbia, Summer 1971. Report on file, Archaeology Branch, Victoria.

Sproat, Gilbert Malcolm

1868 *Scenes and Studies of Savage Life*. Smith, Elder and Co., London. (Reprinted as *The Nootka: Scenes and Studies of Savage Life*, edited by Charles Lillard, Sono Nis Press, Victoria, 1987.)

Stryd, Arnoud H., and Morley Eldridge

1993 CMT Archaeology in British Columbia: The Meares Island Studies. *BC Studies* (Special Issue, *Changing Times: British Columbia Archaeology in the 1980s*, edited by Knut Fladmark) 99:184-234.

Sumpter, Ian D., Daryl W. Fedje, and Fred K. Sieber Jr.

1997 1995/96 Archaeological Resource Management Programme: Pacific Rim National Park Reserve. Report on file, Archaeological Services, Parks Canada, Western Region, Victoria.

Sumpter, Ian D., and Daryl W. Fedge

1997   1996/97 Archaeological Resource Management Programme: Pacific Rim National

Park Reserve. Report on file, Archaeological Services, Parks Canada, Western Region, Victoria.

Suttles, Wayne

1952 Notes on Coast Salish Sea-Mammal Hunting. *Anthropology in British Columbia* 3:10-20. (Reprinted in *Coast Salish Essays*, pp. 233-247. Talonbooks, Vancouver, 1987.)

1962 Variation in Habitat and Culture on the Northwest Coast. *Proceedings of the 34th International Congress of Americanists*, pp. 522-537. (Reprinted in *Coast Salish Essays*, pp. 26-44. Talonbooks, Vancouver, 1987.)

1968 Coping with Abundance: Subsistence on the Northwest Coast. In *Man the Hunter*, edited by Richard B. Lee and Irven DeVore, pp. 56-68. Aldine, Chicago. (Reprinted in *Coast Salish Essays*, 45-63. Talonbooks, Vancouver, 1987.)

1987a The Recent Emergence of the Coast Salish: The Function of an Anthropological Myth. In *Coast Salish Essays*, pp. 256-264. Talonbooks, Vancouver.

1987b Northwest Coast Linguistic History: A View from the Coast. In *Coast Salish Essays*, pp. 265-281. Talonbooks, Vancouver.

Suttles, Wayne, and William W. Elmendorf

1963 Linguistic Evidence for Salish Prehistory. In *Symposium on Language and Culture: Proceedings of the 1962 Annual Spring Meeting of the American Ethnological Society*, edited by Viola E. Garfield and Wallace L Chafe, pp. 41-52. American Ethnological Society, Seattle.

Suttles, Wayne, and Aldona Jonaitis

1990 History of Research in Ethnology. In *Handbook of North American Indians*, vol. 7, *Northwest Coast*, edited by Wayne Suttles, pp. 73-87. Smithsonian Institution, Washington.

Swadesh, Morris

1948 Motivations in Nootka Warfare. *Southwestern Journal of Anthropology* 4(1):76-93.

1949 The Linguistic Approach to Salish Prehistory. In *Indians of the Urban Northwest*, edited by Marian W. Smith, pp. 161-173. Columbia University Press, NY.

1953 Mosan I: A Problem of Remote Common Origin. *International Journal of American Linguistics* 19:26-44.

1954 Time Depths of American Linguistic Groupings. *American Anthropologist* 56: 361-364.

1955 Chemakum Lexicon Compared with Quileute. *International Journal of American Linguistics* 21(1):60-72.

Swan, James G.

1870 *The Indians of Cape Flattery, at the Entrance to the Strait of Fuca, Washington Territory*. Smithsonian Contributions to Knowledge, vol. 16. Smithsonian Institution, Washington.

Swanson, Earl H.

1956 Nootka and the California Gray Whale. *Northwest Quarterly* 47:52-56.

Taylor, Herbert C., Jr.

1974 Anthropological Investigation of the Makah Indians Relative to Tribal Identity and Aboriginal Possession of Lands. In *Coast Salish and Western Washington Indians*, vol. 3, pp. 27-89. Garland Publishing, New York and London.

Thomas, Alexander, and E.Y. Arima

1970 *t'a:t'a:qsapa: A Practical Orthography for Nootka*. Publications in Ethnology 1, National Museum of Man, National Museums of Canada, Ottawa.

Thompson, Laurence C., and M. Dale Kinkade

1990 Languages. In *Handbook of North American Indians*. Vol. 7, *Northwest Coast*, edited by Wayne Suttles, pp. 30-51. Smithsonian Institution, Washington.

Trigger, Bruce G.

1980 Archaeology and the Image of the American Indian. *American Antiquity* 45: 662-676.

1981 Archaeology and the Ethnographic Present. *Anthropologica* 23(1):3-17.

1984 Alternative Archaeologies: Nationalist, Colonialist, Imperialist. *Man* (NS) 19: 355-370.

1985   The Past As Power: Anthropology and the North American Indian. In *Who Owns the Past?* edited by Isabel McBryde, pp. 11-40. Oxford University Press, Melbourne.

1989a *A History of Archaeological Thought.* Cambridge University Press, Cambridge.

1989b History and Contemporary American Archaeology: A Critical Analysis. In *Archaeological Thought in America*, edited by C.C. Lamberg-Karlovsky, pp. 19-34. Cambridge University Press, Cambridge.

1991   Constraint and Freedom: A New Synthesis for Archaeological Explanation. *American Anthropologist* 93(3):551-569.

Turner, Nancy J., and Barbara S. Efrat

1982 *Ethnobotany of the Hesquiat Indians of Vancouver Island.* Cultural Recovery Papers No. 2, British Columbia Provincial Museum, Victoria.

Turner, Nancy J., John Thomas, Barry F. Carlson, and Robert T. Ogilvie

1983   *Ethnobotany of the Nitinaht Indians of Vancouver Island.* Occasional Papers Series No. 24, British Columbia Provincial Museum, Victoria.

Vancouver, George

1984   *A Voyage of Discovery to the North Pacific Ocean and Round the World 1791-1795* (4 vols.), edited by W.Kaye Lamb. The Hakluyt Society, London.

Vayda, Andrew P.

1968 Hypotheses about Functions of War. In *War: The Anthropology of Armed Conflict and Aggression*, edited by Morton Fried, Marvin Harris, and Robert Murphy, pp. 85-91. Natural History Press, Garden City, NY.

Virden, Jenel, and Maureen Brinck-Lund

1980 Ethnohistory. In *Hoko River: A 2500 Year Old Fishing Camp on the Northwest Coast of North America*, edited by Dale R. Croes and Eric Blinman, pp. 32-46. Reports of Investigations No. 58, Laboratory of Anthropology, Washington State University, Pullman.

Wagner, Henry R.

1933   *Spanish Explorations in the Strait of Juan de Fuca.* Fine Arts Press, Santa Ana, California.

Walker, Alexander

1982 *An Account of a Voyage to the North West Coast of America in 1785 and 1786* (edited by Robin Fisher and J.M. Bumsted). Douglas and McIntyre, Vancouver.

Waterman, T.T.

1920 *The Whaling Equipment of the Makah Indians.* University of Washington Publications in Anthropology, vol. 1, no. 1.

Webb, Robert Lloyd

1988 *On the Northwest: Commercial Whaling in the Pacific Northwest 1790-1967.* University of British Columbia Press, Vancouver.

Webster, Peter S.

1983 *As Far As I Know: Reminiscences of an Ahousat Elder.* Campbell River Museum and Archives, Campbell River, BC.

Wessen, Gary C.

1982 Shell Middens As Cultural Deposits: A Case Study From Ozette. Unpublished Ph.D. dissertation, Department of Anthropology, Washington State University, Pullman.

1984 A Report on Preliminary Archaeological Investigations at 45CA201: A "Second Terrace" Shell Midden Site Near Sand Point, Olympic National Park, Washington. Report prepared for National Park Service, Pacific Northwest Regional Office, Seattle.

1988 The Use of Shellfish Resources on the Northwest Coast: The View From Ozette. In *Prehistoric Economies of the Pacific Northwest Coast*, edited by Barry L. Isaac, pp. 179-207. *Research in Economic Anthropology*, Supplement 3. JAI Press, Greenwich, CT.

1990 Prehistory of the Ocean Coast of Washington. In *Handbook of North American Indians.* Vol. 7, *Northwest Coast*, edited by Wayne Suttles, pp. 412-421. Smithsonian Institution, Washington.

1991 Archaeological Testing at the Presbyterian Church in Neah Bay (45CA22), Washington. Reports of Investigations No. 1, Makah Cultural and Research Center, Neah Bay, Washington.

1992   Recent Archaeological Investigations on the Makah Indian Reservation, Washington. Paper presented at the 45th Annual Northwest Anthropology Conference, Simon Fraser University, Burnaby, BC.

1993   Archaeological Activities at and near Sand Point (45CA201), Olympic National Park, Washington. Report prepared for National Park Service, Pacific Northwest Regional Office, Seattle.

1994a Subsistence Patterns as Reflected by Invertebrate Remains Recovered at the Ozette Site. In *Ozette Archaeological Project Research Reports*. Vol. 2, *Fauna*, edited by Stephan R. Samuels, pp. 93-196. Reports of Investigations 66. Department of Anthropology, Washington State University, Pullman, and National Park Service, Seattle.

1994b An Account of the Ozette Shellfish Taxa. Appendix C in *Ozette Archaeological Project Research Reports*. Vol. 2, *Fauna*, edited by Stephan R. Samuels, pp. 333-358. Reports of Investigations 66. Department of Anthropology, Washington State University, Pullman, and National Park Service, Seattle.

Wigen, Rebecca J., and Barbara R. Stucki
1988   Taphonomy and Stratigraphy in the Interpretation of Economic Patterns at Hoko River Rockshelter. In *Prehistoric Economies of the Pacific Northwest Coast*, edited by Barry L. Isaac, pp. 87-146. *Research in Economic Anthropology*, Supplement 3. JAI Press, Greenwich, CT.

Wike, Joyce
1951   The Effect of the Maritime Fur Trade on Northwest Coast Indian Society. PhD dissertation, Department of Political Science, Columbia University. University Microfilms, Ann Arbor, MI.

1958 Social Stratification Among the Nootka. *Ethnohistory* 5(3):219-241.

Wilkinson, Leland, Grant Blank, and Christian Gruber
1996 *Desktop Data Analysis with SYSTAT*. Prentice-Hall, Upper Saddle River, NJ.

Willemar, Rev. J.X.
1870 Report of the Columbia Mission for the Year 1869. In *Annual Reports of the Columbia Mission*. Rivingtons, London.

Wilson, Ian R.
1990 Archaeological Investigations at DgSl 61, Chesterman Beach, West Coast Vancouver Island. Report on file, Archaeology Branch, Victoria.

1994   Archaeological Investigations at DgSl 67, Chesterman Beach, West Coast Vancouver Island. Report on file, Archaeology Branch, Victoria.

Wobst, H. Martin
1978 The Archaeo-Ethnology of Hunter-Gatherers or The Tyranny of the Ethnographic Record in Archaeology. *American Antiquity* 43(2):303-309.

Wolf, Eric R.
1982 *Europe and the People Without History*. University of California Press, Berkeley and Los Angeles.

Yesner, David R.
1980 Maritime Hunter-Gatherers: Ecology and Prehistory. *Current Anthropology* 21(6): 727-750.

Index

Page numbers in **bold type** refer to figures.

Aguilar Point sites, 62, 81, 82-83, 126, 140, 151

Ahous Bay Stillstand, 110, 111, 112

Ahousaht, 221, 223, 224; attacks on Muchalaht, 200; residential school at, 215, 218; warfare, 15, 151, 193, 205; whalers' shrine at, 161

Albatross, 56, 57, 59, 61, 82, 121, 202

Alberni Inlet, 25, 33, 109, 110, 136, 153, 191; archaeological sites on, 75, 203; Tseshaht use of, 26, 28, 203, 205, 208, 211; Ucluelet use of, 15, 211

Amalgamations (to form the historic groups), 13, 28, 36, 128, 193, 196-212, 216

Amos, Pat, 224

Archawat, 99, 101, 164

Barkley, Captain Charles William, 188, 202

Barkley Sound: archaeological research in, 45, 50, 62-83, 108, 113, 119, 130, 201, 203; dentalium beds in, 156; environment of, 25; establishment of reserves in, 191, 203; fur trade history of, 181, 185, 188-91; geological history of, 109-10, 111; halibut fishing in, 18, 141; historic political changes in, 202-11; location of Nuu-chah-nulth groups within, 24-28; Nuu-chah-nulth arrival at, 119, 120, 128; pictograph sites in, 164; warfare in, 143, 147, 152, 193-95, 196; whaling in, 132, 135, 136, 137. *See also* Broken Group islands; Toquaht Archaeological Project

Basketry: as ethnic indicator, 45, 98, 120; ethnographic, 24; preserved in

archaeological contexts, 60, 84, 86, 91, 95, 120; recent, 216

Bear Cove site, 105-6

Benson Island, 82, 126

Blenkinsop, George, 191, 195, 205-6, 209

Boas, Franz, 7, 31, 36, 39

Borden, Charles, 40, 41

Brabant, Reverend A.J., 192, 205, 215

Broken Group islands, 27, 136, 148, 189; archaeological sites recorded in, 62, 129, 130, 131, 148, 211; Tseshaht use of, 26, 203, 205, 207-8

Burials: ethnographic references to, 156; in Late West Coast sites, 57, 82, 145n, 158n; in Locarno Beach age sites, 77, 78, 114, 118, 121, 158; other burial site types, 47, 48, 59-60, 159

Callicum, 187, 198, **199**

Canoes, dugout cedar, 12, 155, 183, **222**, 223

Cape Flattery, 99, 101, 147, 151, 156, 182, 193, 217

Cheewat River sites, 84, 85

Chesterman Beach sites, 79, 80, 126, 140, 143

Chicklesaht: joined Kyuquot, 197, 201n; trade, 153, 155, 156

Chimakuan, 10, 37, 38, 120

Ch'uumat'a: archaeological research at, 70-71, 112, 114-18, 121, 122, 126, 143, 145n, 155, 157, 163, 170-77; ethnographic village of, 69-70, 211; evidence for whaling at, 131, 132, 133, 135; historic artifacts from, 185

Clallam, 6, 37, 85, 93, 151, 154, 209

Clayoquot. *See* Tla-o-qui-aht